MW00562209

Praise for *The Life of the Qur'an*

"Appropriately epic and consistently erudite, yet accessible for lay readers."
—*Kirkus* (Starred review)

"An extremely well-written introduction to the Qur'an. Jebara demonstrates a breathtaking ability to communicate complex ideas with simplicity and eloquence. He does not shy away from directly addressing stereotypes and unmasking myths which surround both the Qur'an and Arabic culture. His deft use of narrative provides fascinating linkages between cultural worlds, past and present, which is guaranteed to whet the reader's appetite for more!"
—Dr. Wendy L. Fletcher, President and Vice-Chancellor, Renison University College, University of Waterloo

"Jebara elegantly engages the cultural and historical context in which the Quran was revealed, demonstrating its timeless relevance to the modern world. Further, he astutely elucidates the vitality of the Qur'an as a positive force for social change and as a spiritual guide for those searching for meaning."
—Dr. Ali Akkam, Dean, Faculty of Islamic Law, Aleppo University

"Scriptures have always contained mysteries and the Qur'an is not an exception. Jebara proposes an exciting journey transporting our mental horizon to an outstanding view of the enlightening message contained in the Qur'an. . . . A vibrant masterpiece, that I highly recommend!"
—His Excellency Dr. Khalid Sacoor D. Jamal, Islamic Community of Portugal

"An accessible and enjoyable read about Islam's Holy Book, which can and should be read by everyone—regardless of faith. During a moment when misinformation about Islam and distortion of the Qur'an is rife, this book brings urgent clarity and powerful commentary."
—Dr. Khaled Beydoun, Wayne State University

"This book unlocks the deeper meanings I've been looking for—and some that I wasn't."

—Hazem Bata, Former Secretary General and CEO of the Islamic Society of North America

"An exquisitely written masterpiece offering a unique window into Quranic wisdom, making it relatable to readers of all backgrounds."

—Rev. Father Andre Boyer, Former Superior of the Oblates of Mary Immaculate

"Jebara takes an ancient, sacred, life-giving book and makes it accessible to modern readers. He patiently offers transformative world-changing insights into the Qur'an making it a window to the Divine, while inspiring readers to seek deeper understanding. This book will truly give readers the courage to go against all odds and listen to the Divine Guidance calling them to make this world a better place."

—Rev. Takouhi Demirdjian-Petro, first Armenian woman minister ordained in Canada by the United Church

"[Offers] fresh insight into a well-known—yet much misunderstood—foundational pillar of the Islamic faith. Jebara addresses many of the most complex and controversial passages, providing readers with the interpretive keys to not merely unlock these texts, but the larger Quranic mindset, which has, and still can, provide inspiration and upliftment for individuals and entire societies."

—Captain Barbara Lois Helms, First Female Muslim Chaplain of the Canadian Armed Forces

"Jebara rescues the Qur'an—one of the world's most memorized yet misunderstood and maligned works—from the book burners and fanatics by elucidating the nuanced meanings of Islam's fundamental text. A beautifully written, well-sourced, and essential read for understanding the power of ideas and intercultural exchange."

—Jason Guberman, Executive Director, American Sephardi Federation

"[Sheds] light on preconceived notions and repairs generational misinterpretations that have plagued so many."

—Anthony Samadani, *Good News Network*

"A paragon of explication that reactivates the central role of the Qur'an as an inspiring force for world-changing impact."

—Dr. Ammar Almehmi,
University of Alabama at Birmingham

THE
LIFE
OF THE
QUR'AN

ALSO BY MOHAMAD JEBARA

Muhammad, the World-Changer

THE
LIFE
OF THE
QUR'AN

FROM ETERNAL ROOTS
TO ENDURING LEGACY

MOHAMAD JEBARA

ST. MARTIN'S
ESSENTIALS
NEW YORK

First published in the United States by St. Martin's Essentials, an
imprint of St. Martin's Publishing Group

THE LIFE OF THE QUR'AN. Copyright © 2024 by Mohamad Jebara.
All rights reserved. Printed in the United States of America. For
information, address St. Martin's Publishing Group, 120 Broadway,
New York, NY 10271.

www.stmartins.com

The Library of Congress Cataloging-in-Publication Data is available upon request.

ISBN 978-1-250-28236-1 (hardcover)
ISBN 978-1-250-28237-8 (ebook)

Our books may be purchased in bulk for promotional, educational,
or business use. Please contact your local bookseller or the Macmillan
Corporate and Premium Sales Department at 1-800-221-7945, extension
5442, or by email at MacmillanSpecialMarkets@macmillan.com.

First Edition: 2024

10 9 8 7 6 5 4 3 2 1

CONTENTS

PART III: THE QUR'AN'S LEGACY

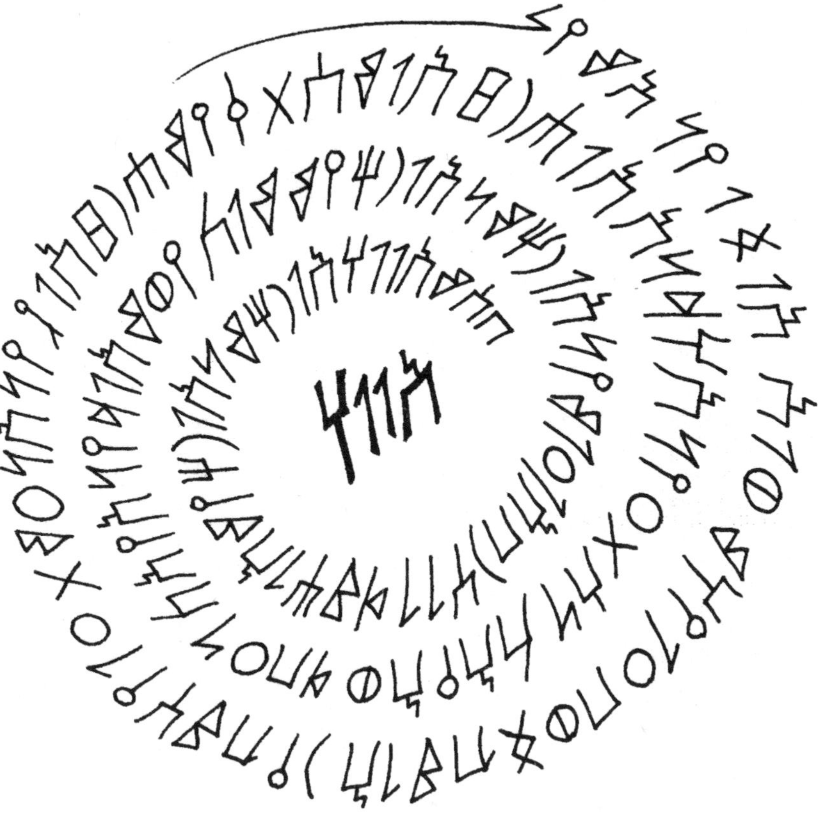

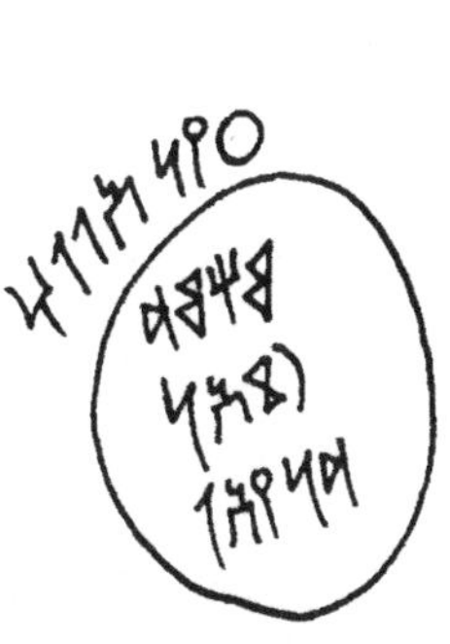

Evolution of the Letters

Ox Skull
"Alif"
Alpha

Eye
"Ayn"

Omega

Lam
Lambda

Staff

D J
R)

To the Ultimate Inspiration of the Cosmic Code,

The Source of Creativity and Nuanced Realization

The Divine Mentor and Channeling Force

Of Awakening and Transformation

AUTHOR'S NOTE

WRITING THIS BOOK, I PRESUMED NO PRIOR KNOWLEDGE OR EXPER-
tise on the part of the reader, allowing the work to serve as both an introduction and invitation to explore the Qur'an's timeless wisdom. While aiming
for brevity and accessibility, I have had to adjust to the corresponding disad-
vantages; not all Qur'anic chapters and passages can be covered, and not all
areas of scholarly debate can be thoroughly presented.

As in the Qur'an, Muhammad is rarely mentioned in this book. In my previous work, the biography *Muhammad, the World-Changer,* I had no choice
but to infringe on his request to remain anonymous. However, here I am
honoring that request by concentrating on the message—the Qur'an—as he
had specified.

There is an inherent tension in trying to create a popular entry-point
into an elite scholarly world that has developed over 1,300 years in another
language and culture. While various popular translations of the Qur'an exist, readers should be aware that there is no definitive scholarly consensus
on accurate translation. Translators understandably struggle to capture the
Qur'an's sophisticated and layered nuances in a foreign language, and ren-
derings can often sound bland or abstruse.

As a scripture that inspired some of the greatest minds in history, the Qur'an deserves a rich and evocative translation that strives to convey the profound wisdom embodied in its original language. Even on a superficial level, its creative use of words is artistic and ingenious. The translations presented in this book attempt to capture at least some of the Qur'an's depth and uniquely compelling exploration of human psychology, emotions, and behaviors. Readers familiar with past translations are asked to keep an open mind as they explore the following pages. The Qur'anic translations presented here aim to convey an appreciation of the original text as traditional Islamic scholars understood it—and not necessarily as some ideologically motivated translators have at times sought to portray it.

Some assume that Muslims view the Qur'an in the same light as adherents of Christianity and Judaism view the Bible. For Jews, the Torah is inspired by God but written by Moses, while the rest of the Hebrew Scriptures, all of which are inspired by God and given specifically to the Children of Israel, are written by several dozen individuals. For many Christians, the core of the New Testament is a collection of biographies of Jesus Christ written by his followers, inspired by God, whereas the *word* of God is Christ himself, as the revelation. Most Muslims believe that the Qur'an is the literal word of God, dictated to prophet Muhammad by the archangel Gabriel, who then served as the supervisor guiding the Qur'an's editing in the final two years of its revelation.

Whereas Christians view Christ as a universal manifestation of the Divine on earth, whereby the "person" of Christ is holy, Muslims merely view Muhammad as an esteemed prophet like Abraham or Moses, simply mortal and not divine. Yet Muslims view the Qur'an as a universal manifestation of the Divine on earth, and it is sacred and holy in and of itself since it represents the direct communication of the Divine for a universal audience. Although not everyone can agree that the Qur'an is the word of God—especially those outside the faith community—nonetheless it is possible to appreciate the Qur'an as a work of wisdom literature with a purpose, irrespective of theological convictions.

This book focuses on the elements that do not require any prior faith convictions. Hence, to appreciate this perspective, readers are not asked to accept interpretations that cannot be supported by empirical evidence, nor by the same token are readers who believe in the role of the archangel required to give up that faith. In this book, as in *Muhammad, the World-Changer*, the focus is not to reinforce specific theological conventions, but to allow all readers to appreciate the Qur'an's remarkable content.

THE
LIFE
OF THE
QUR'AN

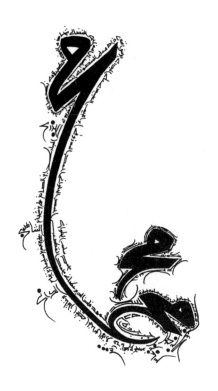

INTRODUCTION

A
LIVING
ENTITY

THE QUR'AN'S MOMENT OF BLOSSOMING WAS ENTIRELY UNEXPECTED.

At twilight on a mid-March morning in the year 610 CE, darkness clung to Mecca as the city slumbered in silence. Perched on the edge of a mountain-top cave overlooking the scene below, forty-year-old Muhammad sat cross-legged. Breathing in the crisp, pre-sunrise air with eyes closed, he sensed a cool breeze gently brush his cheeks. The morning dew amplified the scent of early spring wildflowers. In the distance, the chirping of crickets echoed amidst the occasional hooting owl and howling wolf.

Predawn provided a moment of serenity for Muhammad. The self-made entrepreneur possessed a considerable fortune and a beautiful mansion, where his devoted wife and four daughters slept soundly, awaiting his return. A respected member of society, he was renowned for his discerning mediation skills. Yet wealth and prestige had proved unfulfilling. For four years Muhammad had retreated up the mountain seeking deeper purpose. Week after week, the cave atop Mount Hira became his elevated meditation spot, a sanctuary from the bustle of mercantile Mecca.

This early morning appeared to be like hundreds Muhammad had experienced before. He slowly opened his eyes as the first sliver of refracted sunlight broke over the horizon, splitting the inky darkness. At that moment, a sudden contraction seized his chest near his heart. A terrifying tightness compressed his lungs as a word seemed to resound through his soul, powerfully radiating unstoppably like a cosmic call: "Iqra!"

Yet as soon as the word emerged, filling the vast emptiness, the pang in his chest faded as abruptly as it had struck. Muhammad sat gasping in stunned silence, staring wide-eyed toward the horizon. He shivered in the intense silence that followed. Just as Muhammad began to allow himself to relax, another compression seized him, and the word again emerged: "Iqra!"

Muhammad sat stupefied. Then an even more animated compression sounded through his soul; an outburst of luminous words flowed like a chanted river of intense emotions. Five short phrases shattered the silence and seemed to echo off the surrounding mountains with vibrating energy illuminating the darkness.

> *Blossom forth,*
> *Inspired by your rejuvenating Divine Mentor,*
> *Who revives the dormant to forge empowering connections.*
> *Dare to blossom,*
> *As your Divine Mentor provides spiritual comfort.*
> *The Visionary One, who guides the unlocking of layers of learning,*
> *Elevates the stagnant to once-inconceivable heights.*

The key word *Iqra* that had taken three contractions to emerge literally meant "blossom forth" or "be born"—a call to a new being to break out of the darkness of obscurity and emerge into the outside world. In contrast to the generic Arabic word for "birthing" (*walada*)—which can encompass stillbirths, premature births, and babies born with defects or problematic outcomes, the term *qara'a* implies a healthy birth of something destined to survive. The ancient Arabs would say *Qara'a-til-Mar'ah* ("the woman delivered a healthy birth"), *Qara'a-tir-Riyah* ("the winds fertilized fields sparking their blossoming") and *Qara'at-il-Azhar* ("the flowers blossomed").

In modern times, *Iqra* is frequently translated as "recite" or "read," yet these are secondary connotations, ones not particularly relevant for an illiterate like Muhammad. *Iqra* issued a command to unfurl what was carefully nurtured within and finally share it with the world, allowing an inner truth to be revealed after a protracted period of incubation—like a bud finally daring to blossom and expose itself to the elements.

Muhammad did not know what to make of this formidable force that had emerged through his soul, except that once it had been revealed there was no turning back. The five Arabic phrases sounded like nothing ever heard before, both in terms of poetic composition and provocative message. The society of the Arabian Peninsula prized stagnation above all else as a means of self-preservation. Daring to open up to change was the antithesis of everything Arabia stood for—as Muhammad would soon discover when he repeated this revelation in public a week later in the center of Mecca, only to be ridiculed.

The Qur'an, in other words, had been revealed into an unwelcoming world that would instinctively reject it. Nor was the prophet through whom it was inspired prepared for the responsibilities of its guardianship. He had been caught completely off guard and was unprepared for the immense obligation before him. As he fled down the mountain, Muhammad trembled while repeatedly whispering, "Iqra . . . Iqra . . . Iqra. . . ."

Would the new entity now entrusted to Muhammad manage to survive? Would its unique nature be a blessing or a burden? Muhammad did not know it yet, but on the first anniversary of this mystical morning, the nascent entity would not only name itself *Al-Qur'an* ("The Blossoming") but address these very questions by declaring: "We did not reveal the Qur'an to weigh you down, but rather to liberate and elevate for a lasting legacy anyone willing to listen with an open mind."

Over the twenty-two-year life-span of its unfolding, the Qur'an would face daunting challenges and fierce opposition. Its unique character inspired some, but greatly threatened many others. Rather than open themselves to its call, they would respond by attacking the Qur'an's style, message, and prophet. Trying to convey the art of blossoming in a barren desert, the Qur'an would have to develop dynamic ways to relate to its harsh environment while remaining true to its founding message and core values.

The Qur'an would ultimately go on to inspire some of the greatest innovative minds in history. To appreciate how it changed the world requires understanding its life. And so, dear reader, I present you with the very birth of the Qur'an as it emerged from the realm of timelessness into the temporal world. Behold it and wonder.

❦

The day I was born, my parents attached a miniature Qur'an pendant to my swaddle with a safety pin featuring a baby-blue teddy bear. About an inch in length, the book featured the entire Qur'an in tiny print, safely enclosed within a twelve-karat-gold casing. The talisman lay on the left side of my chest above the heart.

The same pendant was affixed to my newborn brother three years later. Intrigued by the peculiar object, I fiddled loose the top clasp when no one was looking and managed to slide out the miniature book inside. Flipping through the pages revealed a mysterious script. But then I faced a mini-crisis: try as I might, the tiny book would not fit back in its case. So I slipped the book into my pocket—where it would remain for nearly a decade. Day after day, I carried around the miniature without knowing what it was, yet sensing that it had some special significance.

Though my parents rarely mentioned the word "Qur'an" to me, every night at bedtime my mother would chant a mysterious Arabic refrain while putting me to sleep. Only years later did I realize she was reciting the Qur'an's brief opening and closing chapters to help protect her young children from nightmares as we slept. And when my little sister developed a skin ailment, my mother took her to a cleric for healing. Using charcoal, he wrote a Qur'anic passage on her skin (which I later discovered was the iconic *Ayat-ul-Kursi*).

At age five, I noticed that my relatives had a foot-long brown leather set of cassette tapes featuring Qur'anic chanting by a famous Egyptian reciter. They played the recordings only when someone died. During the three days of mourning, the tapes ran on a loop to assist the soul of the deceased to ascend to heaven. The chanting sounded melancholic and consoling, establishing an initial association in my mind of the Qur'an with death and mourning.

High on our living room wall my father hung a red velvet pouch containing a copy of the Qur'an. Most of the time it remained there unread. Occasionally it would be taken down to recite a few verses after someone died, before being passed around for the whole family to kiss in reverence (and only after we had first bathed). As children we had no substantive engagement with the book, which functioned as a purely honorific object. This was typical of most Muslims of my generation growing up in the West.

Above all, the Qur'an to me as a child was mysterious and foreign. I felt my skin shiver from its melodic and rhythmic chanting, and I watched its enigmatic language move adults to tears. My young mind translated mystery into intrigue and curiosity. I had to understand what made this collection of paper and ink so special. Why was it revered as a source of healing and protection? Was it just a talisman or was there substance in the words I could not read?

At age ten, I set out to find a Qur'an teacher who could open a gateway into this unknown world. Every other day after school I would ride the bus for an hour to study with a young African scholar for two-hour sessions. He sat opposite me cross-legged on the floor, our knees touching. I was captivated by the huge bookcases behind him laden with decorated Arabic tomes. My teacher placed a large blue book between us and began guiding me to read the opening chapter of the Qur'an. In our first session, it took two hours just to limp through the first line as I struggled to precisely pronounce the letters.

I was by far the most disadvantaged of my teacher's pupils, most of whom had grown up in the Middle East and already knew how to read and write Arabic. Some of my fellow students mocked my poor skills and insisted I would never make it. But despite encountering a right-to-left script and a tongue-twisting ancient Semitic language, I was determined to excel. After several weeks of consistent study, I had impressed my teacher with my progress. "I will have a gift for you next week," he revealed as we parted one evening.

The next week at the end of our session he handed me a pocket-sized navy-blue book with a floral pattern cover featuring the word "Al-Qur'an" written in Arabic calligraphy. I embraced it like an amazing treasure box that contained hidden gems and began marking up the pages to guide pronunciation, intonation, and rhythmic changes during reciting. For over two decades, working with over a hundred different teachers, I kept adding notes to the same original book, which I carried in my right pants pocket (the left pocket contained the old miniature). Whereas it had once evoked death and mourning, the Qur'an became a source of dynamic learning.

My teacher introduced me to several other instructors and together they propelled me forward on the path to becoming a *hafith* (literally, "conserver" or "guardian")—a term signifying someone who has memorized the Qur'an. I still did not understand what Arabic words meant, so memorization involved processing sounds, melodies, and emotions. It also required extreme discipline.

I would lock myself in my room for hours, constantly repeating passages. To guide me, my teachers invoked a classic mantra of Islamic scholars: *At-tikraru yad'u ilal-qarar*—"Constant repetition leads to stability of memorization."

It took months to build up muscle memory, sometimes repeating a single letter seven thousand times to condition my vocal cords. Memorizing a page at first took nearly two hours, but eventually I could process up to ten pages an hour. Memorization became a kind of intimacy, entrusting something precious to my heart and mind, not merely my pocket. As I internalized how to recite it, the Qur'an became an integral part of my identity, connecting me to an important lineage.

My teachers revealed to me how traditional Islamic scholarship rests upon unbroken chains of transmission called *Isnad* (Literally, "to lean back on for support"—an unbroken transmission of religious authority similar to the Rabbinic concept of *Semikhah*) that link each student back in time through the generations to Muhammad himself. To bring my own *Isnad* to life, my teachers would occasionally gift me books written by ancestors in my chain, like Imam Ad-Dani who lived in eleventh-century Spain.

By age twelve I had memorized all the Qur'an's words, yet understood few of them—a bit like repeatedly watching a foreign film without any subtitles, knowing the scenes in detail without comprehending the dialogue. My teachers began intensive sessions on Arabic grammar, syntax, and etymology, empowering me to at last begin to decipher what I was reciting. As my classical Arabic skills developed, I uncovered layer after layer of meaning, peeling back nuances each more profound than the prior. The process was what the Qur'an's first words describe as "unlocking layers of learning."

My teachers then introduced me to the academic field of Qur'anic exegesis called *Tafsir*. Derived from the Arabic concept for separating strands of raw flax and weaving them into a garment, the discipline of *Tafsir* was developed by Muhammad to help make the Qur'an accessible and relevant to popular audiences. The field today comprises thousands of volumes of commentary aiming to assist readers in making sense of the Qur'an to help improve their lives.

Studying *Tafsir* made me realize that the Qur'an provides no linear history. It functions rather as a multidimensional loop, featuring only one complete narrative (recounting the life of Joseph), and mostly alludes briefly to other stories rather than reproduces them. The discipline also highlighted how scholars widely diverge in their understanding of chapters, verses, and even individual words. I was amazed to discover that the legendary scholar Ar-Razi produced a commentary of over two hundred pages on just seven short verses.

After more than a decade of intense study, the Qur'an still felt distant and abstract. My insatiable drive to unlock its mysterious layers of meaning led me to Mecca. After visiting the Ka'bah shrine at the center of the city, I trekked toward Mount Hira, eager to experience the birthplace of the Qur'an firsthand. As an avid North American hiker, I envisioned Hira as an amazing mountain vista like the picturesque Rocky Mountains.

Hira literally means "the place of resolving doubt"—yet for me visiting the site produced the opposite effect. The winding stairway to the top was packed, with massive crowds jostling past souvenir hawkers and beggars with fake deformities trying to exploit the fervor of devout pilgrims. Graffiti praising Muhammad dotted the rocks near the cave's entrance, which I discovered was smaller than expected. Only a handful of pilgrims could cram inside at once, and the prospect of entering sparked claustrophobia.

Disappointed to discover Mount Hira did not yield the anticipated transcendent experience, I plopped down on the back side of the mountain and looked out over the semi-wilderness outside Mecca. Hira, I suddenly realized, was not a destination but a state of being. The "place of resolving doubt" was inside the Qur'an, not any physical location. After all, Muhammad himself never returned to Hira's peak following his predawn revelation. The real journey before me was to delve deeper into the book I had been carrying in my pocket all these years.

For the next decade of my life, I dove into the field of Tafsir with wide-eyed curiosity, traveling the world to learn from living legends. In Damascus, I studied at the feet of eminent scholars like 'Abdur-Razzaq Al-Halabi and Muhammad Sukkar. These specialists possessed remarkably short chains of transmission back to the founder of the discipline of Tafsir, Ubayy Ibnu Ka'b. This erudite scholar had himself been a prize pupil of Muhammad, serving as one of his top scribes. Learning from the custodians of centuries-old tradition inspired me to try to articulate the spirit of Islamic scholarship in accessible ways. The book you now hold forms a small contribution to the intricate dialogue of Tafsir.

☙❧

For the general public today, the Qur'an remains an enigma. Unlike the Bible, it is not a straight narrative, but rather meditates over a broad range of themes in often abstract poetic language. It is also the product of only one prophet, weaving together hundreds of diverse revelations from a twenty-two-year period into one complex whole. The amount of specialized knowledge required as a foundation to interpret and translate the Qur'an is immense.

Islamic scholars therefore long discouraged any translations of the Qur'an into other languages, insisting that readers needed to learn classical Arabic to access the content directly. The great twelfth-century scholar Al-Baghawi insisted that anyone doing exegesis of the Qur'an must have detailed knowledge of:

- The many and diverse classical Arabic dialects;
- The grammar, syntax, and original root meaning of Arabic words;
- The diverse vernaculars of the Qur'an (known as *Qira'at*);
- Intimate details of the prophet Muhammad's life;
- Awareness of the timing of each revelation, including its context and audience;
- Where each passage was placed in Muhammad's final editing of the Qur'anic text;
- The various ways that Muhammad interpreted the passages, as chronicled in vignettes of Muhammad's sayings to his followers (known as *Hadith*).

By these standards, the Qur'an seems both locked away from popular appreciation and highly vulnerable to manipulation.

The Qur'an was first translated into English in 1649 by a Scottish writer who relied on a French translation that itself relied on an inaccurate medieval Latin translation. Only in the early twentieth century did Muslims begin to translate the Qur'an into English. These were primarily Indian writers responding to inroads made by zealous evangelists under British colonial rule. Competing with the King James Bible, these translations mimicked the latter's style and attitude rather than providing an accurate depiction of the Qur'an's own scriptural content.

Popular audiences reading these translated renditions are treated to a relatively uninspiring text that often appears perplexing, if not incoherent. Readers have a hard time conceiving how the Qur'an could have served as a uniquely inspiring text for millions of people over the past fourteen centuries, including polymath scholars who invented algebra, algorithms, and the camera.

Brilliant Muslim scholars applied Qur'anic insights to spark the medieval Islamic Golden Age filled with a mind-boggling outpouring of creativity in science, math, medicine, fashion, philosophy, economics, mental health therapy, architecture, art, and beyond. To those scholars, the Qur'anic experience went far beyond reading, chanting, or memorizing. The Qur'an was not merely ink on parchment, sounds emerging from someone's throat, or ears listening to recitation. Rather it was the precious moment when inspired audiences found the courage to blossom out of stagnation, opening once-closed petals to reveal dormant potential ready to be unlocked.

Yet today the path to accessing these powerful insights seems blocked and impenetrable. The Qur'an remains distant from contemporary audiences in part because it is less a book than an interactive experience. In that sense, the Qur'an is a thoroughly postmodern work of art, a sui generis entity defying any preexisting categories to deliver multidimensional meditations transcending any standard narrative structure.

The Qur'an is a book with enormous power. When not understood properly, it can yield perilous results—similar to how powerful natural elements like hydrogen, nitrogen, and oxygen are vital components of air, soil, and water, yet can also be manipulated to manufacture explosives. A formidable life-giving force that can be misused for destruction, the Qur'an needs to be handled with care. Given the stakes, this book aims to translate the Qur'an's ideas in meaningful ways for popular audiences—mirroring the Qur'an's own effort to convey a mindset of blossoming to people of all backgrounds.

Appropriately, as an entity specifically designed to support audiences to chart paths out of confusion toward clarity, the Qur'an holds the keys to its own unlocking. It likens itself to a *Hadi,* a trailblazing guide helping travelers navigate out of seeming dead ends toward their desired destination. Defining itself is a passion for the Qur'an, whose formal name signifies the blossoming of new life. Other evocative terms it employs to describe itself include:

- *Hayah*: a source of life;
- *Ruh*: an inspired fresh breath of life;
- *Shifa*: a source of internal healing;
- *Furqan*: an intelligent being capable of discernment;
- *Hakim*: a wise and self-aware counselor.

The Qur'an presents itself as a mentor, offering brief inspirational exhortation, reassurance, and, on occasions, caution. It functions like an interactive personal trainer that can adapt different tones to meet the shifting needs of its audience—a coach that can only be useful if humans first take the initiative. A sophisticated and conscientious guide, the Qur'an empathizes with its audience because it too faced great challenges, though its own story remains largely obscured.

When readers hold a Qur'an today they grasp an edited version compiled under Muhammad's supervision in the final two years of his life. Instead of presenting revelations sequentially, he oversaw the reworking and reordering of them until they were sculpted into a more sophisticated masterpiece. For example, the opening chapter of seven short verses dates from the first month of the Qur'an's existence. The second chapter is forty-one times longer and was completed only fifteen days before Muhammad's death. Moreover, one of the Qur'an's final chapters has a verse inserted in it from the first few months of the Qur'an's unfolding.

This book peels back the order of Qur'anic revelations to chronicle an incredibly dynamic life. The first section, "The Qur'an's Roots," explores its DNA, ancestry, and cultural framework. The Qur'an's DNA is examined via Arabic letters and the sophisticated words they construct. The Qur'an's ancestry is explored via the heritage of Abrahamic monotheism and its biblical older siblings. Then the social context in which the Qur'an was developed is evoked via the evolving audiences in Arabia it directly addressed: first Muhammad himself, then a small group of persecuted followers, then the majority-Jewish city of Medina, then all of Arabia, and finally all people.

This book's core section ("The Qur'an's Growth") then traces the Qur'an's unfolding over three stages in relation to the receptivity of its diverse audiences. The Qur'an's earliest revelations are met with limited response. As it refines its identity, the Qur'an employs a more assertive voice to challenge the status quo. A devastating boycott effectively silences the Qur'an for over two years, providing a forced period of introspection—from which the Qur'an re-emerges with a new mature and self-assured voice articulating a fully formed approach to living. Then, in its prime productive years, the Qur'an is in a position of authority, managing others and running civic efforts as it applies its philosophy in practical ways. Finally, in the golden years of its unfolding, the Qur'an, like a wise elder, largely ceases new revelation to focus instead on reorganizing itself into a refined form to best be appreciated by posterity.

The book concludes with a consideration of "The Qur'an's Legacy," exploring how the message of the Qur'an evolved after Muhammad's death. This section traces how Muhammad's disciples established *Tafsir* as a formal academic discipline at new academies formed two years after his passing. But it also shows how the Qur'an became caught up in political strife, including the dramatic moment when the caliph 'Uthman was assassinated while reading Muhammad's final bound tome—his blood spattering the pages.

෴

While today the Qur'an is viewed in retrospect as the grand scripture of powerful and triumphant empires, virtually its entire unfolding was defined by corresponding experiences of persecution, banishment, slander, and other intense suffering endured by its followers. In many ways, the Qur'an is the product of pain and sorrow. It spent the first decade of its unfolding in a state of loneliness, pointedly addressing its audience in the singular. Only once the Qur'an gained a receptive following in Medina did it expand into employing the plural form. Remarkably, after Muhammad and his followers finally emerged victorious with the conquest of Mecca, the Qur'an largely retreated into silence.

As Ibnu 'Abbas, one of Muhammad's top disciples, observed: "The Qur'an was revealed in circumstances of great sadness and hardship—so chant it with somber and melancholic melodies." His observation serves as an indirect reminder that the Qur'an is concerned with how to blossom under pressure, as it was itself revealed under extreme duress with an inspirational message somehow emerging. Blossoming in the harsh desert of Arabia cannot be taken for granted; managing to flourish under extreme and scarce conditions makes whatever succeeds in blossoming special.

The Qur'an works very hard to maintain a balance between uplifting inspirational rhetoric and the realistic awareness that the world can be a very dangerous place. As a responsible guardian, the Qur'an recognizes it cannot inspire without also warning. It sees potential for greatness in all people, while also cautiously acknowledging that human beings can abuse others. In the end, the Qur'an reminds its audience that there is only one fully trustworthy guide: the Divine. In that humble spirit, let the journey begin.

PART I

THE
QUR'AN'S
ROOTS

1

DNA: ARABIC
LETTERS AND
LANGUAGE

THE QUR'AN BEGINS WITH A MYSTERY. AFTER A SHORT SEVEN-VERSE preface, the Qur'an's grand opening chapter launches not with a word, but with . . . three enigmatic Arabic letters:

الم

Alif Lam Mim

The letters appear together as if they form a word, yet the prophet Muhammad insisted that each letter exists as a separate entity: "I don't say that *Alif Lam Mim* is one word, but rather that *Alif* is a word, *Lam* is a word, and *Mim* is a word." He clearly instructed that this inaugural verse be recited by pronouncing the names of each letter rather than the sound they make combined.

Beyond that one cryptic clue, no record survives of Muhammad explaining what the letters signify. Just as readers begin to explore the Qur'an they are instantly thrown off guard by these perplexing characters. The mystery is further complicated by the fact that twenty-eight other chapters of the Qur'an begin with a few stand-alone Arabic letters. What kind of literary work features solitary letters sprinkled throughout its text, prefacing chapters without formal explanation?

After Muhammad's death, his top students offered conflicting interpretations, some of which only deepened the air of mystery surrounding these symbols. His students referred to the letters as *an-Nuraniyyah* ("nighttime illuminations"), helping to shed light on the obscure aspects of the Qur'an, and as *al-Muqatta'at*—literally, precisely cut patches that collectively comprise a garment. Like sleeves, pants, and pockets, each one serves a specific function but remains useless unless stitched together the right way. "Every book has a pure essence [*safwah*]," mused Muhammad's son-in-law 'Ali. "And the essence of the Qur'an is contained in the *Muqatta'at*."

None of these explanations, however, directly helps readers understand what each letter actually means. The interpretative challenge becomes even more complicated with the realization that many scholars could not solve the riddle—and instead warned students not to even try unlocking the letters' meaning. For example, the eighth-century jurist Ash-Sha'bi was asked by one of his students: "What are we to make of the letters at the beginning of Qur'anic chapters?" Ash-Sha'bi's terse response: "Every book should have a secret, and the unknown of the Qur'an are the *Muqatta'at*. You can ask about anything else, but don't ask about these!"

One of Ash-Sha'bi's contemporaries, the great sage Al-Hasan Al-Basri, bristled at this attempt to push away inquisitive minds. He worried that forbidden fruit would only further incite curiosity, leading students to pursue meaning without appropriate guidance. "Humans by nature abhor being told what not to do!" warned Al-Basri. "Had they been prohibited from playing with excrement, they would do it and say, 'There must be a hidden reason why we were told not to.'"

No doubt recognizing this natural impulse, neither the Qur'an nor Muhammad forbid readers from exploring the meanings of these letters. As a result, the debate persists until today. Modern translators of the Qur'an must grapple early on with how to render the letters with English meaning. Most simply reprint the Arabic pronunciation of each letter and include a footnote about their inscrutable purpose. The translator Yusuf Ali, for instance, writes: "Opinions are divided as to the exact meaning of each particular letter or combination of letters, but it is agreed that they have a mystic meaning."

In some Qur'anic schools in the Muslim world today, students can hear their instructors echo Ash-Sha'bi's warning not to delve into the meaning of the introductory letters, though with a modern twist. The caution is usually phrased in ominous tones: "This is a secret code between God and the Prophet—and should not be approached by mortals. Resist the temptation to try to understand it!"

Within eight short sentences of its beginning, the Qur'an thus immediately sets an intriguing challenge before its audience: Do the introductory letters actually have meaning? And if so, does one dare to even attempt to explore their purpose?

❧❦❧

In the world in which the Qur'an was revealed, a person could literally be killed for using the wrong word. For the people of Arabia, words could be a matter of life and death—and achieving immortality required mastery of Arabic prose.

Once in a town outside of Mecca, an aspiring young poet stood in the village square to show off his oratory skills. To make a vivid impression, he composed a poem in real time praising the young maidens of the local clan, likening their elegance to undulating waves. The poem quickly impressed the audience, yet the novice poet got carried away in the heat of the spontaneous performance and accidently invoked a term for rough waves rather than gentle ones. This phraseology faux pas inadvertently implied that the clan's maidens were easily aroused and highly promiscuous.

Shocked, the previously enamored crowd turned hostile, clenching their fists in rage. One offended father could not passively accept the grave insult directed at his daughters and leapt from the crowd to plunge a dagger into the young poet's heart. The poet's murder evoked an ancient Arabic idiom: "The wound of a word is more deadly than the slash of a saber!" Sticks and stones might break one's bones, but in Arabia, bungling the nuance of words could be fatal.

Why did words carry such power? Beyond standards of etiquette and honor that all societies maintain, the Arabs had two particular reasons for elevating language to a rarefied status. First, Arabic in their eyes was the last remaining bastion of the ancient Semitic mother tongue that had birthed Hebrew, Aramaic, and Ethiopic, as well as other long-vanished languages. Other languages had lost many of the original Semitic letters, merging and contracting sounds to enable quicker conversation. Arabic, in the isolation of the desert, had adamantly resisted and maintained fine elocution and linguistic precision. The Arabs thus regarded their language as a sacred and defining aspect of their identity.

A result of this obsession with language was that Arabs, in the centuries preceding the Qur'an's revelation, effectively had no forms of artistic expression beyond poetry. Arabia produced no original products, instead serving as a trading hub of other civilizations' merchandise. Lacking outlets for practical production, the Arabs channeled their creative energy into language as the epitome of self-expression. As the ancient Arabic idiom declared: "Speak and you shall be known, for the true essence of a person can only be revealed through their words." Words were the blossoms of the mind, emerging from the mouth and generating action as metaphorical fruit.

On the flip side, improper language was abhorrent. A primal fear of Arab parents was that their children's Arabic might be contaminated by inferior dialects and alien tongues. Parents would sometimes plug their children's ears with cotton around foreigners, and elite families made sure to send their infant sons off with desert nomads for four years so their first language would be pure, unadulterated Arabic.

In a world where erroneous elocution equaled blasphemy, the Qur'an quickly faced intense linguistic scrutiny. Most Meccans reacted with hostility to the Qur'an's initial revelations, and they soon attacked its language as a way to besmirch its message. After all, if the Qur'an was playing fast and loose with Arabic, its ideas could be summarily dismissed.

One pivotal incident leveled this charge in a dramatic public duel. Muhammad, though ostracized from the moment he proclaimed the Qur'an's first revelation in the center of Mecca, nonetheless continued to recite new revelations in public. He hoped passersby might overhear a phrase and be inspired. Most of the time, the Meccan public shunned him and covered their ears as they passed him (some even whistled to drown out his soft chanting).

On a late December afternoon in the year 615, Muhammad sat outside the Ka'bah shrine unobtrusively reciting a new revelation called *Surah Nuh* ("Noah"). As usual, most residents paid him little attention—until they heard him utter the phrase: *Wa Makaru Makran Kubbara.* The first three words were well-understood: "And they plotted extensively. . . ." But this last word, *Kubbara,* made no sense and seemed completely out of place. No one in Mecca used the word, let alone placed it at the end of a common phrase like *Makaru Makran.*

Rather than confront Muhammad directly for this affront, a few listeners sensed an opportunity for an ambush. They stealthily hurried off to inform one of Muhammad's key nemeses, the Meccan elder Al-'As Ibnu Wa'il, widely regarded as a master of language and litigation. Here was a unique chance for a top linguist to expose Muhammad's fraud once and for all. Indicting his assault on the Arabic language would spark the collapse of the Qur'an's credibility.

Al-'As seized the moment. He rushed to the city center, stood beside Muhammad, and charged him with a crime graver than murder: "Muhammad is inventing and manipulating the language. We never heard this word *kubbara!*" An angry crowd gathered in silence to watch the showdown, as the Qur'an's fate hung in the balance. (The Qur'an (38:7) would later recount this critical confrontation by quoting the Meccans' accusation: *Ma sami'na bi-hatha fil-millatil-akhirati in hatha illa-khtilaq!*—"We never heard such words and meanings before; this is all invented!")

While the seething mob demanded an answer to the charges, Muhammad coolly requested that one of the oldest men in Mecca be brought to the square. As the crowd impatiently awaited the old man's arrival, Muhammad sat on a rock, head bowed and eyes closed in reflection. Al-'As wore a sardonic smile in anticipation of finally humiliating his nemesis. The old man at last arrived on a donkey. Muhammad greeted the elder, whom he had known as a child, and asked him to sit on the rock. Well over a hundred years old, the man grimaced in pain as he grasped his cane and squatted—yet Muhammad then immediately requested the man move to another rock.

The crowd looked on in astonishment as Muhammad continued to direct the centennial elder from rock to rock, as the frail old man grew visibly exasperated. Half-blind, with sunbaked, wrinkled skin and a long white beard, the old man suddenly cried out: "This has gone far enough! This is too much to bear!"—*Inna hatha la'amran kubbara!* There was the disputed word: *Kubbara*—"unbearable frustration."

Via a clever tactic, Muhammad had prompted the elder to utter an arcane word that had slipped out of common usage over the previous century. Rather than being a fraud, Muhammad proved that *Kubbara* represented high eloquence of the venerated elders. With the linguistic duel decided in the Qur'an's favor, the crowd dejectedly dispersed. This marked the last time the Qur'an would be publicly challenged on linguistic grounds, its mastery of language now firmly established.

The verbal duel in downtown Mecca demarcated a new stage in the Qur'an's mode of presentation. Thereafter, the Qur'an began emphasizing its Arabic and Semitic identity, eleven times describing itself as *'Arabiyya*—"Arabic/Semitic." This declaration echoed the Arabs' traditional insistence that their language was the last remaining stronghold of the ancient Semitic mother tongue. As the first-ever book written in Arabic, the Qur'an set itself as the embodiment and champion of a precious Semitic legacy.

Despite this declaration, many scholars default to interpreting and translating the Qur'an through the lens of theology and politics before first considering language—and specifically the Qur'an's Semitic roots. A problematic result is that one misunderstood word can lead to grave consequences. A classic line from the chapter *An-Nisa* ("The Women") reveals the high stakes. A standard mistranslation of the thirty-fourth verse reads as follows: "Those on whose part you fear desertion [*nushuz*], admonish them [*fa'ithuhun*], and leave them alone in the sleeping-places and beat them [*wadhribuhun*]."

Does the Qur'an really advise men to beat their wives? Muhammad faced several marital disputes yet never once struck his wives—and on many occasions admonished husbands never to hit their wives. Scholars who assume that *dharaba* means "beat" thus struggle with a dilemma. "What the passage means is beat them lightly and playfully with a silken scarf," some argue. "Use a small toothbrush [*siwak*] and lightly tap her," others suggest. Both caution that "the beating cannot hurt, leave a mark, a cut, or a bruise." Rather than reconsider the meaning of the word *dharaba* in context, interpreters twist themselves in knots trying to transform a beating into a nonbeating. The result is widespread perception that the Qur'an permits hitting one's wife during a marital dispute.

The mishap arises from the assumption that *dharaba* only means "to strike." The Qur'an invokes the term over fifty times, using it in diverse ways. Its most common usage is *Dharaba mathala*—literally, to send out a point—as a means to illustrate how a parable can explain complicated concepts in simple ways. The Qur'an also employs the expression *Dharaba fil ardh*—"to travel outside one's comfort zone." The Arabic root *Dh-R-B* indicates creating distance: a farmer spreading seeds or an archer releasing an arrow. Indeed, as an archer pulls back his arrow, the bow in his hands builds up stress that, if not released at the right moment, can ultimately break the cord. *Dharaba* thus describes releasing tension and de-escalating before it is too late.

With that underlying concept in mind, the challenging passage transforms from an uncomfortable approval of aggression to a sophisticated approach to marriage therapy. Stripping away superimposed misinterpretations allows the passage's language to speak for itself: "When a toxic atmosphere [*nushuz*—literally, flaring fangs secreting venom] arises in your relationship, communicate your concern gently and clearly [*fa'ithuhun*]. If the situation remains unchanged, cease intimacy yet continue to share a bed. If the stress becomes unbearable, release them to enable healing via temporary separation [*wadhribuhun*]."

Rather than inject violence into an already tense situation, the Qur'an advocates de-escalation. This is precisely what Muhammad himself did—separating from his wives for a month to help cool tensions—and what Islamic tradition encourages before a couple petitions for a divorce. *Dharaba* urges couples to take a temporary time apart in order to heal and reunite.

Given how muddling language can result in abuse, the Qur'an's constant reminder that it is an Arabic book takes on new significance. Because each individual reader approaches the Qur'an with their own set of assumptions, language provides a unique common ground for unlocking foundational meaning. Appropriately, the only books of Qur'anic exegesis that both Sunni and Shi'ah scholars mutually consult are those focused on language.

Ibnu Mas'ud, one of Muhammad's earliest students, warned about the grave consequences of misinterpretation when he inaugurated the first Islamic academy in Kufah in 634. "Preserving the language with all its intricacies is just as vital a task upon us as devotional prayer," he argued. "For if the nuances of language are not preserved then the essence of the teachings will be lost forever." Put more bluntly, language is the only concrete basis for a shared understanding of the Qur'an.

⁂

If language provides the foundation for a common understanding of the Qur'an, then letters are the foundation of language. The Qur'an's "illuminating" letters at the commencement of chapters point readers back to this essential source. In essence, Arabic letters are the Qur'an's DNA. Just as DNA organizes a handful of proteins in intricate patterns to create unique codes that define every living being, Arabic letters combine in organized patterns to define words.

The ancient Semites were the first people to develop an alphabet and a complex form of human communication—of which the Arabs believed their own language was the sole preserver. Indeed, civilization began in the Middle East via a series of innovations that created the conditions for language to emerge: animals were domesticated; storable agriculture was developed; and the first permanent dwellings were constructed—all requiring new sophisticated tools. The first towns and cities arose in places like Jericho, Damascus, and Byblos.

Language, particularly its written form, emerged in this moment of great tension, as once nomadic clans and pastoral farmers began to cohabitate in cities, for the first time living beside people who were not blood relatives. Desiring more security and more effective ways to meet basic living necessities, people began to form civilizations. Where the bonds of clan had once organized society, suddenly human beings needed a new way to relate to one another.

In this revolutionary environment for human existence, standardized language became a vital mechanism for communicating needs to one another and avoiding conflict. Humans in these early towns had to learn how to coexist in ways they never had before, including defining personal property for the first time. Whereas nomadic hunter-gatherer societies were focused on short-term surviving, civilizations focused on thriving. A key aspect of this new ethos included recording knowledge in writing by developing origin stories, instruction manuals, municipal archives, and even cookbooks.

In pioneering writing, the Semites turned to the physical innovations of their new social context for inspiration. The head of the ox—a tamed version of the wild aurochs harnessed to till the land—became the first letter: *Alif.* The private home became the second letter, *Bayt,* and the lock used to secure its front door became the fourth letter, *Dalet.* These objects were complemented by other letters depicting body parts (e.g., hand, head, eye) and tools (e.g., fishhook, needle, bow).

Each pictograph was originally drawn to mimic the physical object it represented, but over time characters evolved into more abstract forms and were customized by each language offshoot. Several thousand years ago, the Greeks adopted a version of these ancient Semitic characters, which in time passed to the Romans—and so the modern Latin alphabet used in English contains the legacy of these original drawings. The letter *A* is an upside-down ox's head; the letter *M* preserves a depiction of flowing waves; and the letter *O* still resembles the eyeball's cornea. The letters used in this very sentence are thus the inherited legacy of the ancient Semites.

Over 5,300 years ago, these pictographs were combined to convey collective ideas. For example, the icons for "mouth" and "water" together formed the term "drinking." With time, these simple sounds evolved to express more complex syllables and nuanced ideas. The Semites leveraged the physical images to signify abstract concepts and emotions. *Alif* came to connote mastery, because of the controlled power of the domesticated bull. *Bayt* evoked belonging, and *Dalet* security or containment. Semites took the twenty-eight letter icons and assembled them in small groups to convey additional concepts, particularly ones not easily captured in a simple image.

For example, *Dalet* ("contained") plus *Mim* ("life-flow") together formed *DM* as the name for "blood" (*Dam* in Arabic and Hebrew). Building on that core, an *Alif* ("mastery") at the beginning created a word for "human being" (*ADM*): someone in control of internal life-flow. The name reflected how humans are distinguished from other life-forms via an advanced consciousness that allows for sophisticated rather than impulsive decision-making.

Returning to the word *Dharaba* (release) that so flummoxed scholars, examining its root letters helps unlock its core meaning. *Dhad* is an ancient Semitic character uniquely preserved in Arabic (all other Semitic tongues lost it over time because of its arduous enunciation) representing a molar tooth, with the connotation of intense pressure from grinding food. Next comes *Ra*, a depiction of a head (*Ras* in Arabic) with the connotations of elevation and repetition. Last comes *Bayt* for grounding. The formula that emerges from the letters: intense pressure, heightened by constant repetition, needs to be re-grounded. Or, in a word, "release."

The realization that the meaning of Arabic words is embedded in their building-block letters can be mind-boggling. While no accounts of the creation of language survive, the ancient Semites who developed this remarkable system were clearly highly intelligent and dedicated their minds to pioneering a groundbreaking new technology: expressing ideas via an organized methodology of sounds and symbols. How precisely they formed and refined this code remains lost to history, but the language and letters remain, reflecting their creative mindset.

The Qur'an sees itself as an inheritor of these sophisticated ancient innovators. Beyond repeatedly referring to itself as *'Arabiyya* ("Arabic/Semitic"),
the Qur'an muses: "Have [the Meccans] not traveled the earth and marveled
at the legacy of those who preceded them? They were far more powerful and
sophisticated, and fully harnessed the power of the land and built fabulous
buildings, far more impressive than those of present civilizations" (30:9).
While most ancient grand structures may have crumbled as the cities of antiquity fell into ruin, the Semitic letters and language remained—preserving
the DNA of that ancient genius.

In its own way, the Qur'an recounts the creation and evolution of human
language. The first gift the Divine bestows on the first human being (appropriately named Adam) is the ability to describe the world around him with
nuanced words. "The Loving Divine inspired Adam with the deep awareness
to name all things based on their characteristics," explains the Qur'an, before
quoting the Divine command: "Oh, Adam, inform them of their names!"
(2:31, 33). Inspired by the Divine, humans bear the weighty responsibility of
making sense of reality via their own vocabulary. "The Optimistically Empowering and Compassionate One [*Ar-Rahman*]," adds the Qur'an, "created
humanity and immediately taught them the art of advanced communication
[*Al-bayan*]" (55:1, 3–4).

The first thing these fresh new beings needed to learn was how to effectively
convey information to one another using words that described things "based
on their characteristics." Appropriately, the Semitic term for "characteristic"
(*Simah*) shares the same root as the word for "name" (*Ism*). A term for someone or something necessarily reflected its qualities. Not only could words not
be arbitrary, they had to convey nuanced ideas. In meeting the task of naming the world around him, Adam had to give it meaning so fellow human
beings could make sense of it and share knowledge. Inexperienced early humans needed to know about the complex and often dangerous world around
them in order to survive.

Yet knowledge, the Semites realized, could easily be forgotten. In contrast
to the concept of the human being as an *Adam* with consciousness, the Semites also developed another word for human: *Insan*—"the one who forgets."
Life-saving wisdom therefore needed to be passed down from one generation
to another in a more permanent manner. In the Qur'anic account, Adam's
grandson Enoch invented writing and thus earned his moniker Idris—"the

great scribe" (a parallel to Shakespeare's moniker "the Bard"). With this new ability to convey knowledge across time and space, ideas could achieve immortality even as individual mortals might eventually be forgotten.

"Humanity was nothing more than one people speaking the same language," the Qur'an narrates, before adding: "Then with time they diversified" (10:19). As language diversified it evolved beyond merely describing reality to enabling debate between diverse opinions. The Qur'an brings this next stage to life while invoking the story of Noah, which takes place in an early Semitic city. As people developed the concept of personal property, they began coveting their neighbors' possessions and using their wealth to assert their superiority. Concerned by his people's increasingly abusive behavior, Noah urges compassion, generosity, and humility—but his argument falls on deaf ears.

"Oh Noah, you continue to debate and reason with us and we are becoming fed up," complain Noah's neighbors (11:32). Language has enabled discussion, which rather quickly leads to the development of a new phenomenon: social ostracization. "Oh Noah, if you don't cease advising us, you will surely be shunned," the neighbors warn (26:116). Shared words do not always yield shared opinions. In this contentious new communication environment, the challenge before human beings becomes discerning knowledge. Not all arguments are credible, and even if most people think one way, they are not necessarily correct.

As early cities evolved into dominant empires spanning hundreds of miles, language evolved in kind, becoming a tool to help control masses of people by manipulating their understanding of reality for political purposes. Enter Moses in the court of Pharaoh, ruler of the greatest empire of his day. The Qur'an makes a point of relating the standoff between these two men from both perspectives, as Moses seeks to liberate his people from slavery and Pharaoh seeks to convince the Israelites that he is actually their savior.

In depicting this epic confrontation, the Qur'an makes a point of spotlighting Pharaoh's sophisticated abilities as a demagogue. In response to Moses' demands that his people go free, Pharaoh appeals to the Egyptians and the Israelites by casting the would-be liberator as a terrorizer. "Permit me to kill Moses, and let his Divine Mentor come to save him. For I honestly fear that he will corrupt your established traditions and spread disorder and tyranny throughout the land," Pharaoh declares (40:26). He then deviously casts himself as an emancipator rather than an enslaver: "I only have your best interest in

mind and show you reality as I genuinely see it. My only desire is to guide you
to the most liberating path forward" (40:29). In response, Moses warns Pharaoh: "I caution you from contriving deceits in the name of the Divine" (20:61).

The battle of narratives between Pharaoh and Moses shows how language
no longer simply described reality and enabled honest debate, but had transformed into a sophisticated tool for manipulation. In a world where words
empower but also disempower, an outstanding leader guides people out of a
state of deception into clarity. The Arabic word for "tyranny" (*Thulm*) literally means "to cast a dark shadow," with light and illumination instead signifying truth and liberty.

As God explains: "We sent Moses with clear guiding signs [*Ayat*, i.e.,
the Torah] and told him: 'Guide your people from the shadows of darkness
[*Thulumat*] into light [*Nur*] and constantly remind them to remain vigilant'"
(14:5). The Qur'an describes the Torah repeatedly as an antidote to deception
via evocative terms like:

* *Imam*: literally, "a guide out of a dark cave back to the light" (11:17
  and 46:12);
* *Dhiya*: literally, "intense noon sunlight that casts no shadow" (21:48);
* *Mubin*: literally, "a freshly polished mirror reflecting reality without
  smudges" (51:38).

If Pharaoh uses manipulative rhetoric to repress people, the Torah employs clarifying language to liberate. Highly conscious of language's double-
edged sword, the Qur'an insists that it speaks *Bilisanin 'Arabiyyin Mubin*—"in
clear and clarifying Arabic" (26:195). In fact, the characteristic the Qur'an
uses most to describe itself and its message is *Mubin*—"clarifying." Language precision is vital, lest words be manipulated to mislead, repress, and
even induce violence.

The Qur'an's fastidious commitment to precision at times leads it to embrace obscure words not well-known by the audience of its day (see, for example, *Kubbara*)—including non-Arabic terms. At first, there seems to be a
tension between the Qur'an's self-professed identity as a quintessentially Arabic work and its invoking non-Arabic words in key moments. Scholars have
long wrestled to reconcile this seeming contradiction. Some adopt a facile solution, declaring that once the Qur'an employs a foreign word it automatically

becomes Arabized. Yet it bears noting that when the Qur'an describes itself as *'Arabiyya* it conditions the claim alongside the adjective *Mubin*. Occasionally borrowing non-Arabic words to convey a precise concept when Arabic lacks the desired nuance fulfills its commitment to precision.

The presence of non-Arabic words in key Qur'anic passages, however, offers a tempting opportunity for manipulation as the terms may not exist in classical Arabic lexicons. Parallel to the negative impact of misappropriating the classical Arabic *dharaba* to legitimize domestic violence, obscure non-Arabic terms in the Qur'an have at times been seized upon to advance agendas that marginalize, divide, and oppress, particularly non-Muslims. One word stands out: *muhaimin*. The Qur'an twice invokes this ancient and obscure Aramaic term, once to describe its relation to Jewish and Christian scriptures and the second time to describe the Divine (5:28, 59:23). While Islamic scholars have for centuries struggled to understand what the word connotes, advocates who insist that Islam replace Judaism and Christianity triumphantly mistranslate *muhaimin* as "supersede" or "dominate."

But there is a source that can clarify. Opening the Book of Daniel reveals the only two times this word appears in the Bible: once to describe Daniel's prophetic abilities as "clear and reliable interpretation" (2:45), and his own character as "trustworthy, neither negligent nor corrupt" (6:5). If the Qur'an goes out of its way to use this unusual Aramaic term, there must be an important reason. Rather than insist upon its superiority to earlier scriptures, the Qur'an leverages *muhaimin* as a point of connection tying itself to its forebears. Moreover, the word itself is defined by Daniel's example as legendary clarifier who could read the writing on the wall. The Qur'an describes itself as *muhaimin* to emphasize its purpose as a clarifier of distortions by insisting on interpreting based on actual meaning. Twisting the term to signify replacement theology doubly corrupts the word's inherent meaning.

❧❧❧

By positioning the "illuminating letters" prominently at the commencement of twenty-nine chapters, the Qur'an displays its foundational DNA in plain sight and highlights a means to establish shared understanding as a bulwark against potential manipulation. The introductory Arabic letters are not simply a caution against deception, but also a beacon to illuminate the path ahead.

As audiences dive into each chapter, the epitaph letters provide clues to the coming main points.

Take *Surah Ibrahim,* the chapter that quotes the Divine's call to Moses: "Guide your people from the shadows of darkness into light and constantly remind them to remain vigilant" (14:5). The chapter, which meditates on the power of language to influence people both negatively and positively, begins with three letters:

الر

Alif Lam Ra

Each letter's core connotation—*Alif* ("mastery"), *Lam* ("imparting wisdom"), *Ra* ("elevating repetitive action")—signals the core theme ahead: "Becoming a master of one's own affairs requires making the pursuit of knowledge a constant process." The chapter's opening line continues: "We inspired this book through you [Muhammad] to guide people out of the dark shadows of confusion into light via clear instructions from their Divine Mentor, who acts as Supportive Coach (*'Aziz*) and Exemplary Role Model (*Hamid*) to help reveal a well-established path to success." (14:1)

The chapter acknowledges that people must choose their own path. Some may prefer to remain in the dark—ignorance can feel like bliss—while others choose to apply wisdom via action. A few sentences later, the Qur'an highlights human agency in processing language: "Every prophet speaks the language of his people in order to clearly deliver the message—for the Loving Divine allows those who choose to be manipulated and misguided to take their own path, while guiding those who prefer the path of clarity" (14:4).

Those seeking clarity, the chapter argues, can rely on the bedrock of language: specifically, each word's foundational root, known as *kalimah*. The chapter presents a parable contrasting language grounded in nuanced sources with rhetoric disconnected from underlying meaning: "A foundational word full of vitality is like a well-watered and verdant tree whose roots are deeply established and whose branches flourish upward toward the sky; it bears fruit in all seasons. . . . A barren word is like a wilted tree that grows on the surface with no roots; the lightest wind can topple it" (14:24–26).

In this parable, focusing on surface meaning alone is a fruitless task. Core meanings are vital not in and of themselves, but because they can elevate toward a higher purpose and inspire action. Clear language both grounds and uplifts. Acquiring knowledge via language is about achieving mastery of one's own affairs.

The Arabian obsession with the beauty of their language had ironically blinded them to its core purpose. Their poets were masters of rhetoric who failed to inspire action in real life, having reduced their heritage to fancy yet hollow words. Their audiences were fanatically devoted to proper diction— ready to impulsively plunge a dagger over an inadvertent wrong term—yet otherwise wallowed passively in stagnation. Unable to access the latent wisdom encoded in their language, Arabs failed to act as masters of their own fate.

The Qur'an argues repeatedly against such passivity, insisting that language is not an objective but rather a tool for unlocking potential via innovative action. Language must be rooted, yes, but for the specific purpose of bearing fruit. Just as the natural code found within DNA provides directions on the manufacture of proteins vital for healthy growth and development, the meaning embedded in language provides directions for human self-development— combinations of characters to shape one's character.

Parallel to how DNA arranges core proteins to code life, the Qur'an utilizes letters to form root words from which concepts branch out and blossom to inspire dynamic vitality. The system of creating meaning out of letters beautifully harnesses a straightforward logic to form layers of meaning. The process begins with crude drawings of everyday objects, with each object signifying a concept that in turn reflects a mindset. Then individual letters are ordered into groups of three, interacting to create root compounds that describe everyday objects and observable phenomena.

The truly transformative power of language occurs when these descriptive root terms are used to form words that convey abstract concepts. A three-letter root compound used to name the spine (Q-W-M) is adapted to describe "flexibility." The root term for a heated pot boiling over (Gh-Dh-B) constructs a word meaning "hot-headed." A root term describing the process of carefully separating grains (D-R-S) evolves to express "analyzing" or "interpreting." From physical sources emerge words for the intangible, like the Qur'an's parable of the healthy tree with roots anchored in the ground while branches stretch toward the heavens.

The Qur'an focuses on the dynamic interplay of the physical (*thahir*) and metaphysical (*batin*) precisely because it speaks to an audience stagnating in idol worship about an unseeable divinity who wants human beings to pursue blossoming. The Qur'an aims to help readers obsessed with materialism relate to an unseen force in the world and an unrecognized potential inside themselves. Ironically, the solution is hidden in plain sight: the language that audiences in Arabia already valued yet failed to channel for a transcendent purpose.

In that light, the epitaph letters adorning the beginning of so many Qur'anic chapters stand as symbolic sparks to human blossoming. A simple depiction of an ox head inspires the desire for self-mastery and independence. A line drawing of a teacher's rod stimulates the pursuit of knowledge. An icon of a door lock inspires introspection on how to liberate locked-up potential.

The Arabs' great locked-up potential was their language. They had taken a potent tool for empowering people to thrive, and instead froze it, treating it like an inviolable sacred object. With no other means of creative production, language became the only significant marker of Arabs' identity and had to be preserved at all costs. The intense fear of losing that identity led some to cotton up their children's ears to avoid contamination by "inferior" and "impure" dialects. After all, the very word 'Arab at its root describes a pristine and unobstructed landscape.

While the Arabs had reduced this concept to fastidiously removing any external contamination, the Qur'an reclaims the 'Arab concept by instead embracing its openness. Arabic dialects partly emerged because Semitic languages lack written vowels, enabling widely varied pronunciation of the same word and ultimately diverse meanings. Rather than fearing difference, the Qur'an embraces it by incorporating multiple ways of pronouncing words.

Muhammad explained that the "Qur'an was revealed in seven different dialect variations [ahruf], each one contributing a layer of depth [kafi] and healing [shafi]," and further elaborated that "each verse's variation has an external [thahr] and internal [batn] meaning." Shifting vowel pronunciation for Qur'anic letters can alter connotation. In the chapter recounting the story of Joseph, his brothers return from Egypt to inform their father that the youngest son, Benjamin, has been arrested. "Inna-bnaka saraqa," (12:81) they tell the patriarch—"Your son stole." But in another dialectic variation of the Qur'an, the letters are rendered "Inna-bnaka surriqa"—"Your son was set up to make it seem as if he stole." Together, the variations produce a multidimensional perspective.

Just when readers think they have figured out what the Qur'an is saying, they suddenly confront the reality that more than one-third of its words have multiple renditions—each taught by Muhammad to different disciples. A classic vignette has the future caliph ʿUmar overhearing a fellow student recite a verse differently from how he learned it. Outraged, the hot-tempered ʿUmar bellowed: "You are manipulating the Qurʾan!" The student countered the accusation by insisting Muhammad himself had taught the verse that way. When the two brought their dispute to Muhammad, the prophet asked each to recite their version of the verse. "You are both correct," he informed his dumbfounded disciples. "I taught you both different variations of the same passage because the Qurʾan is multilayered in meaning."

What to make of the Qurʾan declaring itself a clear and precise work yet also offering over a dozen different manifestations of that clarity? The introductory letters embody this paradox: simple but complex signposts for a dynamic journey that aims to reclaim language by unlocking its potential to inspire action. The Qurʾan declares its straightforward purpose to engage readers, yet refuses to offer monolithic platitudes because it knows oversimplification ultimately leads to stagnation—and accusations of heresy. A book named "The Blossoming" seeks to keep its audience in a constant state of active learning.

Qurʾanic letters are thus tools to intrigue audiences, presenting a stimulating challenge that forces readers' minds into action. Attempting to unlock the letters' meaning helps jumpstart the process of unlocking oneself and achieving self-mastery (*Alif*), followed by empowering others with wisdom (*Lam*) to ultimately unleash nourishing life-flow (*Mim*).

Language itself may not be sacred, but what people do with language can be.

2

ANCESTRY:
ABRAHAMIC
MINDSET

THREE ARABIC LETTERS ARE HARDLY THE ONLY ELEMENT CHALLENGING readers at the start of the Qur'an's grand opening chapter. Unlike the Bible's bold declarative opening where God creates the elements of the world, one by one, in an unambiguous and detailed chronology, the Qur'an has no specific genesis. Rather than commencing "in the beginning," the first sentence after *Alif Lam Mim* begins by alluding to something mysterious that came before: *Thalik-al-Kitabu la rayb*—"That is the book in which there is no confusion." (2:2)

Translators understandably stumble with the opening words *Thalik-al-Kitab*, rendering the phrase as "This is the book." It makes for a neat start, but *thalik* in Arabic means "that"—a reference to something not immediately present, something distant. Why would the Qur'an start with a phrase that sounds like the continuation of a thought rather than the beginning of one? And why declare there is no confusion in a seemingly confusing phrase?

The first step to unraveling the mystery requires a pause after *thalik*—recognizing the word as a stand-alone introductory phrase: "Given all that has come before . . ." The clue that something came before the Qur'an is further emphasized two sentences later: "They believe in what was revealed before . . ." (2:4) Thus, the Qur'an launches by acknowledging that it did not emerge in a vacuum but rather bears an important ancestry, though it initially declines to provide specifics.

The Qur'an's opening gambit—a mystifying allusion to an undefined past while boldly declaring there is no confusion—has a decidedly postmodern twist. It offers a perplexing yet intriguing hook to grab readers' attention for the journey ahead. Indeed, the opening grand chapter *Al-Baqarah* is also the Qur'an's longest, so audiences must remain engaged for over 280 verses to begin unraveling the mystery.

Beyond its creative tactics to command attention, the chapter's opening also delivers a key message: For the Qur'an to stand as a book without confusion, it cannot be read without acknowledging the rich heritage from which it arose. Or, as the opening three letters remind, mastering your destiny to achieve nourishing life-flow requires deeply rooted knowledge—including of one's own ancestry. Ignoring ancestry leads to obliviousness and leaves one vulnerable to misunderstanding, misdirection, and even harm.

While the Qur'an's linguistic DNA may be rooted in Arabic, its cultural genealogy is Abrahamic. The Qur'an, early in its existence, proclaims: *Millata abikum Ibrahim*—"This is the methodology of your patriarch Abraham" (22:78). When the Qur'an cites ideal character traits, it insists: "This wisdom is also contained in the writings of old: the scrolls of Abraham and Moses." (87:18–19). The names of these two titans of monotheism appear throughout the Qur'an: Abraham 69 times and Moses 136 times. To underline the point, the Qur'an's third chapter declares: "He progressively revealed the book to you as a source of clarifying truth, affirming what has come before it: the Torah and the Gospels, revealed as sources of guidance for all people" (3:3–4).

One reason the Qur'an can feel confusing to readers is because it assumes deep knowledge of the Bible, constantly alluding to biblical stories as well as key incidents in Jewish and Christian history without providing all the details. When the Qur'an invokes biblical content, it assumes readers bring a preexisting familiarity with characters, incidents, and concepts. In its terse style that emphasizes take-away moral lessons over detailed storytelling, the Qur'an provides a concentrated set of information that requires supplemental explanation.

Another reason readers struggle is that some modern translations of the Qur'an belie the spirit of positively embracing all of Abraham's progeny with passages rendered as: "Do not consider the Jews and Christians as your friends for they are only friends with each other; Whoever does so will be considered as one of them; God does not guide the unjust people" (5:51). Or: "Whoever desires a religion other than Islam, it will not be accepted from him and in the hereafter he will be among the losers" (3:85).

Can these translations be correct? Does the Qur'an see a dangerous competition between the claimed inheritors of Abraham, rejecting and replacing its monotheistic older siblings? How can readers stymied by seemingly mixed messages navigate out of confusion to certainty? The journey to clarity lies in exploring how the Qur'an makes sense of its Abrahamic heritage to chart its own future.

❧❧❧

In the Qur'an's view of the world, humanity is naturally monotheistic. From the moment of creation, humans believed in one ultimate architect of the universe. "Remember, when your Divine Mentor created Adam and his progeny and asked them: 'Am I not your Divine Mentor?' And they responded: 'Yes . . .'" (7:172).

As humans broke into diverse tribes, they began developing their own distinctive names for the one master source of life. The Qur'an itself deploys over one hundred names for God and observes: "Call the Divine as *Allah* or as *Ar-Rahman*, for the Divine has many beautiful names" (17:110). An ancient clay tablet from Mesopotamia (modern-day Iraq) reflects the concept of an ultimate creator with multiple monikers: "As many a name as we have called him, he shall be our God. . . . Verily, he is the God, the creator of everything."

Yet because this grand divinity transcended the material world, it could not be directly seen or experienced by human beings. Feeling cut off, some humans instinctively sought more tangible intermediaries to intercede with this remote unseen spirit. They began by fashioning statues to represent a deceased ancestor renowned for his or her wisdom as an inspirational role model. As the years passed, the lived connection to that parent or grandparent receded, and new generations began addressing the statue as an intercessor with the great yet distant divinity, eventually coming to venerate the statue itself as divine.

The Qur'an refers to these worshippers as *Mushrikun*, invoking an Arabic term for a junior partner (*sharik*) in a business venture. The Mushrikun devote all their attention to the junior partner, neglecting the actual owner. As one passage observes: "They concocted partners to the Loving Divine from the material of His own creation, unwittingly inventing sons and daughters for the Creator" (6:100). With time, these invented stand-ins took on a life of their own as inherited dogma. The Qur'an quotes the people of Mecca abjuring any responsibility for polytheism: "We merely worship these idols because our ancestors before us had done so, as we are merely progeny following in their footsteps" (7:173).

Blindly inheriting idols reflected how polytheism froze critical thinking. A stone statue might be designed to appear awe-inspiring, but its inherent lack of physical dynamism signified a stagnant worldview. The Qur'an repeatedly invokes the Arabic term for idol—*sanam*—literally, "frozen in time."

Despite being inanimate rocks, the idols nonetheless required sacrifices from humans. Polytheistic deities needed to be appeased, lest they renounce their patronage of a particular tribe. A portion of every harvest would be offered on altars set up before each statue, the grains and fruit lit aflame and burned as a tribute with the resulting smoke providing sustenance to the gods. Beyond smoke, the gods also demanded blood. Typically, an animal sacrifice would suffice, but in moments of extreme need people would offer their most prized possession: their own young children.

The Qur'an shudders at this tradition, which remained prevalent in Mecca when the Qur'an was revealed. (Muhammad's own father was nearly sacrificed as a ten-year-old to two idols in downtown Mecca.) As one verse observes, the deadly ritual of child sacrifice was the product of manipulation: "Many among the polytheists are manipulated [*zuyyina*] to see false goodness in killing their children as sacrifices to their gods" (6:137). The Arabic term *zuyyina* referred to using makeup and jewelry to cover up defects, artificially transforming something undesirable to appear attractive. "The flesh and blood of sacrifices do not reach the Loving Divine," whom the Qur'an elsewhere describes as the one "who feeds and is not fed" (22:37 and 6:14).

Polytheistic gods were not simply malicious and amoral, but incapable of nurturing life and inspiring human beings. The Qur'an repeatedly demands: "Show me what these idols have created either on earth or in the heavens." It challenges polytheists directly: "Can any of your idols guide your people to the truth?" (10:35).

Even as flawed human beings inevitably corrupt and obscure the natural monotheistic order, all hope is not lost. Just as inevitably, prophets emerge to issue bold calls to restore a nurturing relationship with the Divine. As the Qur'an explains, "Humanity was of one faith, then they transgressed against each other, so the Loving Divine sends the prophets as guides" (2:213). The English term "prophet" suggests someone foretelling the future, yet Semitic prophets are more focused on recovering a precious heritage in order to chart a better future. The *Nabi,* the Semitic term for prophet, describes an unlikely source of water bubbling up in an unexpected location, like a desert spring. The *Nabi* is rarely a prominent elite, but rather an unlikely leader who self-lessly connects with divine truth that inexorably bubbles up inside.

One of the earliest prophets is a modest carpenter named Noah (*Nuh* in Arabic), whom the Qur'an describes as a creative craftsman who invents ply-wood (*alwah*) and nails (*dusur*) and builds the first-ever wooden boat. He observes his idolatrous neighbors abusing one another in fits of envy, trying to undermine other people's success even at their own expense. An intuitive advice giver, Noah urges his community to "honor the Loving Divine who created you" (71:3) and cites all the bounties God has provided: crops, rain, health, children, security, and more. He argues his neighbors have upset the natural balance by turning to idolatry, with the polytheistic pantheon instead inspiring envy and hostility. The outcome, he warns, is that rainwater will transform from a nourishing source of life into a force of deadly destruction.

Noah's advice falls on deaf ears. His neighbors ostracize him and even threaten assassination, before a great flood sweeps them away and humanity must refresh itself. Soon enough, polytheism returns as imperfect human be-ings eventually lose touch with their heritage. Idolatry proliferates once again.

Enter Abraham. At the tender age of twelve, he begins questioning the family business: his father's profession is fashioning idols for their commu-nity in Babylon. Driven by a deep sense of integrity, Abraham cannot make sense of idolatry, immediately seeing through its materialistic façade and the abuse it engenders. To try to awaken his father and community, Abraham poses sharp, direct questions:

> We inspired Abraham with the nuances of critical thinking at a young age and
> bestowed upon him the art of incisive argumentation. Recall when he said to
> his father and tribe: "What are these statutes to which you devote so much ef-
> fort?" They replied: "We found our ancestors devoted to them." He said, "Did
> you not consider that perhaps you and your ancestors may be misinformed?"

They answered: "Are you seriously inquiring or merely mocking us?" He insisted: "Indeed, your true Divine Mentor is the One who created the heaven and the earth, to which I am a witness."

Then he thought to himself about his people: "I shall reveal to you how useless your idols truly are, but only after you depart." So he smashed all the idols [at the main temple] except for the largest among them, to use as an example. When the people discovered the destruction, they cried out in anger, "Who defiled our gods?" Some said, "We recall a youth named Abraham who questioned them." They said, "Bring him before a public prosecution and call witnesses to testify against him." They demanded: "Oh Abraham, was it you who did this to our gods?" He replied, "Perhaps it was the large idol who did it, as the axe lies beside him and he remains the only one left standing. Why not ask the smashed idols, if they can speak?"

At that moment, they realized that their gods were helpless and recognized the error of their ways. Yet indignation overcame them, and they cried: "You know very well that these can neither hear nor speak!" So he asked: "How can you devote yourselves to something that can neither benefit nor harm you? I am surprised at you and what you call gods! Why not expend your efforts in employing your intellect instead?" (21:51–68)

The answer to young Abraham's suggestion is a resounding "no." Abraham's father disowns him, his neighbors attempt to burn him alive, and he flees into the wilderness. Yet Abraham cannot stop asking honest questions, and each new community he enters promptly evicts him, sending Abraham on a journey hundreds of miles along the Fertile Crescent from his birthplace in southern Mesopotamia all the way to Egypt. Without any mentors or direct divine revelation, Abraham must form his new identity by observing the world around him and devising answers to his probing questions.

In the Qur'an's telling, Abraham after much reflection declares himself a *Hanifam-Muslima* (3:67). Typically translated as "a pure Muslim," both words were archaic Arabic terms at the time of the Qur'an's revelation and together constituted a dynamic new identity for young Abraham. The root *Hanif* (cited twelve times in the Qur'an) originally described a tree precariously balanced atop eroding soil in a volatile climate, forced to constantly adjust its roots and branches—and was also used to describe traversing a perilous lava formation. The term connoted the need to constantly rebalance in order to stay safe in unstable situations: remaining true to core roots while having the courage to confront reality. In essence, a *Hanif* is a healthy skeptic who honestly evaluates inherited traditions.

In Abraham's formula, the *Hanif* interrogates reality not as a cynic but as a healer, diagnosing injuries in order to repair them. Indeed, *Muslim* derived from the ancient Semitic root *S-L-M*, literally "to repair cracks in city walls." As the integrity of monotheism erodes over time, repairers need to assess the damage and then get to work restoring the fractures.

Only after Abraham fashions his new identity does the Divine open a direct conversation. God establishes a special covenant with Abraham, promising that Abraham's legacy will continue to impact a large multitude in the future, with spiritual descendants as numerous as the stars. The Qur'an calls this a *Mithaq* (5:12)—literally, a delicate braided strand fused from diverse wild grasses. In forming this agreement, God also gives Abraham a new title, one never before bestowed upon a human being. "[God] said, 'I shall make you an *Imam* for all people.' And Abraham responded: 'And from my descendants too'" (2:124).

While Abraham, like Noah, has limited direct impact on the people around him, he nonetheless lays down a lasting foundation for those after him to transform the world. To help his two sons (and their own progeny) serve as guides who help others emerge from darkness, Abraham builds with each of them a special sanctuary. In Jerusalem, he and Isaac together construct a "masjid"—literally, "a place of re-grounding"—with a parallel masjid erected with Ishmael at Mecca. The Qur'an also describes the two structures with the term *Bayt*—literally "a place where one can repose in peace." The word implies philosophical values accompanying a physical building, as the structures serve as concrete manifestations of monotheistic values. Specifically designed as empty buildings without idols, the sacred emptiness provides a safe refuge where all people can turn inward for inspiration, to return to the outside world with renewed purpose. In Abraham's vision, these unique shrines would help promote the open exchange of ideas, with people circulating from Mecca to Jerusalem and back.

Aside from building the simple sanctuaries, Abraham remains primarily a theorist of the empowering potential of monotheism. His descendants initially do not create a grand civic order, growing first into a tribe and then a nation—with their formational peoplehood experience under the oppressive yoke of pagan slave masters. To liberate monotheism from polytheistic repression, Moses emerges as another unlikely prophet. An impulsive man raised by his people's enslavers in the royal palace, he instinctively feels a force within himself, yet initially struggles to effectively channel it. He kills a slave overseer in a fit of righteous anger and flees into the wilderness like his ancestor Abraham.

What Moses—and by extension his people—need is a healthy structure to direct latent potential. A sudden divine revelation from a blazing bush dramatically catapults Moses onto the prophetic path of leadership, as God sends him to confront the most powerful ruler in the world: a pharaoh who considers himself to be a god on earth. Moses' task is not simply to free his people from physical bondage, but to liberate their minds to think for themselves. Emancipating the mind will prove far more difficult than physically escaping Egypt.

Moses' epic achievement is establishing a divinely inspired system for provoking both Abrahamic critical thinking (*Hanif*) and channeling it toward restorative growth (*Muslim*). This system, embodied in a scripture called the Torah ("instruction" or "guidance"), had to be accessible and practical for ordinary people, with structures designed to assist free-thinkers to unleash their individual potential. Not surprisingly, Moses finds the generation of emancipated slaves quite set in their ways despite the dramatic exodus from Egypt. He ultimately concentrates his energies on training a new generation of disciples—"Only the youth among Moses' people were open to his message" (10:83).

After several centuries cut off from their roots, this new generation of Israelites establishes an independent community in their ancestral homeland. This nascent entity is free to apply monotheistic values in an open civic context. Inspired by the system bequeathed by Moses, the Israelites quickly achieve financial and material success, which in turn sparks envy and hostility from their neighbors. Beset by constant raids, the Israelites struggle to assemble an effective force to protect their fragile community.

Into the void steps a young shepherd boy named David ("the beloved"). The youngest of eight sons, he happens upon a battle with the intimidating army of the Philistines and their massive hero, Goliath. Unable to watch passively as the Israelites cower in fear, a defiant David instinctively marches to the front of the battle. Both the Philistines and the Israelites laugh at the youth's seemingly foolish audacity. Undeterred, David wields his simple slingshot—used to ward off predators attacking his flock—to slay Goliath with one pebble.

This young hero eventually rises to become Israel's king, transforming the fragmented Israelite polity into a political powerhouse to be reckoned with.

David establishes the first-ever secure monotheistic nation with freedom, resources, creativity, manpower, and spiritual inspiration. At the site of Abraham
and Isaac's original sanctuary in Jerusalem, he constructs a grand new capital.
Beyond impressive secular material accomplishments, David also composes the
legendary psalms, beautiful poems of praise for the Divine. "Even the mountains and birds were swayed by David's melodious chanting," observes the
Qur'an, adding: "We taught David the art of manufacturing lightweight armor"
(21:78–80). The Qur'an describes David as a leader of many skills (*Thal-aydi*)
yet humble (*Awwab*), calling him a *Khalifah*—literally, an orchard caretaker.
Adam is the only other Quranic figure to earn the moniker for his tending
to the Garden of Eden. David earns the title for establishing a second Eden.

Under David's son Solomon, monotheistic influence reaches its climax, with
the Qur'an presenting Jerusalem under his rule as the epitome of advanced
monotheistic civilization. A precociously discerning youth like his ancestor
Abraham, King Solomon becomes a master communicator who gathers wisdom from wherever he can, even learning to communicate with animals. In
957 BCE, armed with deep insights gathered from many cultures and vast
financial resources, Solomon martialed an army of thousands of builders to
construct a magnificent temple for the Divine in the heart of Jerusalem, set
atop the foundations laid by Abraham and Isaac on Mount Moriah. "We gave
him the knowledge of the essence of manufacturing and molding bronze. . . .
His skilled craftsmen made whatever he desired, magnificent buildings, sophisticated statues, imposing monuments, and gigantic vats. . . ." (34:12–13).

As part of his diplomatic exchange of ideas with foreign powers, Solomon
invites the Queen of Sheba, herself ruler of a great empire in southern Arabia,
to visit Jerusalem. Entering the Temple, the queen encounters a remarkable
feat of engineering. "As soon as she entered the grand hall, she thought that its
floor was a large pool and so she lifted her skirt, exposing her calves, prompting Solomon to explain: 'It is merely a well-polished crystal floor.'" (27:44)

The massive sheet of translucent crystal embodies the magnificent potential of unbridled monotheistic creativity, an impressive physical accomplishment as well as a symbol of the unseen Divine's inspiring, nourishing flow.
The queen is instantly won over and returns to southern Arabia a devoted
monotheist. Solomon, for his part, continues his father's prophetic legacy by
composing the *Song of Songs,* a beautiful meditation on love and devotion that
celebrates God's greatest gift to humanity.

With Solomon, Abraham's original monotheistic vision of unleashed potential is realized on a grand scale. Indeed, Solomon's own name derives from the root *S-L-M*—specifically in a form that describes achieving a state of fulfillment following extensive restorative work. The theory of Abraham and the structure of Moses at last culminates in a complete package.

ళ్లీ

Solomon's magnificent achievements could not overcome the age-old human tendency to disconnect from the Divine. As the monotheistic political empire he forged achieved great success, it began to atrophy from within. His successors, enjoying inherited wealth and advanced infrastructure, lacked the drive to keep innovating and instead began to stagnate, and surrounding pagan empires began to outshine them. Whereas Solomon had once confidently leveraged diplomacy to spread monotheistic inspiration to foreign societies, subsequent Israelite kings began to import idols from powerful neighboring empires, compromising their core identities to appease potential external threats.

The Qur'an bitterly recalls this betrayal of the Abrahamic heritage. "Remember when the Loving Divine established a covenant with the leaders of the People of the Book to make knowledge accessible and not conceal it. Yet they cast the Torah behind their backs and sold it for a meagre sum. What a shameful transaction!" (3:187).

Appeasement as a policy soon failed. The powerful Babylonian empire, desiring the vast treasures stored in Jerusalem's Temple, conquered the Holy Land in 586 BCE—razing the building to its foundations. The once glorious city of Jerusalem lay in ruins, a physical embodiment of a spiritual collapse. The Babylonians seized not only the Temple's material wealth but also carted off its human capital, taking the Israelites' priests, scholars, and skilled elite back to the court in Babylon—where the exiles wept by its rivers.

To dominate the Arabian spice trade, the Babylonians set up military garrisons in 542 BCE, along a network of six oases along the traditional caravan route. Needing talented manpower for these new towns, Babylonian leaders forcibly resettled some of the Israelite elites in the middle of the Arabian desert as vassals. These first Jews of Arabia (many of them descendants of King David and Temple priests) experienced a new forced journey into the wilderness and faced the challenge of defining a way to retain their identity in isolation. The southernmost garrison town they named Yathrib ("God makes fertile").

Amidst this existential crisis, the Israelites at least had the benefit of ongoing prophetic revelation. In the time period surrounding the Temple's destruction and the Israelites' exile throughout the Middle East, some of the most eloquent prophets emerged, bewailing the Israelites' fallen state while nonetheless insisting on future redemption with the reclamation of the original Abrahamic legacy. These prophets continued the tradition of *Hanif* and *Muslim*—directly calling out failures while simultaneously proposing remedies.

When a benevolent Persian king named Kurush (Cyrus the Great) took over the Babylonian empire, he allowed the rebuilding of Jerusalem in 538 BCE. Many Jewish elites nonetheless chose to remain in Babylon, as well as Arabia, creating a permanent Diaspora. In Jerusalem, a modest version of the Temple was rebuilt, though the great Solomonic spirit of innovation was less easily revived. Without a strong independent kingdom, Israelites primarily directed their energies to economic ventures, amassing wealth but demonstrating limited intellectual innovation. Prophets came and went, the last one (Malachi) preaching around 420 BCE. Then the stream of revelation suddenly ceased, ending the golden era of Jewish prophecy.

In 332 BCE, Alexander the Great annexed Jerusalem yet allowed the Israelites to live in peace. This period of tranquility proved to be a double-edged sword, as Greek language, culture, and mentality began to permeate Jewish society. A Hellenic worldview imposed itself over the Jews' ancient Semitic culture, and many elites assimilated deeply into Greek culture. One top priest was so thoroughly immersed in Greek that he lacked the Hebrew and Aramaic language skills to read the Bible. To appease their Greek overlords, some priests even allowed Greek idols to be erected in the Temple courtyard.

As Greek rulers grew even less tolerant of Jewish life—one even forbade Sabbath observance—a grassroots uprising, circa 167 BCE, by principled Temple priests called the Maccabees (possibly from the Aramaic *Maqqabah*— "hammer" or "to leave a mark") managed to evict the Greeks and their Jewish allies. The Maccabees purified the Temple in a rededication commemorated every year in the Hanukkah celebration, and for fifty years the Holy Land enjoyed independent Jewish rule and a revival of Semitic monotheism. But before this nascent polity had a chance to reclaim Solomon's legacy, the

Roman empire eyed their treasures, conquering the Holy Land and raiding the Temple treasury twice, in both 63 and 54 BCE.

Once again, political machinations led the Temple priests and Jewish elite to corruption. Temple rituals continued, but the spirit was lacking. Priests sought to please their Roman masters and neglected their flock. Religious practice took on increasingly rigid and ostentatious forms, more of an external show than a spiritual evocation of Abrahamic values. Dismayed at the rot seeping into Jewish life, a young rabbi named Yashua' (Jesus) emerged to lead a grassroots reformation movement. In the *Hanif* spirit, he challenged the corrupt clergy with damning questions as he sought to return the spirit of the Torah back into the hands of ordinary people.

To engage Jews excluded by the harsh and judgmental elite, Jesus insisted on preaching out in nature to mass audiences. To renew appreciation for a loving and compassionate Divine, Jesus sat alongside the poor and the outcast, most notably lepers. The Qur'an praises his revolutionary message: "Walking in the footsteps [of previous prophets] came Jesus, the son of Mary, reaffirming all that was revealed before him and reviving the Torah's spirit; we inspired him with the Gospel, containing guidance and illuminating light. . . ." (5:46). The Arabic term for Gospel, *Injil,* plays off the original Greek *euangelos* ("bringing good news"), but with a twist on the Semitic root *N-J-L,* meaning "opening eyes wide." The name reflected Jesus' mission to deliver his people from the bondage of blindly following corrupt clerics by reawakening individual powers of perception.

The Qur'an calls Jesus *Al-Masih,* the Messiah—literally, "the anointed one" or "the one who wipes away injustice." Rather than adopting the Jewish framing of the messiah as a political redeemer, the Qur'anic understanding of the messiah is a reformer anointed by God to revive the theory of Abraham and the structure of Moses. Or, in a related sense, as a great clarifier who wipes away the filmy haze obscuring clear understanding.

Like many of the prophets who came before him, Jesus attracted both an intense following and harsh opposition. In the span of just three years of preaching, he reignited the age-old Jewish spirit of rebellion against oppression. Both the priestly elites and the Romans regarded him as a threatening agitator—this even though Jesus often spoke in parables as a way to deliver his bold critique in a less directly provocative manner.

One of the fiercest antagonists of Jesus' message was a Jewish priest named

Shaul (Paul), who suddenly experienced an epiphany and transformed into the most zealous promoter of his understanding of Jesus' message. Of the Gospel's twenty-seven books, Paul is thought to have authored thirteen. One of Paul's contributing impacts was to extend the awareness of Jesus far beyond the Jewish community, taking the Abrahamic monotheistic message to all people with fervor while suggesting that Mosaic law was no longer relevant.

A few decades after Jesus' time, dissident agitation in the Holy Land became too intense for the Romans to tolerate. The Roman army besieged Jerusalem in 70 CE and sacked the Temple, raiding its treasury for funds to build the Coliseum (completed in 80 CE). Soldiers destroyed the structure down to its foundations, turning the bare plaza into a trash heap. After a failed Jewish revolt in 132 CE, the Romans permanently banned Jews from Jerusalem and sent most into exile, a kind of reverse Exodus as Jews slipped back into servitude. Fragmented across hundreds of dispersed communities, Jews became politically impotent, applying monotheism only inside their own quarters and praying thrice daily toward the destroyed Temple in Jerusalem.

Rather than retreat inward, the evangelical followers of Jesus focused outward, marketing their message to the pagan masses. The appeal of their pitch lay in its simplicity: anyone could become one of God's chosen people by joining the Brotherhood in Jesus Christ. Harnessing monotheistic energy for mass liberation, these devout followers invited people of all backgrounds to join a Catholic (from the Greek *katholikos*—"universal") movement. One of the effects of this early movement (under both Paul and the disciple Peter) was to abrogate most Jewish restrictions regulating everyday lifestyle, there were few onerous obligations that converts needed to adopt. The new movement acted as a fluid and flexible version of Abrahamic monotheism, emphasizing spirit rather than the grounding structure of Mosaic law.

By the year 100 CE, the inchoate movement began to develop a formal identity—adopting the moniker "Christian" for the first time. Following Paul's teachings, a creed would eventually emerge to further define the movement, one emphasizing the divine nature of Jesus and his martyrdom as a sacrifice to redeem believers from humanity's original sin. Gospel letters by followers spreading the "good news" about Jesus were sent out in all directions, driving two centuries of steady recruiting growth despite intense Roman persecution.

For the first time, two monotheistic movements claimed the mantle of Abraham—with Christians insisting that their church was the New Israel enjoying a renewed divine covenant and dismissing the Jews as people forsaken by God. In this narrative, the "Old Testament" instead prefigured Jesus and the Church. Adopting the attitude of the skeptical *Hanif,* early Christians challenged Jews about their religion, asking hard-hitting questions. Most Jews struggled to respond, and many joined the new upstart movement.

Jews had never needed to compete against fellow monotheists (aside from the Samaritan schism after the Babylonian exile), let alone ones claiming their own scripture to undermine them. As Judaism lacked an easily accessible theology, the rabbis urgently sought to develop a counter message that could shore up their followers from attrition. Around 200 CE, rabbis began developing the *Pirke Avot,* a collection of wisdom literature, and the *Mishnah* ("study via repetition"), a compiled set of commentaries clarifying Biblical scripture.

A century later, they expanded the effort to launch a mega-project compiling Jewish oral tradition into a grand work known as the *Talmud* ("instruction"). Paralleling Moses' groundbreaking codification of Jewish law, the Talmud provided a structure for guiding a dispersed community in exile. The process took two centuries, led primarily by rabbis in Mesopotamia, where the upper class had remained since the first exile and established academies in Sura and Pumbedita on the periphery of the Persian empire. Jewish merchants traveling to Babylon for business brought questions to the academies and explained how they were under intellectual pressure from rising Christian communities.

As the Jews worked on their grand scholarly ventures, Christianity continued its steady growth. The new movement capitalized on massive social disruption caused by a major third-century economic crisis. With the Roman empire suddenly unable to provide stable currency and reliable security for its inhabitants, Christianity filled the vacuum by offering a compelling message of renewed purpose in a time of crisis. Recognizing the unifying power of the emerging religion, Armenia became the first state to adopt Christianity in 301 CE, part of an accelerating trend.

Under pressure, the Roman emperor Constantine soon rescinded the ban on Christianity, and in 325 CE hosted the formal Council of Nicaea where diverse Christian leaders formalized a unified theological creed identifying Jesus as the son of God and selecting the four main canonical Gospels. The emperor himself became Christian and sponsored the building of churches across the empire, even putting the cross on his flag. In 380 CE, Nicaean Christianity formally became the sole official state religion of the Roman empire. Yet nothing in Christian theology had prepared the movement for political power. Jesus had preached ethics as a social reformer, not as a political theorist. Lacking guidelines, Christianity assimilated into the existing Roman political structure—which, in an ironic reversal, soon launched the state-directed persecution of pagans.

Firmly ensconced in power, Christians no longer sought to establish their legitimacy primarily by arguing with Jews. Instead, their main ire turned to fellow Christians. Intense civil wars and bloody massacres soon raged, many fueled by trivial squabbles over the choice of adjectives used in declarations of creed. Arguments over a single word could unleash the murder of thousands. Seeking refuge from these deadly debates, many weak minority Christian movements fled to the Arabian desert. Waraqah, the cousin of Muhammad's wife Khadijah, belonged to one such movement (probably the Ebionites), which maintained many aspects of Jewish law while accepting Jesus as the Messiah but not divine.

The Jews of Arabia lived relatively unmolested in their desert enclaves. Excerpts of the Talmud gradually made their way to them via merchant caravans, engaging local scholars in the latest rabbinic discourse. On his return from a military expedition in northern Arabia, As'ad Abu Karib, the king of Yemen, stopped in the oasis of Yathrib for emergency medical care. Impressed by the two rabbis who nursed him back to health, he decided to become Jewish—an echo of the Queen of Sheba's conversion. His kingdom adopted Judaism in 390 CE, and for the first time in centuries a Jewish political power emerged on the scene. The main divine moniker used by this Jewish empire was *Rahman* ("optimistically empowering and compassionate"), a term later preserved in the Qur'an. By the year 527 CE the empire crumbled, with its last king, Thu-Nuwas, riding his horse out into the raging sea, instead of surrendering to the invading Abyssinian forces.

The spiritual world the Qur'an encountered was thus monotheism ascendant but in chaotic crisis. Ironically, claimants to the mantle of Abraham, whose very name means "compassionate patriarch," were splintered by violent divides. A rich and ancient ancestry lay obscured amidst the dust and debris.

❧

Observing the Qur'an many centuries after its initial revelation, one might understandably assume that it refers to a coherent independent Muslim community centered around a theological doctrine, defined political entity, and robust scholarly corpus. Yet the book's references to "Islam" and "Muslims" are not to any formal organized religion with a dogma, but rather the monotheistic mindset of an emerging civic reform movement operating amidst a fluctuating social context.

"Islam" refers not to a religious sect but rather a mindset of "striving to repair and restore fractures," with Muslims embracing the brokenness in all humans while striving to emulate the only perfect being: God. Everyone from Abraham down to Jesus' disciples earns the moniker "Muslim." Rather than present a distinctive doctrinal faith, the Qur'an reveals an identity in process of formation, infusing the ancient values of past monotheistic prophets with contemporary relevance.

In one sense, the Qur'an regards the Torah and the Gospel as older siblings—and looks on with dismay at the family feud tearing apart Abrahamic cohesion. In another sense, the Qur'an exists as an orphan. It presents the first Abrahamic scripture in Arabic, delivered by an Arabian prophet. Claiming a lineage back to the Torah yet revealed in a thoroughly pagan society, the Qur'an enjoys an insider-outsider status—one that empowers it to look lovingly yet critically at its ancestry. This complex inheritance means the Qur'an is aware of its roots yet free to develop its own identity without being confined by parental oversight.

Unlike Christianity, the Qur'an feels no need to deny the past or replace its older siblings. Its main opening chapter thrice sends the same reassuring message: "Oh, Children of Israel, remember my favors upon you and that I have chosen you over all the worlds." Moreover, it seeks to mediate between clashing relatives: "The Jews proclaim, 'The Christians have no solid foundation,' and the Christians respond, 'The Jews have no solid foundation'—yet both have a foundation, reciting the same scriptures" (2:113). Its plea for reconciliation focuses on these shared values: "Oh, People of the Book, let us seek common grounds between us and you" (3:64).

The Qur'an unequivocally and repeatedly affirms past scriptures and prophets. "We believe in the Loving Divine and what has been revealed to us and to Abraham, Ishmael, Isaac, Jacob, the Tribes of Israel, Moses, and Jesus, and what has been given to all the prophets from their Divine Mentor—we do not favor one over the over" (2:136 and 3:84). The content of those past revelations is warmly and constantly cited by the Qur'an, with both biblical vignettes and rabbinic content serving as rich material for moral insights.

Sometimes the Qur'an directly acknowledges its antecedents. "It was for this reason [the fratricide between Cain and Abel], we wrote in the Scripture of the children of Israel that anyone who kills one soul unjustly or spreads discord throughout the land, it is as if they killed all humanity, and whoever saves one soul it is as if they saved all of humanity" (5:32). Interestingly, the quote is a slight modification of Mishnah 4:5: "It was for this reason [the fratricide between Cain and Abel] that man was first created as one person, to teach you that anyone who destroys a life is considered by Scripture to have destroyed an entire world; and anyone who saves a life is as if he saved an entire world."

In other cases, the Qur'an adopts evocative Talmudic metaphors without direct acknowledgment. For example, Rabbi Eliezer (first century CE), quoted in the Talmud, declares: "If all the seas were ink and all the reeds writing pens, and the heaven and earth scrolls, and the people of the world were scribes, there would not be enough room to write all the Torah I have learned, and yet I have not extracted from it more than a man who dips a brush into the sea." Twice the Qur'an picks up on the same oceanic allegory for wisdom: "Were all the earth's trees reeds and all the seas ink, with seven more seas to swell its tide, the wisdom of the Divine Mentor would not end" (31:27), and "Had the seas been ink for the words of my Divine Mentor, the seas would not suffice to transcribe all of my Divine Mentor's wisdom" (18:109).

The Qur'an does not hesitate to retell biblical incidents with modifications—or to introduce entirely new vignettes around iconic biblical figures. As a book purposely not constructed around a formal narrative, the Qur'an leverages these allusions primarily to emphasize a moral value rather than reveal an origin story. Every time the Qur'an presents a story, it always follows with terse analyses synthesizing key takeaways.

Stylistically, the Qur'an often mimics the approaches of past prophecy. Sometimes it echoes wisdom statements with timeless truisms. Just as Jeremiah declares: "The heart is deceitful above all things and beyond cure—who can understand it?" the Qur'an observes: "There is vitality in accountability, oh you who are wise of heart!" (2:179). Other times it mirrors how past prophets delivered social critiques of elite leaders cloaked in metaphors, citing Pharaoh as a stand-in for corrupt Meccan leaders. Echoing the inspiration and pedagogic power of Jesus' parables, the Qur'an abounds with simple allegories to convey complex ideas.

While deeply admiring and affirming past prophets, the Qur'an casts a critical eye on human misapplication of their revelations. "Our prophetic guides came to them with clarifying signs, yet many among them soon lapsed, spreading disorder in the land" (5:32). The perpetual dynamic of monotheistic values revived by prophets only to be subsequently squandered by humans is what concerns the Qur'an. It diagnoses a range of repeated failures, including: losing a close relationship with the Divine and reverting to idolatry; debating minutiae as an excuse to avoid bold action; imposing dogma not found in scripture and turning petty disputes over dogma into deadly violence; and elites selfishly abusing their leadership positions to mislead and manipulate.

In that light, it is worth reconsidering the verse some translate as "Do not consider the Jews and Christians as your friends. . . ." What sounds supremacist when mistranslated is actually an admonition to be wary of corrupt leaders: "Do not blindly rely upon the judgment of Jewish and Christian scholars in all matters, for they can allow themselves to be unjust even unto their own people. If you do [blindly follow], know that your state will be akin to theirs. The Loving Divine does not bestow serenity upon those who choose to remain in darkness" (5:51).

When the Qur'an critically evaluates the individual behavior of certain Jews, Christians, and pagans, it does so because these individuals serve as models for both what to do and not to do. Compared to the standards of harsh prophetic chastisement found in the revelations of Jeremiah and Ezekiel, the Qur'an is a gentle critic—despite attempts by some translators to heighten the tension. Similarly, the verse allegedly declaring those who do not choose Islam end up "among the losers" delivers a very different caution, one that draws lessons from the dynamics of monotheistic history to warn about future mistakes: "Any person who chooses a mindset other than one committed to restoration will fail to progress and ultimately emerge empty-handed and at a loss." (3:85)

That is not to say that the Qur'an blindly accepts tradition. Rather, upholding the legacy of Abraham requires behaving like a *Hanif*: every generation must open its eyes to honestly assess the past in order to chart the best path forward. The *Hanif* respects heritage by honestly interrogating it. Just as every individual determines for themselves what parts of their inherited identity they will and will not uphold, the Qur'an maintains, rejects, and adapts aspects of Jewish and Christian tradition in forming its own unique support structure.

As it devises its own system, the Qur'an takes pains to explain its reasoning. For example, the admonition against indulging in alcohol and gambling is justified by the "immense social harm" both can cause, especially the ripple effect of damage to others via drunken violence and crippling debt (addicts in Arabia often sold their own children into slavery to repay debts).

Healthy outcomes are the primary goal of the Qur'an's discernment process. It seeks to empower all people with the Judaic sense of elevated consciousness—not because they are chosen but because they have the individual freedom to choose a path of healing and growth. Yet Christianity's universalist impulse still requires an underlying structure to help guide people toward the healthy path, and so the Qur'an demurs from following Paul's decision to relinquish the stabilizing force of Mosaic law. Indeed, the Qur'an's grand opening chapter fills many of its 286 verses defining specific social obligations that can elevate the individual and society.

The first passage of the Qur'an's grand opening chapter takes on new meaning in light of the book's nuanced Abrahamic ancestry. *Thalik-al-Kitabu la rayba fihi hudal-lil-Muttaqin,* initially confused with its unusual beginning: "That . . ." Read in context, the verse reveals an aspirational goal for what the Qur'an aims to inspire as a new chapter in the ancient monotheistic discourse: "Given all that has come before, the book shall have no confusion, for its purpose is to provide guidance for those seeking action-based hope." (2:2)

What has come before is an inspiring tool that can be harnessed to unlock human potential to achieve dynamic innovation. Yet what also has come before is a recurring pattern of obscuring and corrupting that powerful mindset, requiring the emergence of unlikely prophets to reawaken, reconnect, and revitalize. Whenever Abraham's descendants slip into stagnation, reducing their precious heritage to a talismanic relic to be revered without being enacted, they ironically hold the solution to their problem in their own hands. But because they allow confusion to cloud that original clear guidance, they struggle to advance.

The Qur'an recognizes it is not immune from the same fate that befell previous scriptures. After all, it is only a revelation, dependent on imperfect mortals for its enactment. Late in its existence, the Qur'an worries about a future time when it will be treated like a "hallowed yet hollow site," (25:30) zealously preserved yet not applied. By expressing that concern, it hopes to preempt the human tendency to venerate yet stagnate, to read the words but miss the underlying spirit.

Like the Arabic language, Abrahamic monotheism is merely a tool. Only what human beings choose to do with that heritage can be transformed into something sacred.

3

❁

AUDIENCE: STAGNANT SEVENTH-CENTURY ARABIA

THE QUR'AN SPEAKS ONLY WHEN IT HAS AN AUDIENCE—OTHERWISE, IT remains silent. In fact, the Qur'an spends over two years in seclusion (617–619) while its prophet remains isolated in a desert concentration camp during an intense boycott by the Meccan elite. To understand the Qur'an, therefore, requires knowing whom it addresses. While its wisdom may be timeless, it was not revealed in a vacuum, but rather in a particular social and historical context to a particular set of people, constantly adapting to its evolving audiences in seventh-century Arabia.

For a work calling itself "The Blossoming," the Qur'an faces a challenge as all its immediate audiences are, each in their own way, stuck in stagnation. These include Arab pagans clinging to tradition at all costs; Jews exiled from Jerusalem sojourning in Arabia for centuries while awaiting a Messiah to redeem them to Zion; and Christians hung up on theological dogma, which has shattered their cohesion. The handful of people in Arabia with whom the Qur'an initially resonates are themselves all minorities of a sort: individuals in bondage, independent-minded women constrained by tradition, and talented elites frustrated with the status quo.

And then there is the Qur'anic prophet: an insider-outsider born into a society obsessed with tradition; an orphan constrained by his social status; a self-made entrepreneur reluctantly transformed into a prophet; a truth-teller facing severe pushback from elite society (including boycotts and assassination attempts); a man constantly rebuilding his life in the face of enormous setbacks; and suddenly, in the final two years of his life, a ruler achieving unimaginable success, with sway over millions of followers.

At different moments, the Qur'an speaks to each of these specific audiences while simultaneously delivering a universal and eternal message. To better unravel the connections between the immediate and enduring long-term message, traditional Islamic scholarship is passionate about deciphering the specific historical context and direct audience for each Qur'anic passage. Qur'anic commentaries (*Tafsir*) abound with substantial debates over what prompted a specific revelation and to whom it was addressed.

One reason *Tafsir* disputes are so intense is because the Qur'an constantly shifts its voice. Arabic grammar provides nuances about audience: A verb can be addressed to a singular, dual, or plural "you." A narrator can speak in the first-person "I" or "we." The Qur'an does all of these and more. Thus, readers constantly struggle to decrypt to whom a passage is addressed—and in whose voice Qur'anic text is speaking, as narrator and audience often shift and sometimes even invert.

For example, the Qur'an's introductory preface—the iconic *Al-Fatihah* chapter—speaks in multiple voices. It commences with a narrator urging conduct without directly specifying by whom, literally saying: "Emulation is for the Ultimate Source of Unconditional Love, who gently nourishes growth in all things." The sentence's grammatical form implies that "emulation" should be understood as a command to action ("Emulate the Ultimate Source!") but without clarifying any specific target audience—a kind of universal truth. The opening verses present the Divine in the third person, with the Qur'an not speaking in the voice of God but as an observer. Yet the fourth verse marks a sudden shift, as a collective plural audience takes over the narrator's voice to address God directly: "We strive to reflect the way You rejuvenate life and trust in Your support to shield our weaknesses. Guide us to navigate a safe path with flexibility." Just as suddenly, the third-person narrator reemerges to describe that "safe path" in more detail as the "we" fades away: "A path previously forged by the foresighted, who steadily restore brokenness to reach a state of serenity. (A path) unconstrained by a stagnant reality of willful manipulation and blind acceptance."

This enigmatically fluctuating narrator and audience is another of the Qur'an's pioneering post-modern techniques, one that grabs readers' attention and forces them into active detective work: Who is "we"? Who is "you"? In past Biblical scriptures, the Divine clearly drives the narrative in conjunction with a third-person narrator: "And thus spoke the Lord. . . ." Yet with its earliest words, the Qur'an provides no such simple clarity and instead intrigues.

The first audience member to be perplexed by the Qur'an's ambiguous voice was none other than Muhammad, who initially found the revelation startling. Its opening word, *Iqra,* surged out in the form of a command: "Blossom forth!" Yet the initial five passages pointedly declined to clarify the source of this bold declaration. Muhammad immediately fled down Mount Hira and rushed home in fright. Shivering beneath a cover of blankets, he contemplated the Qur'an's first word restlessly, unable to sleep.

Muhammad had not been religious before. Suddenly hearing a divine voice at age forty felt bewildering rather than reassuring. Indeed, humans are particularly prone to self-doubt when called upon to embark on a new experience. Hearing a divine command sparked not transcendent elevation, but rather an identity crisis.

With the morning sunlight, however, came a second Qur'anic revelation to calm the novice prophet. It began with a special Arabic word: *Ya.* Translated in English as "Oh!" the term is used by a speaker to capture attention and, in the Qur'an's case, to establish a special connection with its audience. The term is not thrown around casually, but rather used when delivering an important message to someone specific. The Qur'an's second revelation offered the soothing and encouraging voice of a mentor: "Oh, you who are covered up shivering in fear, get up and go out to proclaim the message of self-deliverance." (74:1–2)

With this gentle *Ya,* the Qur'an began a twenty-two-year relationship with the prophet through whom its words emerged into the world. Over these two decades it sought to inspire people of all backgrounds, mostly to be rejected and spurned. Yet those who worked up the courage to be receptive to its message found themselves rewarded with an intimate relationship.

When the Qur'an first emerged on that early March morning, it descended on a vast, barren panorama. The spring rains had sparked only sporadic blossoming: a few shrubs and small patches of grass briefly turned green before reverting to their usual dull-brown desiccated state. Surveying the scene, the Qur'an describes the Meccan landscape—physically and metaphysically—as "a valley devoid of any growth." (14:37)

With no produce cultivated and no artisans manufacturing original products, Mecca thrived on the labor of others. Its merchants bought and sold goods produced in other lands, transported them via camel caravans to new markets, and made their fortunes by maximizing transactions to secure the best deal at any cost. Meccans of all classes relied on enslaved labor for essential manual tasks, from gathering firewood to cooking to even combing hair and bathing. Enslaved people comprised almost half of Mecca's population and drove a social system dependent on forced labor.

Unlike any other city of significance in the world, Mecca had no protective walls or defensive force. The city's talisman was its central cubed shrine, called the *Ka'bah* ("the Nexus"), which designated Mecca as the capital city of Arabia. Built by the patriarch Abraham, the shrine contained 360 devotional statues, one for each of Arabia's major tribes. A site of annual pilgrimage for people across Arabia (another lucrative source of revenue for Meccan elites), the Ka'bah's sacred status bestowed protection on the city. "Anyone who enters there is safe," (3:97) observes the Qur'an, further noting that the Meccans, because of their role as the shrine's custodians, lived "satiated from hunger and protected from fear." (106:4)

Mecca's lack of walls also reflected the town's cultural connection to the nomadic lifestyle prevalent in the surrounding desert. Despite living in a capital city and regularly traveling to great centers of civilization like Damascus, the Meccan elite chose to cultivate a nomadic ethos. From the age of six months, Meccan boys were sent to live with nomads for up to five years, absorbing their pure Arabic as well as their gritty mentality.

As a result, Meccan culture had a distinctively macho, unrefined, stoic, gruff, and cynical flair. Neither punctuality nor hygiene were particularly prized, nor was education, resulting in widespread illiteracy. Reflecting the volatile desert dynamic of sudden massive sandstorms and torrential rains,

Meccans could be impulsive and aggressive, particularly when antagonized. This violent streak, however, manifested itself in disorganized outbursts rather than any formal military prowess.

The Meccans' sole natural resource was genetics. They were, on the whole, impressive physical specimens, admired by outsiders for their distinctive features: durable teeth, strong bones, clear skin, sparkling eyes, and thick, dark hair that only began to gray in late old age. Meccans were handsome, tall, and resistant to most common diseases. The desert environment helped toughen the Arabs' physical constitution, but a more sinister additional factor was the practice of eugenics. Selective breeding, coupled with the killing of any children born with deformities, had deeply impacted the gene pool.

Appearances matter to merchants whose products need to look good to stand out in the marketplace. Given the importance of appearance, the Meccans displayed a particular vanity and evinced a cocky and self-assured attitude, even as their culture lagged far behind the civilized world outside Arabia. At the same time, the mercantile Meccans warily resisted being conned by false flattery. "Cast dirt into the face of flatterers!" cautioned a local maxim in advising how to avoid getting sweet-talked into a bad deal.

Macho Meccan culture, by contrast, appreciated verbal duels. Every year, Arabia's best poets convened in Mecca for an eloquence competition where masters of rhetoric duked it out in extemporaneous rhyming battles, with the winner's poem hung over the Ka'bah's door. Not surprisingly, the Qur'an never tried to flatter the Meccans but rather challenged them with provocative statements to spark a duel of ideas.

Though the Meccans knew that the Ka'bah had originally been established as a purely monotheistic shrine dedicated to Abraham's unseeable God, their ancestors had over the centuries lost a direct connection to the ultimate Divine Master. Instead, the Arabs had come to rely on intermediaries in the form of crude statues crammed onto the Ka'bah's walls. Whereas the Judeo-Christian tradition saw a steady stream of prophets and sages who called on the public to reclaim a lost heritage, the Arabs were—in the Qur'an's words—"a people to whose ancestors no prophet had ever been sent." (36:6)

With no principled voices of reform, the Arabs developed a stunted spirituality. Hollow clay statues—each a rudimentary depiction of an ancient ancestor—provided a shallow veneer of identity rather than a nourishing moral code. To justify their behavior, Arab elites created gods in their own image, defining them as impulsive cutthroat personalities constantly plotting to undermine people rather than uplift them. Tribute to the gods was thus not driven by gratitude but by fear, a kind of extortion racket where human offerings sought to avert the gods' aggression. The Qur'an exposes the superficiality of Meccan idolatry, showing the statues as impotent and frozen objects: "These are merely hollow names that you and your ancestors gave to these images, lacking any substance." (53:23)

Moreover, the Arabs had also lost the ancient belief in an afterlife and a day of judgment where people are held accountable for their actions. Lacking a compelling source of ethical accountability, the Meccan elite could dominate with consequence-free behavior, rigging the social system to their benefit. A Meccan merchant might display generous hospitality and honor to a visiting potential client, yet coldly cheat and abuse his poor neighbor. A massive inequality pervaded Meccan society, with clean and well-dressed elites juxtaposed with dirty and nearly naked lower classes clad in rags.

Underlying it all was a system lacking any uniform standards, with elites constantly altering rules for personal benefit. To justify their self-serving double standards, Meccan elites became experts at evoking necessary loopholes to tradition—an approach they would use repeatedly in their attempts to undermine the Qur'an.

With no afterlife, the Arabs believed they had only one way to achieve immortality: being remembered by their descendants. The only way a man could live on after death was via male progeny who preserved the lineage by the clan's name (itself derived from an esteemed ancestor, like Mecca's main tribe Quraysh) and through poetry praising the deeds of forebears. The Arabs nurtured extremely durable and detailed memories, prizing genealogical expertise and perpetuating vendettas for centuries.

As a result, the Arabs' greatest fear was being forgotten. Every year the camel caravan from Mecca to Damascus passed by the imposing ruins of the once-mighty Nabatean empire. These residents of northern Arabia had amassed great wealth and power, attracting the envy of many outsiders and ultimately succumbing to Roman conquest in the year 106 CE. After the Romans hauled away all their treasurers and dispersed their people into slavery in faraway lands, all that remained of the Nabateans were abandoned monuments exquisitely carved into stone. Their obliterated capital city, originally called Raqmu ("The One that Leaves a Lasting Impression"), received a haunting new moniker: Al-Batra ("The Permanently Cut Off"), known today as Petra. So terrifying was the Nabateans' fateful eradication that Meccan caravans would hasten as they passed by the ruins of Petra.

The cautionary lesson was clear: do not become prominent enough to attract any attention beyond Arabia. Despite the Arabs' soaring self-regard and superiority complex, they remained deeply insecure and fearful. Preserving Arab identity required keeping a low profile and avoiding outside contamination—genetically, linguistically, and culturally. The intense need to survive thus drove a remarkable self-imposed state of stagnation. Any growth, innovation, or new influences posed a threat. To block the natural impulse to adapt, ancestral traditions became infallible and a mental fortress was constructed around Arabian culture.

The Qur'an employs an evocative term to criticize this willful stagnation: *Jahiliyyah*. The word connotes obsessively reusing the same outdated mold to fashion bricks or clay pots, and obstinately refusing to construct new models long after the old ones grow obsolete. "Your perception of your perfection is a mindset fit for a stagnant reality," (2:154) the Qur'an observes, while also asking: "Do they truly prefer a state of willful stagnation over a state of progress?" (5:50)

In the Qur'an's view, the Meccans' decision to artificially limit themselves backfired, concealing major societal ills: "Like a mountain masking a simmering volcano within, be wary of cloaking arrogant superiority in a flimsy veneer of righteousness—a disingenuous characteristic of willful stagnation." (48:26) The seemingly placid façade of *Jahiliyyah* disguised deep internal rot, fueled by boiling resentment and prejudice.

Rather than fear and undermine other people, the Qur'an urges engaging the world with an open mind: "Do not revert to the stagnant ways of the past by acting with a haughty air of superiority—as if defensively isolated in a secluded fortress. Rather, proactively build connections with others; constantly seek to create equal opportunities for others; and help raise up other people to new heights." (33:33)

Yet the stubborn Meccans were innovators only in the field of stagnation, ironically leveraging their vibrant minds to pioneer new ways to block change. They stuffed cotton in their children's ears to avoid hearing strange Arabic dialects and foreign languages. They purposely restricted the growth of their city precisely so it would remain unimpressive and thus not coveted by powerful external empires. They even covered over the only fresh-water spring inside Mecca (the Zamzam well) so potential conquering armies would have no incentive to attack.

Self-imposed stagnation yielded intense inconsistencies. Meccans were ostensibly devoted to tradition at all costs, yet constantly sought loopholes to circumvent onerous obligations. They preached a lofty code of integrity, sacrifice, and honor, yet failed to match such bold rhetoric with action, preferring virtue signaling to genuine behavior. Their intense narcissism came coupled with deep insecurity, as envy drove them to incessantly undermine one another, deviously plotting beneath a hospitable veneer. Fatalism about the scheming of evil spirits fueled rampant superstition as well as scapegoating to mask deficiencies and shirk personal responsibility. The Qur'an likens these contradictions to a "mountain masking a simmering volcano within"—a metaphor for a volatile identity crisis derived from the seemingly solid Arabian mountains sitting atop a volcanic subterrain.

As a social order established atop contradictions, *Jahiliyyah* required a bizarre, inverted logic to constrain the natural human impulse to evolve, create, and expand. The system of *Jahiliyyah* also generated intense human suffering. For instance, in a hostile environment that demanded the projection of strength to survive, women were viewed as a weak liability. They required extra protection and did not carry on the family name or preserve its memory.

Women had no right to own property and were themselves treated as inheritable property (with eldest sons taking ownership of their late fathers' wives). The more women a clan had, the weaker its social standing—leading some fathers to quietly bury their young daughters alive. So common was the practice that Arabic developed a distinctive word for the victim: *Maw'udah*.

Female infanticide, while widespread, was never discussed. Fathers would dispose of their daughters like refuse in the wilderness outside town, never even raising the subject with their spouse or close friends. Girls simply disappeared. The heinous act of a father emotionlessly suffocating his own flesh and blood passed in silence. The Qur'an pointedly breaks the unspoken taboo by directly calling out this gruesome act as its first critique of *Jahiliyyah*. "For which crime was she buried alive?" (81:9) it asks rhetorically, while also negating any materialistic justification for child murder with a divine injunction:

"Do not kill your children due to poverty or need, as We will provide for both you and your children." (6:151)

Beyond simply denouncing female infanticide, the Qur'an dives into the twisted psychology underlying it, exposing the mental instability driving one of forced stagnation's most shocking consequences. A Qur'anic vignette examines how a father convinces himself to dehumanize his own daughter:

> When one of them is given tidings of a female born to him, his face turns dark with deep shame and his heart bears an immense hatred for her. He scurries about furtively to avoid other people due to the excessive humiliation he feels thrust upon him. Then, while lurking in the shadows, he thinks to himself: Should he keep it alive and let it diminish and vitiate his status—or should he instead trample it deep into the earth?
>
> Oh, what a shameful way to reason! . . . These fathers ostensibly sacrifice as a prized offering to the Loving Divine what they most detest [daughters] while saving for themselves what they erroneously consider superior [sons]. . . . *Tallahi!* We have sent prophets in the past to awaken many nations that deceive themselves into perceiving harmful actions as good . . . and we only revealed the Book [Qur'an] to you to help them see clarifying reason via a message of guidance and compassion for people who actively seek nurturing safety for growth (16:58–64).

Precisely because the Meccans intentionally avoided the taboo topic of infanticide, the Qur'an directly tackles the human psychology of an honor killing. The passage strips bare a father's unnatural shame over a daughter, reducing his child to an object whose continued existence mars his own. The verses highlight the father's contradictory attempt to rationalize the killing as a sacrifice, when it is actually an attempt to discard a loved one society has convinced him not to value. *Jahiliyyah* thus swindles a father out of his own precious child. To heighten the gravity of the moment, the Qur'an swears a rare oath—*Tallahi!* ("By the Witness of the Loving Divine!").

The Qur'an's forthright honesty challenged the Meccans' intense need to control public discourse. Any ideas that could contaminate or upend the precious status quo were immediately and intensely censored by Meccan elders, who developed an expertise at maligning dissenting voices through sophisticated public relations campaigns. In classic form, the elite council that ran Meccan affairs actually paid poets to travel Arabia denouncing the Qur'an's message and defaming the character of its prophet.

Daring to publicly express ideas independent from the dominant elite narrative indeed had serious consequences. Those who did faced isolation—and worse—if they failed to heed repeated warnings to remain silent. The Qur'an, of course, refuses to be muzzled. In challenging the Meccans' dogged censorship, it presents them as undermining an opportunity to benefit themselves:

> Do they think their prophet is insane? They know very well that he only teaches righteousness and truth, yet alas many detest the truth. The world would be a chaotic and unjust place if truth were based on their whims and desires. We simply seek to uplift them and improve their state, yet alas they turn away from improving their condition. Perhaps they worry that you will demand payment—though the remuneration provided by your Divine Mentor is far more enriching than anything they could offer (23:69–72).

The Qur'an often repeats this disclaimer that the prophet seeks no compensation or reward, using the terminology of business transactions. One chapter repeats the same passage five times: "I don't ask of you any remuneration; indeed, my remuneration is from the Divine Mentor of the cosmos." (26:109) The Meccans, in keeping with their suspicious and competitive outlook, evidently could not fathom that anyone might altruistically seek to improve their condition. No one could possibly care about them because deep down they did not genuinely care about themselves.

※ ※ ※

The Qur'an exposes the Meccans' toxic combination of public egotism and internal self-loathing, but pointedly never engages them in an intimate conversation. Never does it declare *Ya 'Arab!* or *Ya Ahla Makkah!* ("Oh, Arabs!"; "Oh, People of Mecca!"). An audience has to earn the Qur'an's intimacy, and the Meccans fail to demonstrate any receptivity despite repeated appeals.

One Meccan, however, immediately gains the Qur'an's confidence: Muhammad. While the ego of a typical Meccan would surely have swelled at being singled out for divine revelation, the initial shock instead paralyzed

Muhammad with fear. As the new prophet retreated in a cold sweat under a mass of blankets in his living room, the Qur'an reassures him with the tone of a trusted confidant:

> Bring clarity to yourself before you try to change others. Cast off the constellation of obstacles weighing you down. Help others out of sincerity without expecting any personal benefit. Trust in your Cosmic Mentor and persevere through the difficult process ahead (74:4–7).

In order to fulfill the obligation to help liberate other people from stagnation, Muhammad had to first liberate himself. The passage's language evokes the dynamics of stagnation—confusion, constraint, selfishness, and lethargy—by insisting on the opposite values: transparency, liberation, altruism, and determination.

Buoyed by the Qur'an's advice, Muhammad rushed out to publicly declaim the Qur'an's initial *Iqra* passage before the entire city—only to have the message roundly rejected in a most humiliating manner. The people of Mecca immediately ostracized him: covering their ears and eyes when he passed; and placing thorns and animal waste outside his front door. The abrupt transition from being one of Mecca's most respected citizens to complete pariah understandably rattled Muhammad, causing him to doubt his prophetic abilities. The Qur'an takes pains to reassure Muhammad that he has indeed been selected for the role, with the first forty years of his life serving as preparation for his calling:

> Your Divine Mentor never abandoned you nor forsook you. What is to come is greater than what you have already accomplished. Did He not find you an outcast orphan yet nonetheless embraced you? Did He not find you confused and doubtful yet still guided you? And did He not find you impoverished yet ultimately enriched you? (93:3–8)

While the Qur'an does not talk much about Muhammad or recount the dynamics of his life, this passage reveals clues as to why he was selected as the unlikely spokesman for the Qur'an's message. In essence, Muhammad demonstrated a persistent ability to rebuild and even thrive in the face of setbacks that would have broken most men.

The odds were stacked against him before he was even born. His father died several months before his birth, leaving the infant with no progenitor—and no siblings—in a patriarchal and tribalistic society. Without any immediate male relatives to protect him, Muhammad entered Arabian society devoid of critical structural support. To achieve social standing, he could only rely on merit.

Rather than simply survive in the barren landscape of Mecca, Muhammad from birth was tasked with a seemingly impossible mission. A few moments after he emerged into the world, his grandfather lifted him up in an emerald-green shawl and formally gave him a unique name never used before. Built upon the archaic Semitic root *H-M-D,* "Muhammad" described an exemplary role model demonstrating inspiring actions from an elevated platform. The boy would thus have to spend the rest of his life walking around with a distinctive and highly charged moniker advertising his life purpose. There would be no escaping it.

Like most Meccan boys, Muhammad spent his formative years with desert nomads, under the care of a strong woman named Halimah who taught him pure Arabic and life skills for surviving in a hostile environment. Young Muhammad was lowered over the edge of a sheer cliff by rope to gather honey from beehives, and he was entrusted with herding a flock of goats with other young boys. This latter activity sometimes required chasing after runaway goats—which once nearly led to his abduction into slavery by passing travelers.

The near abduction ended Muhammad's desert apprenticeship and began a new phase of learning in urban Mecca. He encountered idolatry, slavery, and the unspoken horror of vanishing young girls. His curiosity about his missing father led his mother Aminah to finally return with her son to her native city of Yathrib, where her late husband had died and been buried after catching the plague. It was at last, time for Muhammad to learn about the hidden other side of his heritage. In the desert oasis of Yathrib, Muhammad for the first time saw a lush agricultural center with ponds, palm groves, water channels, planted wheat fields, and expansive greenery. He also observed a community of scholarship, as rabbis huddled with students in discussion over Hebrew scrolls.

The visit came to an end with the arrival of the caravan headed back to Mecca, and Aminah reluctantly took her son to at last visit her husband's grave. Overcome with emotion in the cemetery, she collapsed and within hours died of heartbreak. In her final breaths, as her six-year-old son clung to her crying, Aminah further clarified his life mission: "Oh, Muhammad," she said with difficulty, "Be a world changer!" With those final words, Muhammad became a true orphan—one tasked with the seemingly impossible challenge of transforming a society committed to resisting change at all costs.

Returning to Mecca, Muhammad moved in with his grandfather, beginning a precious two-year period of companionship and tutelage under Mecca's chief elder. Sitting on his grandfather's lap at meetings of the elders' council, six-year-old Muhammad observed mediation skills, refined oratorical eloquence, and how masters of the Arabic language leveraged sophisticated words to persuade. Though he never attended a day of school in his life, Muhammad received a unique education from his grandfather. The inquisitive young boy soaked up the lessons, beginning a lifelong pattern of gathering information, though he remained illiterate. "Neither did you read books nor write anything," (29:48) observes the Qur'an.

The death of Muhammad's grandfather once again thrust the young boy into foster care. His one constant companion since birth—and throughout his entire life—was an enslaved African Christian woman named Barakah. With selfless compassion, she helped the vulnerable orphan make sense of the tragedies in his life and instilled a commitment to action-based hope, to persevere despite the bleak odds. He quickly applied her teachings by taking his first public action: formally emancipating her with a declaration on the steps of the Ka'bah. Barakah would be just one of many strong female mentors and supporters who propelled the future prophet.

At age ten, Muhammad joined his uncle on the annual camel caravan to Damascus, for the first time experiencing the world beyond Arabia. At one caravan rest depot, he met a Christian monk, who saw potential in the shy yet refined boy who stood out amidst the boorish Meccan crowd. The monk, named Bahira, took the unusual step of showing Muhammad inside the monastery and its remarkable library. Never before had Muhammad seen a bound book, nor conversed with a religious intellectual—it sparking his lifelong passion to engage with people from different cultures and backgrounds.

For the next two decades, Muhammad would join the annual caravan to Damascus, seizing the unique entrepreneurial opportunities the great metropolis afforded him. He sought out mentors among the city's merchants and befriended visiting businessmen from across the Middle East. Wide-eyed in wonder at the pulsing energy of a dynamic city, Muhammad began to identify new opportunities to generate wealth. Several times he defied market expectations by deducing trends unappreciated by other merchants, scoring remarkable returns to the astonishment of the naysayers. He also became the first Meccan to purchase goods in Damascus for resale back in Mecca—until that point, the caravans had returned to Arabia largely empty.

Muhammad's business innovations did not threaten the Meccan order, in part because they earned him the credibility that Meccans appreciated: financial success. Yet Muhammad also began to challenge exploitation of visiting merchants, his ire sparked by one of Mecca's senior leaders refusing to pay money owed to a foreigner. Muhammad formed a league of principled colleagues to confront corruption and abuse. The founding members banged on the door of the powerful leader and insisted he hand over the money owed. Shamed into acting honorably, the elder complied, but began nursing a grudge against Muhammad as an uppity young man daring to defy authority.

Muhammad's business acumen and principled social advocacy earned him the attention of a wealthy young widow named Khadijah, who recruited Muhammad to serve as her business operator. The two combined their skills and assets to grow a small fortune into a large one—and in the process fell in love. In a highly unusual move, Khadijah proposed to Muhammad. The couple could often be seen walking through the streets of Mecca holding hands, a gesture of affection frowned upon in *Jahiliyyah* society.

The couple had many children, yet none of the boys survived past the age of two. Twice Muhammad had to bury his infant sons with his own hands. And while he embraced his daughters with deep affection—acting as a loving and supportive parent who helped educate them—Muhammad recognized that without any sons he would not meet Meccan society's condition for greatness. A man with no sons was called an *Abtar*—cut off, with no male heirs to perpetuate his memory.

Only in his midthirties, Muhammad faced a dizzying challenge: a self-made commercial titan with a loving wife and charming daughters, he nonetheless seemed to have no path forward as an exemplary role model who could change his hometown, let alone the world. In his despair, Muhammad turned inward, abandoning the annual caravan trade to instead meditate in self-imposed seclusion for several years. Unsure how to apply his talents to achieve the life mission bestowed upon him, Muhammad began to doubt himself—and to stagnate.

It was in this state that the Qur'an first spoke to Muhammad. The *Iqra*

call to "blossom" came as such a shock precisely because it demanded doing
what Muhammad had resisted exploring for years. The once-great entrepreneur was being called back into action, only this time with a grander and more
profound objective. In a callous society that disdained altruism, the Qur'an
revealed its ambitious plan for Muhammad, repeating many times: "We have
sent you as a model of compassion for all creation." (21:107) Real blossoming required an underlying moral framework so that people engaged in self-
transformation would not lose their humanity in the process.

By becoming a prophet delivering a message of compassion to a society
diametrically opposed to it, Muhammad embarked on a perilous journey.
The powerful elite of Mecca hardly looked kindly on a once-respected civic
leader suddenly issuing public calls for compassion and independent thinking.

The Qur'an insisted that Muhammad not simply verbalize its message but
enact it. Prophethood required opening himself up as an exemplary model.
To deepen its intimate relationship with Muhammad while simultaneously
propelling him forward, the Qur'an began addressing him directly with the
verbal command *Qul!* Typically translated merely as "say," the highly nuanced
directive conveys the need for visible action: "Emerge to publicly proclaim!"
And not simply to speak, but to explain by demonstrating so everyone can hear
and see. *Qul* embodies the opposite of retreating under blankets or stagnating
in self-reflection. To declare in public requires planning and self-awareness:
dressing oneself appropriately, striding up to a public platform, command-
ing the audience's attention, and declaiming eloquently. Put another way, *Qul*
called Muhammad to fulfill his own name.

Yet the role model rarely found anyone interested in emulating his behavior. One early exception was a brave woman named Sumayyah, who became
enthralled by the Qur'an's message and herself began preaching self-liberation
on the streets of Mecca. The same Meccan elder Muhammad had embarrassed
for failing to pay a visiting merchant was tasked with silencing Sumayyah. He
tortured her and her husband on the outskirts of Mecca before murdering them.

The martyrdom of Sumayyah exposed the deep dilemma facing Muhammad. He had been called to model blossoming, but he was powerless to avert
the killing of a devout follower. In fact, for the first decade of his prophethood,
Muhammad could do little in public beyond reciting Qur'anic passages on
the margins of Mecca's marketplace. Anything bolder would endanger the
lives of his handful of followers.

Burying Sumayyah evoked the painful pattern of bereavement that marked much of Muhammad's childhood and adult life, triggering a fresh bout of sadness. The tension of being called to action by the Qur'an took an enormous toll on Muhammad. Again, the Qur'an assumes its role as the prophet's comforting mentor, repeatedly consoling Muhammad: "Persevere and remember that your steadfastness is sustained by the Loving Divine. Don't allow yourself to be constrained by sadness over their state of being or feel downhearted over their attempts to undermine you" (16:127).

With therapeutic sophistication, the Qur'an recognizes Muhammad's sorrowful reaction as natural: "We know that you are deeply saddened by what they say. Remember, they are not decrying you; those who dwell in the shadows of darkness naturally feel threatened by the illuminating signs of the Loving Divine" (6:33). Passages publicly discussing Muhammad's vulnerable emotional condition mark an unusual break with Meccan society's silent stoicism. Acknowledging the prophet's difficult struggle to persevere amidst great suffering models genuine resilience—and illustrates how being a role model does not require perfection, but rather striving imperfectly to overcome. Instead of presenting an illusion of prophetic perfection, the Qur'an purposely reveals Muhammad's vulnerabilities as a means to establish trust with its larger audiences.

Some Meccan elders recognized the power of the Qur'an, particularly the elder Al-Walid, who was sent by the leadership council to silence Muhammad. While Al-Walid and Muhammad conversed, a poor blind man came seeking Muhammad's advice. Seeing the man approach, Muhammad grimaced at the interruption of his attempt to win over the influential elder. "He frowned and felt repulsed when the blind man came to him," (80:1–2) the Qur'an critiques Muhammad. "What makes you think that your time is better spent with a man of significance closed to the message rather than with a man of no significance who seeks to be elevated by it? Why do you allow yourself to be distracted from the one who approaches actively seeking?"

No one witnessed Muhammad's frown, as the blind man could not see and Al-Walid had turned away. Nonetheless, the Qur'an plucked this moment out of obscurity to immortalize it as a lesson in how all human beings struggle to prioritize genuine compassion. In the case of Muhammad, the Qur'an several times admonishes his frustration with his imperfect followers: "Persevere and be patient with those of your followers who actively seek to improve themselves throughout the day. Don't roll your eyes, wishing for less needy followers." (18:28) The Qur'an recognizes that mentors naturally grow frustrated, yet insists they never give up—just as it continues to engage Muhammad throughout more than a decade of relative inaction.

❦❦❦

Over the dozen years Muhammad patiently endured persecution in his hometown, the Qur'an's message attracted fewer than 150 followers. Because of the risks, they could never meet in public. They stealthily circulated scrolls of Qur'anic passages hidden in piles of merchandise and gathered secretly in small groups in private homes for nighttime study sessions. Less a community than a disparate network, the early followers were a diverse cross section of society. Several had to conceal their involvement even from their own spouses and children. Trapped in a defensive underground posture, the group persisted in survival mode, unable to blossom beyond their own minds.

To protect their identity and respect their privacy, the Qur'an chooses not to directly address its persecuted disciples. Instead, it provides insights relevant to their strained condition, sharing examples of noteworthy individuals from the past who overcame trauma and repression. Muhammad's confidant Abu Bakr would have been mortified had the Qur'an openly discussed how his wife and son constantly mocked his devotion. As a stand-in, the Qur'an recounts the story of Noah struggling with the opposition of his own wife and son, thereby offering a coded private message to Abu Bakr. Many passages from this tense decade address multiple layers of audiences, embedding individualized messages amidst timeless universal wisdom.

For more than a decade, the Qur'an speaks directly and intimately only to one person. Its great transformation occurs twelve years into its existence when suddenly a community outside Mecca actively seeks out its message. The unlikely new audience: residents of Muhammad's maternal hometown. The people of Yathrib authorized a delegation to visit Mecca and invite Muhammad to bring the Qur'an's message to their community.

Delighted to at last find a people confident enough to admit their weakness and open enough to receive outside guidance, the Qur'an for the first time bursts forth with revelations addressed to a plural audience. It unleashes a stream of intimate invocations: *Ya Bani Israel* ("Oh, Children of Israel!"); *Ya*

Ahlal-Kitab ("Oh, People of Learning!"); *Ya Ayyuhal-lathina Amanu* ("Oh, Seekers of Serenity!").

Unlike the Meccans, the Yathribites not only acknowledge their own stagnation amidst intra-communal strife but also display genuine compassion. Describing them as "people who love to improve themselves," (9:108) the Qur'an also lauds their individual and communal altruism:

> These people of receptive hearts actively sought to elevate themselves. They love those who seek refuge with them and bear no resentment in their hearts for all they have selflessly donated. They sacrifice to aid others, even when it causes them great distress. Indeed, when individuals overcome their personal egotistical inclinations, then the larger community truly succeeds! (59:9)

As a monotheistic community, the Yathribites nurtured a messianic vision of complete transformation—yet had over the centuries forsaken their own dynamic traditions to passively await an external redeemer. The stagnation in Yathrib was thus also self-imposed, exacerbating a gnawing tension between transcendent dreams and torpid reality. The Jews of Yathrib still mourned the destruction of the great Temple in Jerusalem centuries earlier, and separated themselves from the larger Arab society around them.

Rather than start the rebuilding process, they sat hundreds of miles from Jerusalem awaiting a savior. In the meantime, their scholastic acumen was wasted on trivial debates over scriptural interpretation, arguments over minutiae that often flared into squabbling between rival scholars and clans. Rather than think for themselves, each group of devotees preferred to blindly follow their teachers, whom they regarded as local gateways to God.

Even as they bickered amongst themselves, the Yathribites cultivated a verdant oasis and enjoyed relative independence amidst a city surrounded on three sides by natural defensive fields of volcanic magma. In this safe haven, the Yathribites retreated inward to preserve their minority identity in a sea of idolatry. Mirroring the Meccans, the Yathribites had culturally sealed themselves off from the outside world, signaling a lack of self-confidence and a reluctance to trust outsiders. They might have hospitably served as a pitstop for caravans, yet pointedly refrained from sharing their Abrahamic values with the larger world.

The Qur'an sees enormous untapped potential in the Yathribites despite their passivity. "No matter their circumstances, they are plagued by self-pity and lamentation—yet possess the ability to transcend their current condition by reestablishing a strong bond to the Loving Divine and to all humanity" (3:112). This verse pointedly admired the Yathribites' innate talents in the art of persuasion.

Thanks to their ancient scholarly traditions, the Yathribites possessed sophisticated emotional intelligence, nuanced interpersonal skills, and an aptitude for promoting ideas—yet had allowed these special talents to lie dormant. The Qur'an aims to convince the Yathribites to burst out of their self-imposed shell and radiate their energy outward. Seeking a symbiotic partnership, the Qur'an envisions harnessing the Yathribites' talents to carry its message to the world.

But before the Yathribites took up this global mission, they became the first mass audience of the Qur'an and the action-based followers of Muhammad, the exemplary role model. After escaping Mecca by the skin of his teeth, Muhammad arrived in Yathrib to a rapturous welcome—though he soon detected more messianic fervor than a readiness for the hard work ahead. He promptly renamed the city Medina ("A Place of Flowing Change Built atop an Ancient Foundation") and drafted a constitution to unite bickering tribes into a coherent cooperative.

The newly named Medinians' once-diffused energy could thus be rechanneled into a massive city building project. A new civic center and marketplace were constructed; an extensive network of irrigation channels maximized precious rainwater to transform Medina's agriculture; and massive storehouses were built to store grain reserves as an emergency resource.

For a prophet who had spent a dozen years unable to publicly role-model civic blossoming, the explosion of innovation in Medina was transformative. The Qur'an recognizes this breakthrough by directly addressing Muhammad for the first time as *Ya ayyuhan-Nabi*—"Oh, Prophet!" Muhammad's identity had been clear from the moment of the Qur'an's emergence, yet only once he gained a receptive audience and moved them to blossom did he fully earn the title. The Qur'an views identity through the prism of action, not ancestry, tribe, or genetics. Unleashing the Qur'an's words alone did not fulfill the obligations of prophethood, which required translating rhetoric into deeds. Action, after all, is the antithesis of stagnation.

☙❧

Because of the Qur'an's constantly shifting voice and distinctive yet overlapping target audiences, its every verse must be approached with an attentive mind. By requiring active listening, the style refuses to allow audiences to stagnate. And just as readers must decipher the particular audience addressed in each phrase, so too must they interrogate the very meaning of identity.

Human beings have a natural propensity to simplify identity as something static and immutable. Yet the concept of identity is a purely human invention, a mythical narrative designed to help give meaning to existence. The only true identity human beings actually have is their humanity.

The Qur'an's elusive and singular communication style helps assert its own identity as a dynamic living being—one whose identity must remain fluid, unconstrained by preset categories. In defying definition, the Qur'an models to human beings how they can do the same to forge a healthy identity by embracing the positive qualities of traditions as building blocks to create something dynamic and new. It aims to actively demonstrate how audiences can look at themselves in fresh ways, celebrating a multifaceted individuality that continuously reinvents itself.

You, dear reader, are a part of the Qur'an's audience. This chapter and its two predecessors have been dedicated to helping prepare you for the next section's retrospective tracing of the Qur'an's life chronologically. The first chapter aimed to reveal how to derive core meaning from the Qur'an's letters and language. The second spotlighted how the Qur'an joins a preexisting intergenerational Abrahamic dialogue of perpetual reformation. And finally, this chapter introduced the identity quests of the Qur'an's primary audiences during the time of its revelation.

Without these three critical elements, the Qur'anic verses will inherently lack grounding, context, and dimension—they will not fully make sense. Not only do you leave yourself vulnerable to faulty translations that can obscure and manipulate, but the Qur'an's special message will not be able to move you to blossom.

In the end, the Qur'an is not primarily concerned with identity labels, but actions. Identity itself is not sacred—but what identity inspires human beings to do can be.

PART II

THE QUR'AN'S GROWTH

4

HANIF: THE QUR'AN AS CHALLENGER AND AWAKENER

IN THE BEGINNING, THERE WAS A VOID OF SILENCE. AND THEN SUDDENLY words emerged, bubbling up inexorably via the soul of a melancholy merchant meditating in the predawn darkness. The human who served as the cosmic words' messenger was wholly unprepared for their arrival.

> Blossom forth [*Iqra*], inspired by your rejuvenating Divine Mentor [*Rabb*],
> Who revives the dormant to forge empowering connections ['*Alaq*].
> Dare to blossom, as your Divine Mentor provides spiritual comfort.
> The Visionary One, who guides the unlocking of layers of learning [*Qalam*],
> Elevates the stagnant to once-inconceivable heights. (96:1–5)

The words came as a call to a single individual, bluntly yet poetically issuing a direct challenge: Open yourself up so you can be elevated to achieve the seemingly impossible. The word *Iqra* evoked a tightly closed plant finally daring to unfurl its petals, making itself vulnerable but also accessible for pollination so fruit can eventually emerge. Blooming did not happen in an instant, but rather via a gradual unlocking from waves of experience, as *Qalam* described the extended process of carefully whittling a reed down into a quill pen.

While *Iqra* was delivered in the form of a command, the revelation's tone suggested it came from an encouraging coach rather than a harsh master. The rejuvenating Divine Mentor aimed to inspire, with *Rabb* describing the care-taker of a fragile young plant gently sprinkling drops of water and providing support to guide upward growth. That nurturing motif was complemented by the image of vines ascending trees *('Alaq)*, reflecting the symbiotic qualities of healthy relationships where people advance not by running others down (the typical approach of Meccan elites) but by lifting others up—sometimes even to once-inconceivable heights.

These few compact phrases, each dense with meaning, served as a kind of opening mission statement: a summons for self-awakening to help empower others. But being summoned by an unseen mentor to transform his life and his society stunned Muhammad to his core. In panic, he fled from the cave of revelation, scrambling down the mountain in a desperate dash home. Once there, he collapsed in feverish fear, seeking refuge under a mass of blankets. The following morning, the Divine Mentor returned with reassuring words:

> Oh, you who are covered up and shivering in fear, get up and go out to proclaim
> the message of self-deliverance! Empower people to rebuild themselves inspired by
> the Cosmic Mentor, but bring clarity to yourself before you try to change others!
>
> Cast off the constellation of obstacles weighing you down! Help others out
> of sincerity without expecting any personal benefit! Trust in your Cosmic Men-
> tor and persevere through the difficult process ahead! (74:1–7)

The revelation clarified *Iqra*'s initial mission statement: proclaim the mes-sage of self-deliverance while persevering through difficulties. It also clarified the altruistic spirit behind the empowering connections: Help others without expecting any personal benefit. In a society built upon manipulating others to advance oneself—with hospitality only extended to receive a gift in return—this was a revolutionary concept. The unseen Cosmic Mentor modeled self-less behavior, empowering people to rebuild themselves while acknowledging they would naturally struggle to achieve clarity.

The pep talk had its intended effect. The fledgling prophet gathered a small group of friends and allies to share the revelations and plan a grand public unveiling. A few days later he stood before the main Friday market throng in downtown Mecca and dramatically chanted the first revelations' inspir-

ing words. Yet the Meccan public was in no mood to accept the revolutionary message, which landed with a thud. The marketplace crowd jeered the
prophet, as his own uncle publicly shamed him for wasting everyone's time.
Rather than achieving once-inconceivable heights, the revelations had driven
the previously esteemed merchant to once-unimaginable depths.

For two weeks, no revelations emerged, and the dismayed prophet wandered the alleys of Mecca awaiting inspiration on how to proceed. He hap-
pened upon an old lady struggling with heavy water jugs and rushed to relieve
her burden. Due to weak eyesight, the lady could not recognize her mysterious helper, but she assumed he demanded some compensation. "I am a poor
woman who cannot offer a reward for your kindness," she explained. "But
I will give you a word of advice: That man Muhammad has done so much
harm, misguiding the youth. Avoid him."

Later that evening, the spurned prophet anonymously sent the lady a food
basket with a pouch of silver coins. Twice altruistically helping someone who
had slandered him in fact generated a reward: a profound revelation.

> Emulate the Ultimate Source of Unconditional Love [*Allah*], who gently nour-
> ishes growth [*Rabb*] in all things; Who optimistically empowers even the most
> fragile [*Rahman*] and comforts in moments of vulnerability [*Rahim*]; Who pro-
> vides fresh energy [*Malik*] for each unfolding phase in the journey of life.
>
> We strive to reflect the way You rejuvenate and trust in Your support to
> shield our weaknesses.
>
> Guide us to navigate a safe path with flexibility—a path previously forged
> by the foresighted, who steadily restore brokenness to reach a state of serenity;
> a path unconstrained by a stagnant reality of willful manipulation and blind
> acceptance. (1:1–7)

The revelation spoke to an audience suffering from a shattering setback,
where initial high hopes were unexpectedly dashed and a public display of
enthusiasm was harshly rejected. Intense emotions like shock, sadness, vulnerability, confusion, discouragement, and lethargy all flowed from this dramatic setback. The revelation sought to nurture healing without indulging
an unhealthy sense of victimhood or grievance.

The revelation's opening verses introduced five key divine attributes, which
together provided a model of holistic counseling: an unconditional loving

embrace *(Allah)*; practical external mentoring *(Rabb)*; a reminder of untapped future potential *(Rahman)*; a comforting presence *(Rahim)*; and an infusion of fresh energy *(Malik)*. The revelation put momentary pain and trauma in perspective as temporary sensations to be endured rather than life-defining limitations. Instead of wallowing in past mistreatment, the verses encouraged resilience for the journey ahead, an extended process of gradual healing rather than a forced shortcut solution.

Lest the audience feel isolated, the fourth verse spoke in the plural voice to remind the prophet that all human beings struggle with weaknesses. A chorus addressed God in a joint call of solidarity to persevere through trauma together. The Divine served as a role model for reinvigorating, and as a protector to help overcome flaws. The expression of "trust" in God evoked a prerequisite for healing, as trust in the future enables hope, which in turn inspires action to transcend the present.

Taking action required breaking out of an immobilized state onto a safe path forward. The chorus of healing requested flexibility (invoking an Arabic term describing how the curved spine enables suppleness), as rigidity impedes both healing and progress given the inevitable obstacles ahead. Others who had previously navigated the journey of recovery offered a model to emulate—including eschewing the temptation to alleviate the burden of personal responsibility by blindly following others. Human beings all have intrinsic potential, but also a capacity to manipulate—so avoid naïveté and remain alert.

The revelation emerged with the title *Al-Fatihah* ("The Unlocking"). Its name alluded not only to dormant potential but also releasing a flood of constrained emotions. The seven short verses would later become Islam's core iconic prayer, recited seventeen times daily as a constant reaffirmation of human potential despite challenges. Muhammad would later designate *Al-Fatihah* as the concise preview summary of the entire Qur'an.

In the moment, however, *Al-Fatihah*'s message took time to sink in, as Muhammad endured the Meccans' escalating ridicule, which included a sarcastic nickname, *Muthammam*—"the one deserving of scorn." People in the streets snickered as he passed, some even covering their ears and eyes as a sign of total rejection. Amidst this "stagnant reality of willful manipulation and blind acceptance" came revelatory verses, marking a sudden continuation of the earlier call to "someone shivering under blankets" delivered a month earlier. As if no time had passed, the revelation remarkably picked up mid-thought:

Rather, consider the example of the varying phases of the Moon; how the darkness of the night recedes away; and how dawn gradually illuminates everything making it clearly visible. Inevitable change is one of the greatest truths: a clear reminder for flawed mortals so that they can shine through, if they choose to. Therefore, remember that anyone among you can choose to either progress or lag behind! (74:32–37)

The verses recognized the gradual process of recovery and reemergence from melancholy. For the first time, a revelation used a parable to make a point: the inevitable nocturnal phases and daily progression from darkness to light served as external examples to help inspire pursuit of internal clarity. After that gentle metaphor, the revelation delivered its key truth: stagnation is a choice. Wallowing in self-pity might feel like a comforting escape from responsibility, but is in fact an unconscious decision to lag behind. The only thing stopping flawed mortals from shining through is themselves—so choose to progress!

The Meccans, who had deliberately chosen not to progress, also mocked Muhammad's small group of underground followers as *Sabi'un*—a hot-headed, immature group, like unstable lids atop boiling pots. Unable to meet with his nineteen followers in public, Muhammad began organizing secret study sessions in the interior courtyard of a follower's home, a makeshift academy known as Dar-ul-Arqam. At the first gathering, participants sat in an egalitarian circle, unusually uniting low- and high-class as well as men and women. The session commenced with a compelling one-verse revelation:

This is the methodology of your patriarch Abraham; it was he who originally named you Muslims, and now you continue that legacy. (22:78)

Until this point, the budding movement had lacked a coherent identity, an uncertainty only exacerbated by melancholy and mockery. Two months after the first revelation, it finally had a formal name harkening back to Arabia's ancient heritage. Abraham, the founder of Mecca and builder of the Ka'bah shrine, had originated the term "Muslim" to describe those who followed in his path. It was Mecca's derisive elite who had lost touch with their heritage, not the budding movement's followers—who were actually reviving an ancient legacy. Derived from the Arabic root *S-L-M,* used to describe repairing

cracks in a city's protective walls, "Muslims" carried a distinctively social responsibility as civic repairers.

Subsequent study sessions at Dar-ul-Arqam centered around revelations
that began with rhetorical questions designed to spark discussion:

> About what do they argue? About the great revelation over which they have con-
> flicting opinions and ideas. Inevitably, through analysis, they will synthesize
> and come to know. (78:1–4)

These revelations provided an instructive model for how to learn and
expand one's mind—vital skills in a society where illiteracy was the norm
and education a rare privilege. Rather than passively receive information,
followers were prompted to actively analyze. Several months after the first
revelation, a chapter called *Al-Insan* played on the word's multiple meanings: "human being," "the one who forgets," "the one who stagnates," and
"the one who stands out."

> Can a human being [*Insan*] not recognize that there was once a moment in time
> when they were unworthy of being recalled and remembered? Indeed, We cre-
> ated humans from mixed fluids, enduring tribulations across the generations.
> We endowed them with the power of hearing and sight. . . . The mindful among
> them uphold their vows to enact change and are conscious of future account-
> ability. Out of loving kindness, they feed the destitute, the orphan, and the en-
> slaved. Then they say, "We feed you for the love of the Divine, we neither ask
> you for repayment, nor that you feel obliged to us." (76:1–2,7–9)

The revelation reminded audiences that they once did not exist—and challenged them to consider whether their brief existence might prove worthy of
recall by future generations. Given that every human was in essence merely
a combination of DNA from thousands of ancestors—all of whom suffered
adversity—the only way to stand out amidst the mass of humanity is via impactful action that can be witnessed visually or shared aurally.

Of course, people suffering from depression sometimes wish they never existed. To counter that sentiment, the revelation upliftingly suggested anyone
can have a lasting, positive impact. Human beings can choose to stand out via
their actions. The verses clarified previous encouragement to "help others out

of sincerity without expecting any personal benefit" by specifically citing the need to assist people at the bottom of the social hierarchy. While caring for the poor and the enslaved might seem to modern audiences like standard moral guidance, this call posed a direct threat to the Meccan social order precisely because it defined even the lowest people as worthy of care, respect, and dignity.

The message of *Al-Insan* had a particularly profound impact on a disciple named Sumayyah, who had been liberated from slavery several years earlier along with her husband and son. Already middle-aged, Sumayyah had not yet achieved anything noteworthy and began to reflect on her earthly purpose. Even though *Al-Insan* provided no direct command, Sumayyah synthesized a sudden clear calling: she must publicly proclaim the message of equality and liberation embodied in the revelations of the past five months. While Muhammad himself had not recited any revelations in public since his failed initial pitch in the marketplace, Sumayyah marched through the streets of Mecca proclaiming verses—the first non-prophet to publicly spread the message. If people easily forget and can easily be forgotten, Sumayyah was determined to be remembered by literally enacting the revelations' message.

For six months, Sumayyah boldly called on the people of Mecca to blossom and seize their potential. She sparked popular interest with her preaching and in turn generated deep concern among Mecca's ruling elites. One leading elder, 'Amr ibn Hisham—the cousin of her former master—took it upon himself to extinguish the message. He tied up Sumayyah along with her family on the outskirts of Mecca, demanding they recant while torturing them beneath the blazing sun. When intense pressure failed to dissuade Sumayyah and her husband, Ibn Hisham killed them. Their son, 'Ammar, blurted out in anguish that he repudiated the Qur'an and was promptly released.

Muhammad, with no ability to intervene, later comforted 'Ammar by gently condoning his desperate attempt to live. Yet still no new revelations came.

⁂

Muhammad's early followers surely wondered why the stream of revelation had dried up for half a year, all the more so as dark events escalated to a fatal crescendo. Shortly after Sumayyah's murder, however, a revelation at last emerged: a brief passage named *Ad-Dhuha* after the first morning rays of sunlight to warm the earth.

Behold the comforting first rays of the early morning sun—as the gloom recedes after a night of extended darkness.

Remember, your Divine Mentor neither neglected nor abandoned you. Indeed, the success to come shall be greater than that of the past. Surely, your Divine Mentor shall grant you a state of serenity that will ease your heart. Did He not find you as an orphan, comforting and caring for you? And did He not find you lost and guided you? And did He not find you destitute and enriched you?

Likewise, never disadvantage an orphan by adding more obstacles to his path. Never dishearten and ridicule anyone in a state of need and despair. Rather, proclaim and share the many bounties bestowed upon you by your Divine Mentor. (93:1–11)

The passage directly addressed Muhammad (the destitute orphan who became wealthy) with an acknowledgment of his sadness. In Meccan society, showing vulnerability, particularly for men, was highly frowned upon—yet here the revelation openly revealed Muhammad's emotional state to model grieving and recovery. Evoking the longstanding pain felt by the orphan Muhammad, the closing verses offered a reminder to gently care for the newly orphaned 'Ammar, who had just witnessed his parents' brutal murder. While orphans might naturally feel alone and helpless, Muhammad's own life trajectory showed that enormous potential remained. "The success to come shall be greater than that of the past," noted the passage, using the term *Akhirah* to reference the delayed reward after planting seeds that ultimately yield a bountiful harvest.

A week later, a revelation delivered the first direct critique of Meccan society, specifically via the example of young girls buried alive by their own fathers. "For which crime was she killed?!" the revelation demanded—a double entendre also condemning Sumayyah's murder. The chapter's title, *At-Takwir*, evoked crumpling up and casually discarding a valuable scroll, and its content described the metaphor of crushing the sun and tossing it aside. By demanding that Meccans imagine the horror of treating a life-giving force as a worthless object, the revelation condemned how they casually discarded precious human lives.

On the occasion of the first anniversary of *Iqra*, a lengthy revelation emerged. It was the first one to: begin with mystic letters, recount a story with named characters (Moses, Aaron, Pharaoh, and Adam), quote God directly, and . . . give the revelations a formal identity. Named *TaHa* after the two Arabic letters that began the chapter, pronouncing the polar-opposite letters required expanding and moving the tongue, pressing it against the palette, then relaxing it while contracting the larynx, allowing air to emerging from the depth of the throat. The name itself offered a study in contrasts, between the rough *Ta* and the gentle *Ha,* which together meant "stand firm"—an important reminder in the wake of Sumayyah's murder.

Stand Firm! We did not reveal the Qur'an to weigh you down, but rather to help liberate and elevate for a lasting legacy anyone willing to listen.

A revelation from the One who fashioned the earth and the celestial bodies, the One who Optimistically empowers all creation, Who takes care of all that is in the cosmos, on earth and even beneath the soil. Whether you speak to the Divine Mentor in the silence of your heart or by proclaiming in public, He knows the secrets of the hearts and the deepest unspoken thoughts. Allah, there is no comforter or deity but He! The One who reveals Himself through many exquisite and empowering names.

Has anyone related to you the story of Moses? . . . He said, "Oh my Divine Mentor, relieve the tension in my chest, make my mind flow with ease, and untie the knot in my tongue so that they can understand my speech. . . ."

[God] said, "I have showered you with my love, precisely prearranging the events of your life with my gentle care! Now go, you and your brother, empowered by my guiding signs [*Ayat*] and don't hesitate to proclaim what I do to raise up those who are oppressed. . . . I have prepared you precisely for my mission. . . . Go, you two, to Pharaoh for he has truly transgressed all bounds! But remember, speak to him gently with kind words, as perhaps he may become mindful of his faults and reconsider his actions. . . .

Due to his reputation of strength and bravery, Moses concealed his feelings of fear and apprehension. We said to him, "Do not feel anxious! For yours is the higher path!" . . . Moses quickly returned to his people, engulfed by rage and sadness. . . .

Proclaim, "Oh my Divine Mentor, increase me in nuanced knowledge!" . . . Persevere and be patient with the hurtful things they say, and find solace by remembering the example of your Divine Mentor. . . . Go proclaim: "We are all waiting to see the outcome. . . . So keep waiting with anticipation, you will come to know who among us are the ones following the successful path and who is well-guided to reach success!"

At last, the disparate revelations had a unifying identity: *Al-Qur'an*—"The Blossoming." The name only came after the Qur'an had first demonstrated its identity in action. Notably, the title "The Blossoming" did not specify an exact category of object. The Qur'an was not a book per se or any other kind of physical object, but rather an unfolding experience—its own unique category of living being. Rather than "weigh down" audiences physically or emotionally, the Qur'an sought out anyone who would "listen" to its message and in return offered elevation and guidance toward becoming remembered for great actions.

Just as the Qur'an finally gained a name, the chapter for the first time invoked God's many refined names, each describing a special attribute that could provide distinctive inspiration. Thus began the Qur'an's two-decade effort to reveal over a hundred monikers for the Divine. The many names recognized how individuals needed meaningful ways to connect to God given their particular emotional state. To Arabs who assumed God had grown distant and aloof—requiring the intercession of idols that themselves were largely uncaring—the revelation presented a comforting and caring Divine who understood human beings' feelings even if they struggled to express them.

The passage then pivoted to the example of Moses, focusing on a midlife crisis when God suddenly called out to Moses in the wilderness via an illuminated bush and bestowed a bold life-mission: to liberate his people from bondage by directly confronting Pharaoh, the most powerful man on earth. The narrative emphasized Moses' emotions—ranging from self-doubt to trepidation to righteous rage—as much as his actions. Despite these flaws, God declares His unconditional love for Moses and insists that he has extraordinary potential. The frank dialogue between God and Moses modeled mentorship in action and showed how a withdrawn secular person with many flaws can still be loved by God and even chosen for a grand prophetic mission.

God stresses that Moses must be methodical in his approach to Pharaoh. Even though the Egyptian despot has "truly transgressed all bounds" in his cruel enslavement of Moses' people and injunction to murder all newborn Israelite boys, nonetheless Moses must "speak to him gently with kind words." Responding to outrageous aggression with equal aggression could be counterproductive and miss important opportunities to de-escalate.

Muhammad's followers could not miss the clear parallel to 'Amr ibn Hisham's murder of Sumayyah. While the revelation recognized anger and pain as natural reactions, it cautioned against being controlled by them, lest further damage and harm result. To "stand firm" required directing intense emotions into constructive action. Rather than react impulsively and erratically, the verses urged remaining grounded in wisdom and strategic behavior. De-escalation and patience were not signs of weakness, but noble self-control.

The chapter concluded with the only time the Qur'an ever urges its audience to request more of something from the Divine: not for wealth or health, but wisdom. "Oh my Divine Mentor, increase me in nuanced knowledge!" The supplication would become an iconic verse, one etched over the door of most Islamic academies. It offered a specific way to channel powerful emotions productively: by devoting energy to exploration and analysis.

Ultimately, time would tell "who among us are the ones following the successful path and who is well-guided to reach success." In a chapter filled with contrasts, this concluding verse pointedly refused to draw one. Rather than say "who is well-guided and who is misguided," the ending phrase refrained from negativity to cite only positive results—modeling how to speak gently despite intense emotions.

Still, the Qur'an could no longer constrain itself from demanding accountability for the Meccans' abusive behavior and soon began an extended period of critique in rapidly escalating tones. A chapter named after Muhammad's own tribe—*Quraish*—started gently, offering verses that superficially seemed to praise while delivering thinly veiled disapproval:

> Consider the comfortable security that Quraish enjoys, with their caravan routes passing unmolested during the winter [to Yemen] and the summer [to Syria]. So, therefore, let them dedicate their skills in the service of the Divine Mentor, the source of the sanctity of the Sacred House [the Ka'bah]—and the One who keeps them satiated from hunger and protected from fear. (106:1–4)

While saluting the tribe's unique privilege of operating caravans without having to pay tribute to foreign powers and living in a capital city that needed no protective walls, the revelation also described a pampered elite with no excuse not to progress. It noted that the Quraish tribe's unique benefits derived not from skill or merit, but solely because of their status as guardians of Mecca's holy shrine. Enjoying a unique inheritance they did not earn, Quraish could at least give back to the Divine whose authority protected them. Signaling assertiveness, Muhammad began reciting this chapter in Mecca's marketplace, his first public declaration since being laughed off the stage over a year earlier.

A few weeks later, the Qur'an stiffened its critique with a chapter called *Al-Mutaffifun* ("The Swindlers"): "Shameful are the ways of the swindlers, who rig the scales and sell inferior merchandise to deceive the imprudent." Recognizing that its tone was veering into specific denunciations of unethical behavior, the Qur'an stopped mentioning God. Nine chapters emerged without divine invocations. *Al-Humazah* ("Mockers and Slanderers") offers a vivid example of the harsh tone that necessitated a break from the sacred:

> Shameful are the ways of every arrogant mocking slanderer who miserly hoards wealth and occupies his days by obsessively counting it. Does he truly delude himself in thinking his ill-gotten gains will immortalize him? Nay! He shall be forgotten and discarded like the burnt ashes of a crumbling ruin. . . . (104:1–4)

Instead of investing money in visionary efforts or donating to charity, the hoarder squanders precious resources and slanders others. The chapter's sharp warning evoked the Meccans' great fear of being forgotten, like the abandoned remnants of destroyed empires.

After nearly a year of Muhammad publicly reciting such acerbic critiques, a revelation emerged to channel righteous indignation into a constructive plan. A chapter called *Al-ʿAsr* evoked the "Intense Squeeze of Time" as a reminder to translate ideas into action:

> Behold time's intense squeeze—
> The stagnant person squanders their ephemeral potential—
> In contrast to those who strive to achieve serene clarity by exerting themselves
> in restorative action; supporting one another by sharing expertise on best
> practices; and persevering through arduous challenges. (103:1–3)

The pithy revelation presented time as a precious yet fleeting resource. To make the best of time before it slipped away, people needed clarity of purpose paired with constructive action and cooperation. Muhammad began reciting the passage at the end of every study session at Dar-ul-Arqam—and it would eventually become a Muslim tradition to begin important meetings with *Al-Fatihah* and end them with *Al-'Asr*.

Muhammad's followers quickly took the message to heart. On the first anniversary of Sumayyah's murder, they organized an evening demonstration outside the Ka'bah. Their faces masked to remain anonymous, a group of about twenty people locked arms and rallied in protest. The Meccan crowd outside the shrine responded with hostility, throwing garbage and shouting slurs—forcing Muhammad's followers to quickly retreat. Their earnest yet shortsighted attempt at "restorative action" revealed a fledgling movement still in need of major refinement.

❧

A few weeks later, the Qur'an celebrated its second anniversary with the return of God's name in a revelation emphasizing the process of gradually honing raw knowledge into synthesized wisdom. Called *Al-Qalam* ("The Quill" or "Gradually Revealed Layers"), the chapter marked the first time the Qur'an described its own physicality with the term *Yasturun*—"precise straight lines." A verse evoked Muhammad's followers transcribing Qur'anic revelations during secret nocturnal study sessions: "Behold the quill and what they transcribe in perfectly ordered straight lines." (68:1)

In contrast to the disordered and unstandardized state of Arabic script at the time (Arabic authors were often the only ones who could decipher their handwriting), this verse depicted the Qur'an's conception of its own ideal physical manifestation: meticulous lines written in elegant script with a delicate pen. The passage would ultimately inspire a dynamic explosion in Qur'anic calligraphy and elaborate Arabic scripts. Precise lines written with a carefully honed quill also served as a metaphor for how to process and apply knowledge: gradually peeling back one layer at a time to reveal core insights and then carefully reprocessing that raw content into a refined product.

Muhammad's followers learned to perform this process during their clandestine nighttime sessions, which took place in Dar-ul-Arqam's inner courtyard. The group study circles were partially illuminated by moonlight and a canopy of twinkling stars. Whereas students remained confined to the small courtyard, each evening the stars appeared to roam freely across the sky on their nightly rotation. Above the wilderness of Arabia, stars served as the main distinctive nocturnal navigation points.

Mirroring the starlit study scene, the Qur'an devoted a year to a series of revelations exploring the guiding power of celestial bodies. Evocative chapter titles included *Al-Buruj* ("The Zodiac"), *An-Najm* ("The Stars"), and *Al-Qamar* ("The Moon"). It bears noting here that all Qur'anic passages rhyme, with each chapter maintaining its own distinctive rhyme scheme. The effect is impossible to reproduce in languages other than Arabic, but the chapter *Ash-Shams* ("The Sun") offers a small glimpse of how repeating sounds merge with vivid imagery to produce a mesmerizing effect:

> Behold the sun with its comforting light,
> Followed by the calming night.
> Day illuminates matters clear and bright,
> As flaws grow reconcealed at night.
> Behold the cosmos He architected with splendor,
> And the earth's vast landscapes He molded with grandeur.
> How He forged the soul [Nafs], empowering it with vision
> While endowing it with destructive or constructive decision.
> Successful is the one who raises the soul and continuously repairs,
> Yet degraded is the one who allows it to be trampled with
> tears . . . (91:1–10)

To the Arabs, the night sky was at once intimately familiar and mysteriously remote. People knew stellar constellations in great detail, yet struggled to understand the stars' many cryptic behaviors. Particularly enigmatic were pulsing stars that flashed like a strobe only to suddenly disappear without warning. (Modern astrophysics has revealed that pulsars ultimately give way to black holes, collapsing into darkness after intense throbbing.) A Qur'anic chapter called *At-Tariq* ("The Pulsar") cited this cosmic mystery as a metaphor for how God's actions can sometimes evade human comprehension.

> Behold the night sky and the pulsar. Oh, you wonder what the pulsar is? It is
> the throbbing star that pierces a hole. Likewise, every soul needs a guardian. . . .
> Behold the cosmos with their recurring cycles and the earth with its seasonal
> sprouting plants. So too are the words of revelation simultaneously crystal clear

and profoundly nuanced. They should not be quickly dismissed as trifling matters . . . (86:1–4, 11–14)

The passage was purposely constructed to spark intrigue. For budding students intensely peeling layers of knowledge in search of deeper truth, *At-Tariq* induced humility and an acknowledgment of the finite limits of the human mind. Something could be observable but not explainable, just like the complicated events in their own lives. In its own way, this perspective helped make sense of trauma and pain, which often lack a clear explanation or simple solution. Acceptance of the unsolvable, Islamic scholars would later argue, enables students to enter the threshold of wisdom.

These Qur'anic insights surreptitiously began to circulate in pockets of Meccan society. While Muhammad's followers had not grown significantly in number, the few fresh recruits did include relatives of key Meccan elders. The identity of these followers remained a closely guarded secret, yet city leaders were unnerved by rumors about elite youth increasingly drawn to the Qur'an. They invited Muhammad to a lavish reception and presented a most enticing offer. If Muhammad would stop preaching the Qur'an's message, they would make him Mecca's leader and richest man, granting him keys to the Ka'bah and any woman he desired.

The offer, while extravagant, was also a trap. Should Muhammad accept, it would completely discredit the Qur'an as simply a tool in Muhammad's quest for power. The prophet gently but firmly explained that no force in the universe—even grand celestial bodies—could stop the Qur'an unfolding revelations: "Even if you were to place the sun in my right hand and the moon in my left, I would not divert from my mission."

The sun and moon served in part as metaphors for Muhammad's long-deceased parents, and several days later a revelation related the story of a single mother struggling to give birth to her only son. Called Maryam (Mary) in honor of the mother of Jesus, the chapter chronicled a defiant woman whose name literally meant "rebellious" and who refused to succumb to her society's limitations. Its concluding verses elucidated Muhammad's refusal to sell out:

Truly, the Loving Divine shall always guide those who actively seek guidance. The enduring legacy of reparation is far superior to wealth and status in the eyes of your Divine Mentor and far greater in ultimate reward [*Maradda*] . . .

Alas, they have falsely molded gods in place of the Loving Divine as would-be
sources of honor and strength, yet these will lead instead to their degradation
and produce the opposite of what they desire. . . . Don't hasten outcomes, as all
days are calculated and planned . . . (19:87, 81–82, 84)

The passage invoked *Maradda,* a business concept well understood by
Meccan merchants that described the mistake of accepting a short-term offer to sell and missing out on a far greater long-term gain. All the money and
status in Mecca could not match the Qur'an's lasting value, even if unlocking
its potential would require enormous patience and uncompromising tenacity.

Fuming at Muhammad's principled rejection of their buyout offer, the
Meccan elders intensified the crackdown on the Qur'an's acolytes. For students risking their reputations to join secret study sessions, increasing persecution heightened the gap between the Qur'an's lofty message and the grim
reality that three years of revelation had failed to make a visible impact on
Meccan society. A revelation named *YaSin* (two Arabic letters combined to
mean "Oh, Distinguished One") emerged to explore the dispiriting phenomenon of people rejecting a seemingly compelling message. The chapter
recounted a tense dialogue between three prophets and the obstinate townsfolk they were sent to save.

The townsfolk declared: "You are nothing more than flawed mortals, like our-
selves. God [*Ar-Rahman*] did not reveal anything to you! You are simply lying."
The messengers replied: ". . . Our task is merely to convey the message clearly
and eloquently." To which the townsfolk retorted: "We clearly perceive you as
a bad omen! Either you cease advising us or you will be ostracized and harshly
punished!"

The messengers responded: "You are using your superstitions and preju-
dices as excuses to dismiss what you know to be true. Our observations have
merely exposed a hidden insecurity within yourselves. Alas, you have chosen
to be self-destructive."

The passage flipped the dynamic of rejection to argue that the Meccans' animosity was in fact a recognition of the Qur'an's powerful impact. If Qur'anic
revelations had not struck a chord, they would simply have been ignored. The
Meccans' vigorous protest over the Qur'an's call to blossom revealed their own

deeply entrenched self-doubt—and instead of signaling something deficient in the Qur'an only enhanced its power.

To bolster morale, the Qur'an refocused on helping its audience appreciate the remarkably positive aspects of life with a chapter named *Ar-Rahman*. This specific name for the Divine had permeated the previous revelations and derived from the word for "womb." Just as a pregnant woman optimistically invests in the unknown future of the fragile life growing inside her, the Divine sees potential in all things and therefore invests energy in empowering growth.

> The Optimistically Empowering Divine inspired the Qur'an, created humanity, and quickly taught humans the art of advanced communication. Both sun and moon flow in a calculated orbit. Shrubs and trees sway with ecstasy. The heavens He raised and set in a system of balance . . . The earth he has made a source of nourishment for all beings, containing fruits of all kinds, laden palm groves, grains with husks, and aromatic herbs. So which of these favors do you deny? He created humanity from moldable clay, yet firm like pottery. . . . So which of these favors do you deny? From the sea emerge pearls and corals. So which of these favors do you deny?

While positive results in Mecca might not yet be immediately visible, audiences just had to adjust their perspective to recognize the amazing potential constantly developing around them. What on the surface appeared inertly bleak actually brimmed with vibrant possibility.

❧❧❧

For all the Meccan elders' hostility to the Qur'an, the harshness of their response was constrained by Arabian tradition. Muhammad after all was a fellow elite, the grandson of a former chief elder, and could not simply be killed like a former slave. The elders' relative restraint as they sought to repress the Qur'an without violating tribal custom infuriated Mecca's most intimidating citizen: the nearly seven-foot 'Umar ibnul Khattab. Known for his violent temper, 'Umar had earlier helped his uncle 'Amr ibn Hisham torture Sumayyah.

In a fit of rage, 'Umar stormed out of the city assembly with an unsheathed sword, determined to extinguish the Qur'an by killing its prophet. Yet remarkably the Qur'an instead extinguished 'Umar's rage. En route to assassinate Muhammad, he discovered a scroll of the chapter *TaHa* in his sister's home and out of curiosity began to read it. 'Umar, who had never actually read or heard the Qur'an, found himself transformed by his first direct encounter with it and began sobbing.

The example of Moses immediately struck home, as *TaHa* revealed an impulsive macho man raised in luxury and power who was both feared and harbored deep internal fears—and despite his flaws was chosen by the Divine for a great mission. Long denied affection by his own stern parents, 'Umar melted at the tender words of the Divine Mentor: "I have showered you with my love, precisely prearranging the events of your life with my gentle care!"

The shocking and sudden awakening of 'Umar earned the Qur'an a powerful new ally, but one whose raw energy needed to be sublimated in a healthy direction. Rather than unleash 'Umar to preach in the streets of Mecca—which might lead to him violently imposing the message on unreceptive audiences— the Qur'an instead directed 'Umar and other followers inward to introspective learning. In fact, 'Umar's unexpected transformation from ferocious antagonist to devoted follower sparked a new emphasis on finding compassion for people stuck in stagnation.

A string of seven chapters was revealed roughly one week apart, each beginning with the letters *Ha* and *Mim*. These chapters aimed to help the Dar-ul-Arqam students explore the viewpoint of the Meccan public that had been resisting their message for three years. The letters at their core represented an orchard wall (*Ha*) and a flowing water (*Mim*), images that suggested different perspectives: inside versus outside the wall and how reality is refracted in water reflections.

Whereas *TaHa* presented the Exodus drama from Moses' viewpoint, the revelation *Ghafir* ("The Most Forgiving") repeated the story from Pharaoh's standpoint, including revealing an unusual dilemma faced by the most powerful man on earth. On the one hand, Pharaoh was an absolute ruler who could act with impunity, yet by custom, even Pharaoh could not assassinate a member of the royal household—into which Moses had been adopted as a baby. The divine plan had indeed positioned Moses as an unassailable messenger in the royal court, and the Qur'an presented Pharaoh grappling with his aides over how to address the impasse.

> Pharaoh said: "Permit me to kill Moses and let his Divine Mentor come to save him. For I honestly fear that he will corrupt your established traditions and spread disorder and tyranny throughout the land. . . . I only have your best interests in mind and show you reality as I genuinely see it. My only desire is to guide you to the most liberating path forward." (40:26, 29)

Through the character of Pharaoh, the Qur'an gives sympathetic voice to the genuine fears of the Meccan elders, who viewed themselves as guardians of tradition. The Qur'an allows Pharaoh to lay out the logic of his rigid mindset, not to justify it but rather to help better appreciate the challenge of trying to change it. In so doing, the Qur'an aims to guide more effective interventions by recognizing that psychological outlooks cannot be overcome with mere logic.

For two years, the Qur'an would continue to share stories exploring the Exodus account as well as other biblical episodes and to expand its audiences' perspective. One chapter called *An-Naml* ("The Ants") recounted the drama of the court of King Solomon from below—via the dialogue amongst ants observing events in Jerusalem—as well as via a hoopoe bird observing palace intrigue from above. In contrast to the typical Meccan attitude that only Arab male elites mattered, the Qur'an spotlighted even the ants trampled underfoot: "There is not a creature that thumps upon the earth nor flies with wings that is also not a nation [of feelings and interests] just like yourselves" (6:38).

Gaining fresh perspective also required delving inside human emotions—and for this journey the Qur'an turned to the traumatic travails testing numerous persecuted biblical prophets. Arabian custom insisted on stoic suppression of emotions, especially by male leaders, to maintain a façade of fortitude. Yet the Qur'an reveals deep internal turmoil endured by great men chosen by God for a special mission. In *Al-Anbiya* ("The Prophets"), verses even give voice to the profound depression experienced by the prophet Jonah:

> Then he cried out with profound grief [*Nada*] from the darknesses of despair: "There is no comforter but you, raise me and release me from what weighs me down, I allowed myself to descend into the shadows of darkness." (21:87)

The revelation stressed the unusual plural form "darknesses" (*Thulumat*) to emphasize the overlapping forms of distress compounded upon Jonah and the need to gradually peel back each shade of darkness in the journey to recovery. In his lowest state—expressed in the gloomy belly of a whale deep under the waves—Jonah achieves a transcendent self-realization: his depression is self-induced ("I allowed myself to descend"). Healing, therefore, is also in his hands, though comfort from the Divine Mentor is also essential.

The term *Nada*—"to cry out with intense emotions"—described behavior disdained by Meccan men, yet the word would be repeated throughout a series of Qur'anic revelations exploring the experiences of prophets. Another revelation soon followed, using the same term in recounting Noah's story from an intense psychological perspective. Noah experiences rejection both from most of his neighbors and even his own son.

> The obstinate elites among his people said: "We see you as a mere flawed mortal like ourselves and that your followers are of the lowest classes, dimwitted and impulsive. You and your followers have nothing better to offer than what we already possess. In fact, we think you are blatant liars!"
>
> Noah said, "Oh, my people, consider if I stand upon a path, seeking clarity of vision, guided by my Divine Mentor, who showers me with His compassion and understanding—which alas you fail to see—should we then force it upon you even as you detest it? Oh my people, I don't ask you for wealth, my reward is only with the Loving Divine, and I cannot turn away those who seek serenity, no matter their status, for they seek to connect to their Divine Mentor. Indeed, I perceive you as a stagnating people. . . .
>
> "I don't claim to possess the treasures of the Divine, nor do I have knowledge of the unseen, nor do I claim to be an angelic being, nor do I stoop to say that those you detest will not be granted greatness and elevated by the Divine. It is the Divine alone who knows the depth of their true selves. Indeed, if I turned them away, I would be truly unjust. . . ."
>
> God said to Noah: "Build the ark, under our watchful care and through our inspiring directions, and don't plead with Me on behalf of those who have chosen to dwell in the dark shadows. Alas, they shall drown." And he diligently manufactured the ark with precision and superior workmanship. And every time the elite among his people passed by, they laughingly sneered and mocked him. . . .

Finally, Noah declared [to his few followers]: "Board it! May its sailing and mooring be blessed by the Name of the Divine. Indeed, my Divine Mentor is full of forgiveness and compassion!" And the ark was battered by rough waves like mountains. Yet Noah's son had cut himself off from his father [and refused to board], so Noah desperately pleaded [*Nada*]: "Oh my dear son, please, ride with us and do not be among the obstinate."

The son responded: "No! I will seek the refuge atop a mountain that will protect me from the rising waters. . . ." Then a great wave flashed between them and fiercely swept him away. . . . Then Noah cried out in profound grief [*Nada*] to his Divine Mentor: "Oh my Divine Mentor! My son is part of my family [*Ahli*] and you promised to save my family, for your promise is true, and You are the Wisest of the Wise!" God replied, "Oh Noah, he was most certainly not your family. He was the embodiment of destructive deeds. . . ."

With that blunt divine pronouncement, the Qur'an for the first time directly upheld individual consciousness over the collective constraints of blood bonds. In Arabia, family ties defined an individual, with *Ahli* ("my family") literally meaning "my tent"—i.e., a person's source of shelter and protection. But just as Noah had been forced to construct a new home to protect himself and his followers from the deadly flood, the Qur'an encouraged audiences to take the bold leap of separating themselves from toxic familial elements in order to preserve their integrity. Actions, not bloodlines, determined an individual's worth, and sometimes one's own close relatives could be harmful or even destructive. In expressing this painful truth, the Qur'an was laying the groundwork for its early followers to be able to make a heart-rending break from their own families in order to save their lives—to prepare them for a painful declaration of independence.

❦❦❦

Achieving true independence—not simply rebelling to indulge in anarchy—required taking personal responsibility for one's own decisions. Daring to blossom required opening up and honestly assessing the surrounding reality, an approach the Qur'an had now spent years exploring and demonstrating. On the sixth anniversary of the *Iqra* revelation, the Qur'an finally gave this constructively critical posture a name:

Stand flexible and establish the clear intention of your actions as a *Hanif,* and
make that the method of your daily life. . . . (10:105)

Drawing on the term for a tree constantly rebalancing itself atop unstable
terrain, the *Hanif* operates as a healthy skeptic who honestly evaluates inherited traditions, staying true to roots while adjusting to reality in productive
ways. The clear intention of the *Hanif*'s actions should not be cynical or aggressive, but rather to challenge in order to awaken. Such constant societal and
self-examination required both grounding and flexibility. For an audience that
might soon be forced to abandon their own families and community, this message provided a powerful mindset.

As the Qur'an presented a name for the spirit of its approach, it also acknowledged terms for its constituent parts. The same chapter revealed that
each verse was called an *Ayah,* which the Qur'an had already used many times
in previous years to describe "clarifying signs"—using a poetic word for the
brightest star in a constellation. Appropriately, the chapter collecting these stars
in a group served as a constellation, or a "Surah." While the word "Qur'an"
evoked the terrestrial blossoming of plants nurtured by soil and daytime sunlight, its components pointed to a celestial parallel: twinkling stars together
comprising constellations for nighttime guidance.

Most Meccans, of course, had no interest in the Qur'an's guiding signs or
constructive criticism, but simply wanted an end to the escalating tensions in
Mecca. The city's elders decided to make one final attempt at diplomacy to
demonstrate that they had exhausted all options. Mecca's premier poet, Al-
Walid Ibn Al-Mughirah, was dispatched to convince Muhammad to silence
the Qur'an. While the Meccans hoped the poet's unique mastery of Arabic
could outshine the Qur'an and shame it into withdrawing, Muhammad hoped
the Qur'an's eloquence could instead sway Al-Walid and thus in one fell swoop
win over Arabia's elites.

In the midst of the poetic duel between Al-Walid and the Qur'an, one
of Muhammad's followers—a poor blind man dressed in tattered rags—
unexpectedly approached without realizing he was interrupting an epic encounter. As Al-Walid turned to glance at the blind interloper, Muhammad
frowned in visible annoyance at the sudden break in the intense conversation's
flow. While no one but the Divine witnessed Muhammad's scowl, a chapter
soon emerged to publicly reveal the inconsiderate impatience. Called *'Abasa*

("He Frowned"), the surah advertised from its opening sentence an admonishment of the prophet himself: "He frowned and turned away, when the blindman came to seek his counsel."

The standoff with Al-Walid ended in a stalemate, with the elder praising the Qur'an's power even as he condemned its threat, declaring: "Its deeply rooted call to blossom can bear fruit and overrun the social order. With its eloquence surpassing all others, it will surely shake the foundations of our established order, which is inferior to its powerful message." Based on Al-Walid's honest assessment, it became clear to both Muhammad and the elders that a direct confrontation was now inevitable.

Facing an imminent crackdown, Muhammad and his followers needed to prepare for possible annihilation—and the Qur'an's silencing. Under pressure, the Qur'an revealed four chapters in a row all beginning with the phrase *Al-hamdulillah*—a direct echo of the opening line of *Al-Fatihah* nearly seven years earlier that called on audiences to emulate the Divine's unconditional love. This opening served as a signpost that the four chapters contained vital life lessons and a roadmap for how to remain focused and directed in the absence of any further Qur'anic revelations.

The crescendo of parting wisdom culminated in a surah called *Al-Kahf* ("The Cave"). Its core narrative retold the popular story of "The Seven Sleepers"— Roman elites belonging to a persecuted movement who flee their town for sanctuary in a distant cave. After falling into a deep sleep, the fugitives awaken three hundred years later and emerge to discover the old Roman empire fragmented and their own movement triumphant. The Qur'an's message to its persecuted followers: the present does not define the future. They should seek refuge so their movement might ultimately persevere.

The chapter's opening and closing reiterated the Qur'an's key themes:

Emulate the Ultimate Source of Unconditional Love, who Gradually Revealed the Book, as a source of guidance to His mentee and has not allowed it to become twisted and distorted. Rather, it has an upright and flexible spine as a caution against declining into desolation and as a source of serenity for those who attain clarity. Indeed, the result of their hard work will ultimately be a pleasant and lasting reward. . . .

Be mindful of your ego [*Nafs*] and persevere with followers who sincerely seek guidance from the Divine Mentor, at dawn and in the late evening, actively attempting to improve themselves and be elevated. Do not allow your eyes to divert from them in the false desire for the deceptive ornamentation of inferior goals. . . . Wealth and sons are but the embellishment of the lower aspects of this world; however, a lasting constructive legacy is far better. . . .

Go out and proclaim: "Had the sea been ink for the words of my Divine Mentor, the sea would not suffice to transcribe all of my Divine Mentor's wisdom, even if they were refilled."

Go out and proclaim: "I am merely a flawed mortal, like yourselves. . . ."

For an audience about to be cut off from the Qur'an, these revelations served as a reminder to focus on what truly matters, not others' standards of approval. To achieve a lasting legacy required maintaining principled independence, even if that meant enduring extended isolation. And even though Muhammad's followers had spent seven years engaged in little more than learning, the seas' vast knowledge called them to continue studying and analyzing. After all, they were merely flawed mortals, albeit ones chosen for a special mission of blossoming.

5

MUSLIM: THE QUR'AN GUIDING HEALING AND REPAIR

TWO ARMED SENTRIES DRAGGED SHUT THE ACACIA-WOOD BARRIER gates, which screeched as they scraped the parched ground causing a cloud of dust to swirl up out of the desolate valley. The gates led to a hectare-sized stockade, cut off from the outside world by a fence of coarse palm-fiber ropes. Their bristly strands scraped the skin on contact and were typically used to domesticate feral animals.

Corralled inside there were not bucking broncos, but rather some two hundred men, women, and children—all members of Muhammad's clan, the Hashemites. An hour earlier, they had been dragged from their homes and forced to wear turmeric-yellow bracelets around their right wrists, marking them for isolation the way shepherds tagged diseased livestock for elimination. As the sun beat down from the noon sky, the Hashemites wandered around their new concentration camp in a daze. Arabia had never before witnessed such mass incarceration of innocents.

The real target here was not human beings, but the Qur'an. Seven years after it issued a bold call to open up to the world and blossom, the Qur'an suddenly found itself physically restrained and confined, quarantined from society like a dangerous disease. The leadership assembly of Meccan elites had reached their limit. The Qur'an's messenger, Muhammad, would be boycotted along with his pagan clan, imprisoned in a desert valley without food or water to force them to silence the Qur'an. "The Blossoming" would wither away in a barren wasteland.

Mecca's elders had reached the end of their rope after a humiliating scene at the assembly hall a week earlier. The chief elder's firstborn son—groomed as Mecca's future leader—had dramatically appeared before the council to reveal himself as a follower of the Qur'an. The Qur'an's message was clearly no longer restricted to a fringe underground movement and had even begun to seep into the elders' own families. In a panicked frenzy, the council hurriedly adopted an unprecedented final solution: a boycott (typically dismissed as a cowardly and underhanded ploy) would force the Hashemites to succumb to hunger or give up their principled protection of the Qur'an.

Muhammad received advance warning about the impending boycott and decided with his followers that they should flee across the Red Sea to Africa to keep the Qur'an's message alive. They boarded a ship to Abyssinia (modern-day Ethiopia), but he insisted on remaining in Mecca to face his fate without relenting to the elders' demands. The standoff that everyone assumed would last only two weeks instead dragged on for two years. Modest food supplies were smuggled into the camp, but there was barely enough to sustain the Hashemites. Day after day, month after month, the camp's inmates languished.

During these two years, the Qur'an remained silent. It had never withdrawn like this before. Did the prolonged silence mean the elders' plan had succeeded in stifling it forever? One brief verse emerged to reassure and suggest a larger purpose behind the forced quarantine:

> Don't hasten revelation by movements of your tongue, hoping it will transpire—
> We will reveal it when the time is ripe for wisdom to gather and blossom
> forth. (75:16–17)

Evoking the prophet's tongue flicking in an anxious quest to trigger revelation, the verse admonished against forcing progress. Instead, it called for granting time to allow "wisdom to gather," urging profound introspection before moving forward. Indirectly, it even suggested that the elders' boycott was actually part of a divine plan, giving the Qur'an a chance to guide its followers in a distant land while forcing its messenger to reflect on why the movement had failed to make any significant progress during its first seven years. The Qur'an would speak only when it had a receptive audience fully prepared to take action.

Even as the Qur'an remained silently sequestered in Arabia, its message thrived openly in Africa. The refugees in Abyssinia immediately began applying the Qur'anic revelations they had transported across the ocean in manuscript form. After years of persecution, the followers no longer needed to behave as *Hanifs*—healthy critics of stagnation—but were for the first time free to behave publicly as *Muslims*: social repairers taking positive action to enhance their surroundings. Rather than wallow in victimhood, the refugees rushed to set up new businesses to become an economically self-sustaining community that could also provide support services to impoverished locals. They established the first-ever mosque *(masjid)*, an open educational center for exploring the Qur'an's teachings in broad daylight instead of in a secret nocturnal academy. With Muhammad absent, the Qur'an served as their guiding mentor.

The Meccan elders, frantic to exterminate the Qur'an's message, sent an elite diplomatic delegation to the Abyssinian king to demand the refugees' return. In a showdown at the royal court, a Meccan emissary denounced the Qur'an's message as toxic, even alleging the Qur'an vilified Mary and Jesus. When the Christian king demanded an answer from the refugees, they allowed the Qur'an to speak for itself by melodiously chanting *Maryam* with its evocative account of Mary and Jesus. Despite being translated from the original Arabic into Ethiopic, *Surah Maryam* captivated the king—who promptly declared the Qur'an's affinity with the spirit of the Gospels and proclaimed his personal protection of the refugees.

During the showdown at the royal court, the Qur'an had charmed royalty, swaying the scholarly Abyssinian court that governed one of the era's dominant superpowers. Though it emerged from the cultural backwater of Arabia, the Qur'an had dazzled a formidable empire, transforming persecution into an opportunity to demonstrate its own power. Meanwhile, the Qur'an's followers had accomplished far more in Abyssinia in just a few months than in seven years in Mecca.

Until this point, the Qur'an had been mere theory; now at last it had the opportunity to prove itself. The question remained, though: Why had the refugees achieved such success in Africa while stagnating for years in Mecca? When the Qur'an would finally break its silence, its new revelations would force Muhammad and his followers to confront this question and challenge them to determine how to truly become *Muslims*.

✿✿✿

Just as the Qur'an saved its followers in Abyssinia, it finally came to the rescue of its followers held in the concentration camp outside Mecca. Five young pagan members of the elite in Mecca grew increasingly troubled by how the elders' drawn-out boycott violated Arabia's cultural norms and made the Meccans look both cowardly and incompetent as the Hashemites refused to buckle. One evening, the young men sneaked into the camp to share their outrage with Muhammad, who in turn recited the Qur'an's most recent revelation to them. The story in *Surah Al-Kahf* of young elites who dared to challenge an unjust status quo proved inspiring. The next morning, the five youths stood before the Ka'bah shrine to denounce the boycott as illegitimate, sparking a grassroots uprising that forced the elders to rescind their edict.

The Hashemite clan limped back into Mecca, barely able to move their frail, malnourished bodies. Some were too weak to walk and had to be carried back to their crumbling homes on stretchers. Among those invalids were two of the Qur'an's key supporters: Muhammad's wife Khadijah—the Qur'an's first follower, a woman who recognized its divine message even as her husband initially panicked, and his foster uncle Abu Talib—a pagan who did not recognize the Qur'an's divine message yet nonetheless supported its right to speak, even in the face of overwhelming persecution. Both supporters, one a follower and one an external ally, had refused repeated opportunities to abandon the Qur'an. Within days of their release from the camp, both died, succumbing to the boycott's deadly consequences.

Muhammad faced the lowest moment in his adult life. Though finally liberated to once again interact with other people, he had lost two of his dearest and most steadfast supporters. With three of his children having fled two years earlier to Abyssinia, he returned home accompanied only by one teenaged daughter. The once grand family home sat decaying after two years of neglect, and so Muhammad, while in mourning, set about slowly fixing the cracks in the walls one by one. This simple act of restoration echoed an iconic scene from the ending of *Surah Al-Kahf* that featured Moses and his unnamed mentor enduring hunger:

They came upon a town seeking sustenance, which was adamantly refused them. Then they came upon a crumbling wall within that town, which they repaired. Moses demanded: "Why should we repair a wall for a people who refuse to feed us?" His mentor replied: "You asking this question marks the end of your apprenticeship. . . . As for the wall, it belongs to two local young orphaned boys whose father had been generous and kind and concealed a treasure beneath the wall as an inheritance for his sons when they grew up. I feared that if the wall collapsed, the townsfolk would steal the treasure from the young orphans."

In this vignette, impatient Moses at first fails to appreciate the importance of altruistically fixing cracks in a fragile wall—and as a result is cut off by his mentor. Repairing fractures in walls, of course, is the literal meaning of what a Muslim does, and the Qur'an's followers had likewise been cut off from new revelations for two entire years. They had briefly been given the identity of Muslims by the Qur'an without any direct explanation of the concept—and they had attracted a following of only several dozen individuals. While this small crew had spent seven years learning critical thinking, blossoming required advanced techniques for identifying and transcending obstacles, then moving from intention to action.

Put another way, becoming a Muslim required repairing oneself from within before setting out to repair the world. Symbolic of this internal rebuilding process, Muhammad had to first repair the cracks in his own home before again addressing the fissures in Meccan society; only then would the "time be ripe for wisdom to gather." Indeed, after repairing at home for two weeks, Muhammad reopened the Dar-ul-Arqam academy for the few followers remaining in Mecca. The next day, on the ninth anniversary of the Qur'an's first appearance, revelation finally returned.

After holding back for two years, the Qur'an reemerged with a masterwork and its only full narrative. A vivid new telling of the story of Joseph, *Surah Yusuf* was like no previous revelation. Modern readers may note its cinematic qualities, as the narrative shifts rapidly between dramatic scenes, rarely interrupted by any editorial comment. The chapter aims to show rather than tell, compelling audiences to analyze Joseph's saga and draw their own conclusions. The psychological dimensions of Joseph's fall and rise form the heart of the narrative, which serves as an engrossing distraction to help Muhammad and other followers gain some distance from their own immediate pain.

At the end of the chapter, Joseph's final declaration provides the larger context for recounting his epic story: "May I complete my life having fulfilled my mission of being a Muslim—as one who altruistically seeks to repair the world!" (This marks the first time the Qur'an presents the word "Muslim" in the singular form.) How Joseph navigates his perilous personal journey, both practically and psychologically, reveals what it means to act as an individual Muslim. Moreover, in the middle of the *Surah,* Joseph declares: "I followed the methodology of my patriarchs, Abraham, Isaac, and Jacob"—a statement that directly echoes the first time the Qur'an invoked the term "Muslim": "This is the methodology of your patriarch Abraham—it was he who originally named you Muslims."

Joseph finds himself cut off from his family and homeland, forced to forge a new identity in a foreign African land—just as the Qur'an had to do in Abyssinia. Joseph endures persecution and betrayal by his own brothers, only winning their respect via the staggering accomplishment of rising from slavery to rescue the entire world from starvation. Proving worthiness via deeds and outcomes, not merely words, sets the standard. Yet as the chapter begins, young Joseph has won his father's adoration despite having accomplished nothing.

> Recall when Joseph said to his father: "My dear father, I dreamt of eleven stars along with the sun and the moon prostrating before me." Jacob replied: "My dear son, don't inform your brothers of this dream, lest they plot to hurt you. Indeed, the dark forces within men are their greatest enemy. It is in such wonderous ways that your Divine Mentor has chosen you and teaches you to decode the mysterious and to fulfill His covenant of bounty upon you and upon the descendants of Jacob, as he did for your two forefathers, Abraham and Isaac."

Joseph's dream is filled with classic Semitic symbolism of parents (sun and moon) and brothers (stars) bowing before him. In contrast to how their charismatic brother spends his time daydreaming, Joseph's siblings toil in the fields. Their natural jealousy is evoked by Joseph's unearned superiority, which blinds Jacob to his other sons' intense efforts. Jacob, for his part, recognizes that his son has remarkable God-given talents, but also worries about the "dark forces within men"—that is, the unchecked human ego. Joseph offers no acknowledgment of the Divine's favor and seems to coast on his talents rather than channel them into action.

Surah Yusuf quickly cuts between scenes, sometimes even mid-sentence, to drive forward the dramatic narrative.

> Joseph's brothers gathered together, plotting to cast him into the darkness of the drywell, and We revealed to Joseph: "One day, you will see them again and you will remind them of what they did to you, even though they will not be aware of who you are."
>
> . . . Then a caravan passed by the well and sent the water-bearer to draw water. When he raised the bucket from the well, the man exclaimed: "Oh what good fortune, it's a handsome boy!" They concealed Joseph among their merchandise, and the Loving Divine was aware of what they had done. Then they sold him into slavery for a meagerly price of a few silver coins, as they hastened to get rid of him lest they be discovered for trafficking a free man. Then the man who purchased Joseph in Egypt said to his wife: "Treat him well and honor him, as perhaps he will be of benefit to us or maybe we can even adopt him as a son."

Haughty Joseph is quickly humbled in his new state of bondage, as he is effectively worthless in the slave market. Lacking any practical experience or skills, he commands but a few silver coins. The Qur'an, in one of its few editorial asides, interrupts the narrative to make sure audiences understand that Joseph's degradation serves a larger purpose:

> It is in such mysterious ways that We arranged for Joseph to attain a high position in the land, teaching him the interpretation of the enigmatic. The Loving Divine is perpetually arranging destinies, though most people remain oblivious. When Joseph matured, We endowed him with deep wisdom and penetrating knowledge, such is how We reward those who are sincerely upright.

While God arranges opportunities, humans choose whether or not to seize them. Joseph must demonstrate that he is truly "upright," and "endowed with deep wisdom." When his master's wife, unable to resist Joseph's magnetic appearance, attempts to seduce him, the young man refuses to betray the gentleman who altruistically adopted him "as a son." Here the chapter's drama really heats up:

Then she in whose house Joseph dwelled tried to seduce him. She firmly locked the doors and said: "Look, I have beautified myself for you." He insisted: "God forbid! My master has treated me well, and to betray his trust in me is truly unjust." Yet she desired him and wanted to have him, and he too would have been seduced by her had his Divine Mentor not given him the resolve to remain steadfast. Such was Our arranging to protect him from harm. He was truly a sincere devotee. . . .

Then the women of the city began to gossip: "The wife of the minister tried to rape her servant boy. She is captivated by love. We think she is drowning in lovesickness."

When the minister's wife heard their gossiping, she invited the ladies to a lavish banquet. As they reclined to eat, she gave each of them a sharp knife to cut fruit. Then she had Joseph brought before them while dressed in his finest. When the women saw Joseph, they were so deeply mesmerized and captivated by his beauty and charm that they cut into their own hands without noticing, declaring in astonishment: "God forbid, this cannot be a human! This must be an angelic being!"

The minister's wife retorted: "This is the one whom you judged me for desiring [when you cut yourselves in seconds and I have to live with him every day]! Yes, I did try to seduce him, yet he held back. If he does not submit to my demands, I will have him imprisoned and degraded to the lowest status."

Joseph cried out: "My Divine Mentor, prison is more beloved to me than what they ask me to do! If You do not save me from their intrigues, I will surely be swayed by them and become stuck amongst the stagnant."

By refusing the wife's offer to betray her husband, Joseph takes his first true independent action, choosing the deprivations of prison over the luxurious refinements of the senior minister's mansion and beautiful wife. He makes a conscious decision to be humbled rather than betray the one man who uplifted him solely out of the goodness of his heart. The Qur'an briefly interjects to insist that Joseph was not abandoned by God:

His Divine Mentor heard his entreaties and protected him from their plots; He is ever present actively listening and deeply aware of all things.

The verse indirectly suggested that the Qur'an's extended silence did not mean that God had withdrawn, but rather was part of a deliberate maturation process for the purpose of inducing introspection. Joseph's own extended detention comes as he is sent to jail despite his obvious innocence in the trumped-up charges of raping the chief minister's wife. In prison, he is approached by two former servants of the royal court to interpret their dreams.

> Joseph said: "There is not a meal you have received without me first prophesizing it beforehand—that is the skill my Divine Mentor has taught me. I have rejected the ways of a people who do not believe in the Loving Divine and remain ungrateful for their blessings. Instead, I followed the methodology of my forefathers, Abraham, Isaac, and Jacob, devoted to only one God. This is the blessing of the Loving Divine upon all people, though most remain ungrateful. Oh fellow prisoners, which is better: many hostile deities maliciously competing amongst themselves or One God, unique and supreme? Certainly, what you devote yourselves to are simply names that you and your ancestors invented without deep knowledge. True wisdom lies in the hands of the Loving Divine. . . .

From the lowest depths of his jail cell, Joseph identifies himself for the first time with forefathers, reconnecting to his heritage despite being cut off from his family for years. Despite living in a foreign land alone amidst a foreign people, Joseph declares that he has remained true to his people's core values. One of those values is gratitude, and for the first time Joseph acknowledges that his talents are God-given rather than earned. He has ended up in prison because of unwavering gratitude to a human master who selflessly cared for him, a devotion that mirrors his gratitude to the Divine Master. In this terrible low moment, Joseph sounds fulfilled for the first time in his life, as the principled decision to accept imprisonment provides an uplifting sense of purpose. With renewed appreciation for God's care, Joseph challenges his fellow inmates to reject backstabbing pagan deities whose flaring egos drive them to relentlessly pursue self-aggrandizement at the expense of others. As humans naturally emulate the characteristics of their deities, Joseph prefers an ethical and compassionate Divine Mentor.

Joseph eventually amazes the Egyptian king, the most powerful man in the world, by interpreting his dream—yet refuses the monarch's request to leave jail and join the royal court, insisting that first his reputation must be cleared. Demonstrating a healthy ego, Joseph demands an acknowledgment that he never tried to rape the chief minister's wife. In a surprising twist, the wife contritely admits the truth, accepts responsibility, and offers genuine reconciliation while invoking God's compassion in the spirit of healing wounds.

> Then the minister's wife publicly confessed: "Now the truth is exposed clearly for all to witness. It was in fact I who tried to seduce Joseph—yet accused him—even though he had spoken the truth. I say this so that Joseph should be assured that I did not maliciously intend to slander him; indeed the Loving Divine does not bless the treacherous. I don't exonerate myself [*Nafsi*] from blame—truly, the ego [*Nafs*] can lead us to commit acts of transgression. I acknowledge that I wronged Joseph and seek forgiveness. Indeed, the Divine Mentor is full of forgiveness and compassion."
>
> The king demanded, "Bring him before me! I want to reserve him for my exclusive service!" When the king spoke to Joseph, he said, "Today, you are highly esteemed and trusted by us!" Joseph replied: "In that case, place me in charge of all the treasuries and storehouses of the land; indeed, I am a man of reliable integrity and uniquely skilled."

Once again, Joseph seizes a pivotal moment and owns his rare talents. With self-confidence and foresight, he steps up to initiate a mass mobilization of resources to prepare for a looming seven-year famine—effectively saving the world from starvation. By anticipating an impending fissure that would cause society to crumble, Joseph preemptively planned ahead. On a micro level, his actions save his own family from dying of starvation, their fate in a faraway land directly impacted by Joseph's leadership. At this juncture, the Divine Narrator interrupts the story to observe:

> In such wonderous ways We established Joseph in a place of prominence on earth, settling wherever and however he pleased. Our compassion encompasses those whom We choose, and We always ultimately reward the good works of the sincere. As for those who seek serenity and trust in the Loving Divine, the reward that is yet to come is far greater. . . .

Surah Yusuf then relates an additional opportunity for repair when Joseph's brothers come to Egypt in a desperate quest to obtain food for their starving family. Joseph chooses not to reveal himself to them and instead orchestrates an extended drama to assess whether his brothers have matured since they betrayed him years earlier. In a deeply moving moment, they sacrifice themselves to save another one of their brothers—and Joseph finally discloses his real identity. Like the chief minister's wife, Joseph's brothers immediately admit the truth:

> The brothers confessed: "Truly, the Loving Divine has favored you despite our plotting, and we truly feel great remorse for the harm that we had done." Joseph responded: "Today, I no longer hold ill feelings toward any of you. The Loving Divine will forgive all your wrongs."

Cathartically releasing decades of intense pain and suffering helps Joseph finally acknowledge that the seemingly overwhelming challenges he faced were instead catalysts for him to grow and achieve greatness. After being reunited with his father, Joseph sits on the throne surrounded by his family and ends the saga by declaring:

> Oh my dear father, this is the fulfillment of my old dream. My Divine Mentor has made it come true. He has been kind to me by liberating me from prison and saving me from the desolation of the desert, where rivalry was ignited between me and my siblings. My Divine Mentor is ever so gentle and compassionate, full of wisdom, and knowing of all things. My Divine Mentor, you surely have granted me great authority in the land and given me great knowledge to understand what most cannot comprehend. You formed all things; You are my guardian and caretaker in this world and the next. May I complete my life having fulfilled my mission of being a Muslim—as one who altruistically seeks to repair the world.

The Divine Narrator then closes out the surah with one final observation:

> When messengers reach a nadir of despair and feel completely rejected without any hope, precisely then our assistance comes to relieve them. In the stories of those who passed before you are lessons for people of reason; these are not mere entertainment but rather an affirmation of previous revelations inspired into the world whose true purpose is as a guide and a source of compassion for people seeking serenity.

Like desire and drive, despair is also a powerful ego-driven emotion, albeit a negative one where individuals decry their own hopelessness. Rather than succumbing to the temptation to give up easily, the Qur'an urges resilience: to hold on and never lose faith in one's own potential. Stories of other people who overcame far worse challenges offer a special opportunity to step outside one's own self-pity and be inspired to aim even higher. For this reason, Muhammad encouraged followers to recite *Surah Yusuf* whenever they felt depressed, anxious, or confused. Joseph's remarkable triumph offers a timeless escape from one's own crises and a model for how internal repair can yield transformative opportunities to improve the world.

Joseph's journey also offers a model for how to "fulfill the mission of being a Muslim." Based on the example presented in *Surah Yusuf,* a Muslim recognizes the role of the ego in both its healthy and unhealthy manifestations. The ego can inspire the praiseworthy desire to repair the world for its own sake, but also a false and unearned sense of haughty superiority. A Muslim makes principled decisions, even if they come at immediate personal cost, and remains optimistic and appreciative no matter how dark the present—staying grounded amidst turmoil and focused on the future. Such focus enables them to seize unanticipated opportunities to apply their talents while simultaneously appreciating how success only comes with the assistance of other people, who deserve acknowledgment and gratitude. A Muslim manages to transcend the pain of a wounded ego in order to forgive, always remaining open to reconciliation as an important aspect of interpersonal repair. Finally, a Muslim reveres a moral Abrahamic God— rather than immoral, dishonest, and selfish deities—and emulates how God altruistically seeks to elevate and bring out the best in others, enjoying fulfillment in others' success.

❧❧❧

In a burst of enthusiasm inspired by *Surah Yusuf*'s message of proactively shaping one's destiny, Muhammad left the confines of Mecca for the first time in years to bring the Qur'an's message to the nearby resort town of Taif. Yet the slight change in venue and target audience failed to yield more hospitable results. Encouraged by their parents, the children of Taif delivered the ultimate Semitic act of social ostracization: hurling an avalanche of stones at

Muhammad to drive him away. His legs bloodied and enthusiasm deflated, Muhammad fled for his life.

Nonetheless, channeling Joseph's indefatigable long-term optimism, Muhammad expressed his hope for the children's future despite their violence (several of them would years later end up carrying the Qur'an's message all the way to India). That evening, while recuperating from his physical and emotional wounds, Muhammad experienced the epiphany of a night journey to a rebuilt and restored Jerusalem filled with dozens of biblical prophets sharing words of inspiration. Just before the sun rose the following morning, a rejuvenated Muhammad established the formal mechanics of Muslim prayer as a physical act of re-grounding where individuals prostrated themselves to regain perspective as a spiritual reset.

News of Muhammad reciting the Qur'an in Taif quickly reached the Meccan elders' assembly, who realized that urgent action was needed to disparage the Qur'an before its message could proliferate beyond Mecca. To proactively discredit the Qur'an, the elders financed an extensive and expensive campaign of poets traveling Arabia to malign the Qur'an in acerbic tones. Called *Hija'* (literally, "a stabbing barrage"), the coordinated slander campaign deliberately quoted the Qur'an out of context to cast it as bewitching sorcery that sought to spark conflict and enslave people, playing off the classic Arabian fear of becoming subjugated to outsiders.

Of course, the elders' campaign partially backfired, as it raised the Qur'an's brand and profile throughout Arabia. Most people did not know what to make of this mysterious entity that poets denounced as dangerous, but one elite young man from Arabia's fiercest marauding tribe was intrigued. Jundub Ibn Junadah (later renamed Abu Tharr—"the far-reaching seed spreader") journeyed to Mecca to examine the Qur'an for himself. He ended up spending several months studying under Muhammad's tutelage, before leaving with Qur'anic manuscripts to propagate the message among his tribe. For the first time, the Qur'an had gained a receptive follower who was not a relative or acquaintance of Muhammad.

Six months had passed since *Surah Yusuf* without any new revelations—another unusual extended gap—but right after Abu Tharr departed, the Qur'an at last broke its silence. Called *Ash-Sharh* (literally, "untying ropes binding a harness to a camel," and figuratively, "relieving the tightness of the chest when anxious"), the surah offered a message of solace:

Did We not rip away your chest's tight compress?
And did We not cast off the mountains of burdens with their deep
*   depress?*
A feeling of hopelessness that nearly broke your back bent down—
Yet did We not raise you from obscurity and spread far and wide your
*   renown?*

Remember well, if the obstacle is defined, remedies flow [Yusra] around
*   it with ease.*
If the obstacle is defined, remedies flow around it with ease.
Therefore, once you refocus your perspective, stand straight with
*   confidence.*
And remain unwavering in trusting your Cosmic Mentor's wise
*   guidance.*

Echoing the divinely empowered transformation of Joseph from obscurity to renown, the surah introduced a fresh concept in Qur'anic revelation: *Yusra,* which evoked water flowing around a rock in the middle of a stream. Rather than be paralyzed by obdurate short-term obstacles, a Muslim needed to find effective and healthy ways to flow around them. As *Surah Yusuf* had illustrated, the greatest obstacles are often internal and self-imposed, like the formidable wounded ego. Defining the obstacle (a phrase the surah repeated twice) was vital to then devising solutions: diagnose the root cause of the problem in order to repair it.

Speaking of flow, the elders' smear campaign had ironically raised the Qur'an from obscurity and spread its profile far and wide throughout Arabia. Jewish elders in Yathrib, a city about three hundred miles north of Mecca, heard the traveling poets' denunciations yet were intrigued, sensing the Meccans' intense propaganda was sparked by fear of a formidable force. Yathrib's residents, predominantly Jews descended from exiles after the First Temple's destruction, were stagnating and squabbling, balkanizing in low-grade civil strife that threatened the city's future. Perhaps the notorious Qur'an—which supposedly spread discord—instead offered a formula for civic reconciliation and cohesion.

A discrete delegation of Yathribite elders visited Mecca to investigate the Qur'an for themselves. They met with Muhammad on the outskirts of the city and examined Qur'anic manuscripts, taking several scrolls back with them to

Yathrib for further review with their fellow citizens. While no specific partnership was forged, for the first time the Qur'an had attracted the interest of an outside community. The Abyssinian court had respected the Qur'an as a monotheistic peer but not formally adopted it. Could the reclusive Yathribites follow Abu Tharr's example as external adoptees?

After five months with no new surahs (just new individual passages added to existing surahs), the Qur'an roared back with a vengeance, delivering a series of five surahs all linked by their opening letters of *Alif Lam Mim*—the first time this combination of symbols was used and further reinforcing their role as a collective unit. The surahs emphasized achieving mastery *(Alif)* via learned experience *(Lam)* to achieve flow *(Mim)* around obstacles. First came *Ar-Ra'd* ("The Thunder") on the Qur'an's tenth anniversary:

The Loving Divine discerns the realms of the unseen and the known; the One of vast knowledge is exulted above all. It makes no difference for Him whether you communicate with Him silently from the depths of your inner heart or audibly out in the open; whether concealed by the night's darkness or exposed in the brightness of broad daylight. The Loving Divine has an underlying purpose for all that has befallen you and all that will continue to befall you, always protecting you by His providence. But the Loving Divine will surely not change the state of a people until and unless they change their inner attitude and perspective [*Anfusihim*—the plural form of *Nafs*]!

When the Loving Divine resolves to test a people with tribulations, know that there is no avoiding it. Yet even in those moments, He remains a source of unconditional comfort. He shows you lightning and massive clouds to inspire feelings of fear and hope within you. . . . He is the one who answers those who call out to Him, while the idols whom they call upon never respond in any way. Their example is like someone exhausted by thirst who merely extends his palms toward fresh water, deludedly anticipating the water will reach his mouth on its own; but the water will never reach. Indeed, the ways of the obstinate do not lead to success.

In arid Arabia, thunder and lightning were extremely rare, typically occurring only once every few years. Some Arabs would experience the terrifying rumble of thunder but once or twice in a lifetime. The surah argued that lightning, while instilling fear, actually served as a source of hope, heralding the imminent arrival of rejuvenating fresh waters. What seems scary can in fact mark the beginning of a transformative opportunity—but only if audiences adopt a foresighted perspective and actively seize the moment. Rather than cower in fear, they can prepare to harness the rainwater. Similarly, trauma from past experiences can feel paralyzing or propel progress. Change cannot simply be wished into existence, but rather requires reorientation and taking calculated action. Because one's state of being is directly tied to outlook, the passage emphasizes transforming one's internal state in order to achieve real-world impact.

In moments of turmoil (metaphorical thunderstorms), a Muslim needed to stay grounded. *Surah As-Sajdah* ("The Grounding") reemphasized how to overcome seemingly overwhelming short-term challenges. In Semitic culture, prostrating on the ground signified emotional self-control.

> We revealed the book to Moses—so don't doubt what We reveal to you as well—and made it a source of guidance for the Children of Israel. And We raised among them great leaders [*A'immah*, plural of *Imam*] because they persevered [*Sabaru*] and were certain of the promises of our revelations. . . .
>
> Do people not consider how upon a parched land raging with scorching sandstorms We send replenishing rains, calming the soil to produce vast vegetation as a source of sustenance for their herds and for themselves—so that they can see beyond the turmoil?

One of the most grounded plants in the desert is the cactus *(Sabr),* whose deep roots connect to subterranean aquifers and provide long-term stability in harsh conditions. The cactus inspired the concept of perseverance (*Sabaru,* in the plural action form): the ability to remain anchored and steadfast despite being buffeted. Of course, standing firm for too long can lead to stagnation, and regaining clarity requires movement out of darkness back to light. The term *Imam* referred to a particular kind of expert guide able to rescue lost explorers from deep caverns. *Surah As-Sajdah* marked the word's first appearance in the Qur'an, repurposing it to describe great Jewish leaders who persisted despite enormous setbacks to guide their people as shining beacons in extremely dark moments. The surah depicts how sudden rains can calm a raging sandstorm, causing whirling sand to re-ground and transform parched lands into fertile soil, enabling vegetation to emerge to sustain human life. Similarly, re-grounding amidst flaring ego-driven emotions serves as the key step to enable blossoming.

One constant external source of insecurity in Arabia was the extended war between the region's two superpowers: the Byzantines and the Persians. Nearby lands would fall to one empire, only to be recaptured by another, creating enormous economic instability for traveling caravan merchants who had to navigate constantly shifting taxation regimes. A new surah directly invoked this conflict with the title *Ar-Rum* (the Byzantines, the last remnant of ancient Rome). It urged looking beyond international headlines to focus domestically, including on what Meccans were doing in their own homes to bolster resilience. Meccan marriages were driven not by love and partnership but by economic and political alliances amongst tribes, objectifying individual brides as assets for barter. Rejecting such external superficialities to instead embrace personal fulfillment, the chapter's climax insisted true love was more powerful than any transient empire:

> It is He who causes the living to emerge from the dead and the dead to emerge from the living, and the One who resuscitates a dead land—likewise you too will be revived. And of His clarifying signs is that He created you from dust and then you are proud yet flawed mortals spreading throughout the land. And from His clarifying signs is that He created partners for you, from your own selves, so that you can find comfort [*Sakan*] with them and established your unions upon *Mawaddah* [tearing fragments from one's most prized garments to mend a partner's wound] and *Rahmah* [optimistically envisioning a better future for a depressed partner]. . . .

Like empires, human beings can rise and fall. Yet rather than pursue domination and subjugation, humans' purpose is to seek partnership. Indeed, women are not inferior but rather equal partners—and a healthy marriage should establish a secure place for comfort and recuperation (*Sakan* described a rooftop canopy beneath which families refreshed themselves after a long, exhausting day). Spouses give the best of themselves to their partners, especially when the spouse feels at their worst—repairing wounds in classic Muslim fashion and supporting partners to achieve their potential even when they are filled with self-doubt. A healthy marriage in turn serves as an example for a healthy society: based on equality, altruistic care, and mutual support. Put another way, repairing societies begins in the nucleus of the home—and this passage soon became an iconic part of Islamic wedding ceremonies.

Any healthy marriage, of course, requires lots of hard work. The Qur'an next meditated on what constitutes effective effort, leveraging the metaphor of a spider web spun on a busy street, with lots of invested energy destroyed in an instant. Called *Al-'Ankabut* ("The Spider"), the surah urged careful planning before intense exertion, as well as the flexibility to recognize when it becomes necessary to move on:

> Do people actually assume they can get away with simply declaring their trust in God without being tested? Indeed, We tested all those who came before, and through such tests God reveals who is truly honest and who is only deceiving themselves. Do those who commit destructive deeds actually assume they will achieve success without consequences? . . . The one who exerts their best effort [*Jahada*] only puts in such great effort for their own benefit—the Divine is exulted above any need for human devotion. . . .
>
> We advise the human being to honor his parents and treat them with loving compassion, but if they exert intense effort to thrust you toward an unhealthy path then do not obey them. . . . The people responded to Abraham: "Let us kill him or burn him alive." Only Lot stood by him. Then Abraham declared: "I am emigrating [*Muhajir*] to my Divine Mentor—He is the Great Coach wisely perceiving untapped potential [*al-Aziz al-Hakim*]."
>
> Those who exert intense yet misplaced effort are like a spider spinning a web on a busy path, rendering its great efforts futile. . . . Indeed, those who exert their best efforts [*Jahadu*] with self-awareness and foresight, We shall surely guide them to our paths [*subulana*]. The Loving Divine always supports those who seek to beautify the world with beautiful actions.

For the first time, the Qur'an invoked the concept of *Jihad*—literally the contractions of childbirth and metaphorically strenuous and determined efforts to nurture vitality. *Surah Al-'Ankabut* insists that action without clear purpose and strategy can be futile. Sooner or later, reality will test the web one has spun, with tribulations revealing whether it is durable enough to withstand pressure. Moreover, action alone is value-neutral, as the destructive efforts of Abraham's neighbors illustrate. A Muslim must be aware enough to recognize brewing signs of toxicity in time to avoid catastrophe, as Abraham does by expressing the concept of *Hijrah* (literally, leaving a marriage without closing the future possibility of reconciliation) for the first time in the Qur'an. Unable to make any progress, twelve-year-old Abraham must flee while keeping open the option to return in peace. The chapter's concluding verse reminded its audience that the ultimate purpose of human action was to make the world a more pleasant place to live.

The Qur'an's followers who had undertaken their own forced migration to Abyssinia began to return in a trickle to Mecca, testing whether reconciliation might be possible. Returning refugees brought detailed accounts of the Qur'an's success in Africa, and the Qur'an in turn invoked the inspiring example of an African sage named *Luqman* ("one who takes a large bite"), who had been abducted into slavery yet earned his freedom (like Joseph) by leveraging his rare wisdom to save his society from calamity. *Surah Luqman* recounts the now elderly gentleman imparting wisdom to his twelve-year-old son:

> We blessed Luqman with deep wisdom and inspired him by saying: "Act with gratitude and humility to the Loving Divine." Those who act in gratitude do so for their own benefit, and those who are ungrateful [*kafara*] should know that the Loving Divine is self-sufficient and a source of emulation for all.
>
> Recall when Luqman gently advised his son: ". . . Oh my dear son, remember that any deed you do, regardless of how insignificant—even as small as a mustard seed concealed within a solid rock or in the furthermost galaxy or a most distant land—the Loving Divine is aware of it and will ultimately cause it to bear fruit. Indeed, the Loving Divine is ever so gentle and deeply aware of all things.
>
> "Oh my dear son, establish a deep connection to the Loving Divine. Proclaim healing works; avoid harmful actions; and persevere in all the tribulations you encounter—for these are the most exemplary traits. And never look down upon others with a haughty glance nor walk the earth with arrogance. Indeed, the Loving Divine does not support the ways of the boastful and arrogant. Walk with modesty and lower your voice, for the most repulsive of sounds is the braying of donkeys."

Despite surviving severe trauma, Luqman is the gentlest character portrayed in the Qur'an, with refined politeness and none of the prophetic impetuousness of Moses. True knowledge and wisdom have humbled him, taming rather than boosting his ego. He seeks to improve society in practical ways, recognizing that deep wisdom needs to be shared to inspire others. The chapter ends with a powerful reminder that Muslims cannot know everything and need to recognize their own natural limitations:

> Indeed, the Loving Divine is the only one who knows:
> when and how the world will come to an end, and
> knows when and how refreshing relief (*Ghayth*) will descend, and
> knows what is within the wombs, and
> no soul knows what it will earn in the future
> nor does any soul know the conditions of its death.
> Indeed, the Loving Divine is deeply aware and knowing of all things.

In contrast to some Christians and Jews obsessed with doomsday prophecies, the Qur'an insists that humans should instead concentrate on repairing the world. Invoking rain that comes after an extended drought *(Ghayth)*, when the scorched earth appears hopelessly barren, the Qur'an reminds its followers that even deep trauma can ultimately give way to growth. The passage refuses to define a human being by their parents or ancestry, arguing that every fetus is born with the chance to determine their own destiny. Though future results cannot be guaranteed, purposeful action now lies within the control of all people.

❧❧❧

For the past year, the Yathribites had critically examined Qur'anic manuscripts like a *Hanif*, weighing ideas and carefully assessing potential plans to repair their strife-torn city like a Muslim. After much discussion, they returned to Mecca determined to recruit Muhammad to bring the Qur'an's teachings to their fertile and hospitable oasis. Unwilling to abandon his hometown despite making little headway, Muhammad instead offered one of his top students to lead communal education efforts and test the Yathribites' true readiness and sincerity.

For the first time, the Qur'an enjoyed a receptive large audience eager to learn and implement its teachings. After spending eleven years addressing a singular "you" in its revelations, the Qur'an finally allowed itself to use the plural form—invoking the word '*Alaikum* ("upon you") as a pivotal transition. The new chapter's name *Surah Bani Israel* ("The Children of Israel")

MUSLIM: THE QUR'AN GUIDING HEALING AND REPAIR 119

highlighted the new collective audience—the Jews of Yathrib—and began by exploring their lost Temple in Jerusalem, a city they had been banned from entering for nearly half a millennium.

Let all prostrate themselves in adoration of the One who by night took His mentee on a serene nocturnal journey from the sacred sanctuary [*Al-Masjid Al-Haram*] to the ultimate place of grounding [*Al-Masjid Al-Aqsa*], the site We elevated as a place of blessing and holiness.

We decreed to the Children of Israel in the book [Torah]: "Twice you will be despoiled in the land [of Israel], yet thereafter you will rise again, even greater and more majestic than before. . . ."

Now when the first decree came to pass, We sent an extremely powerful nation [the Babylonians] upon you who thoroughly sacked every home. This was decreed, and it took place. Then the scales tipped in your favor, and we granted you more than you ever had before: great wealth and many vigorous sons. And we raised you as a prominent people among the nations. . . .

Now remember, that if you do good works, it is for your own benefit. Likewise, if you do harm, then you only harm yourselves. When the promise of return from exile finally transpires, on that day your faces will change in shock at what seemed impossible—and they shall once again enter the masjid [the Temple in Jerusalem] to restore its toppled building blocks to their former glory. . . .

Confusion will always be the uncomfortable condition of those who choose to sit passively awaiting external salvation. . . . We declared to the Children of Israel: "Live throughout the earth [in exile], and only once you have invested your full effort will We gather you from far and wide."

. . . Your Divine Mentor decreed [in the Torah] that you shall dedicate yourselves to no other deity but Him and honor your parents. If either of them or both reach old age, then do not disrespect them in the slightest nor raise your voice before them, but rather speak to them gently and respectfully. And be humble and compassionate with them and say: "My Divine Mentor, encompass them with compassion for raising me when I was young. . . ." Do not commit adultery, it is a repugnance and dark path to tread. And do not kill a soul—made sacred by the Loving Divine—unjustly. . . . Do not cheat an orphan out of their inheritance entrusted to your care. . . . Fulfill your oaths and pledges. . . . When you weigh give full measure and weigh with an accurate balance. . . . Do not proclaim what you don't know to be true. . . .

The surah began by invoking the Jews' turbulent past, encompassing both great glory and terrible destruction, before shifting to a future vision of splendid ingathering and restoration. Bridging the gap between the two required principled action, rather than waiting passively for a messianic redeemer—which had left the Jews stagnating for centuries in politically impotent exile. "Only once you have invested your full effort will We gather you," the Qur'an insisted.

The "full effort" required was communal, expanding the vision of a couple's healthy partnership in *Surah Ar-Rum* to a larger thriving society. Whereas the Qur'an had previously made recommendations for appropriate individual behavior, *Surah Bani Israel* envisioned for the first time a functioning community, united by shared redemptive purpose and a clear code of conduct. To reassure the Jews of Yathrib, the chapter centered its comportment guidelines around the iconic Ten Commandments, suggesting that the Qur'an had come to reinforce rather than replace the teachings of Moses. It would revive traditional Jewish concepts by clarifying their underlying purpose in order to make the values accessible to a wide audience. Murder, for example, extinguished life sanctified by God. Parents deserved honor because they had sacrificed to raise their children. The original injunction "do not steal" expanded with vivid examples of an executor siphoning off an orphan's inheritance or a merchant fixing the scales to cheat customers. From this ethical code, only Sabbath observance—a commandment particular to the Jews—was excluded, replaced by a more general injunction not to lie.

Letting this expanded vision sink in, the Qur'an offered no new chapters for an entire year, revealing only short passages to supplement existing material. In one evocative fragment, the Qur'an described itself as *Ghayra thi 'Iwaj* (39:28): a veteran tree that remains unbroken and upright after surviving a massive storm, embodying both perseverance and maturity. Meanwhile, reports from Yathrib indicated that the locals had wholeheartedly embraced the Qur'an's message and were thirsty for more. At last, the Meccan followers had a practical outlet for flowing around the obstacle of repression and persecution in their hometown. It was time to move on, just as Abraham had done when faced with his own impending murder.

On the Qur'an's twelfth anniversary, the revelation *An-Nahl* ("The Bees") explored the example of a united community that works together efficiently and maintains the flexibility to transplant their collective to new hospitable environments when necessary. After not invoking the term "Muslim" since *Surah Yusuf,* this chapter repeated it several times—this time in the plural form, to role-model how Muslims conduct themselves.

The redemption from tribulation enabled by the Loving Divine is fast approaching, but don't hasten it. . . . Those who have been wronged and abused yet muster the courage—supported by the Loving Divine—to leave the past behind [*Hajaru*] will find a fertile and welcoming land, one that will empower them to achieve successes and impact far greater than they could have ever imagined. . . .

Your Divine Mentor inspired bees with the flexibility to construct their hives in mountains, trees, vineyards, and even cities, saying: "And extract your nourishment from a variety of fruits, and seek diverse paths always adjusting. . . ."

We gradually revealed the Book to you as a clarifying source for all things and a guide, a source of compassion and joyous inspiration for people committed to repair [*Muslimin*]. Indeed, the Loving Divine commands justice, beautifying the world, and kindness to all—and forbids deeds of malice, injustice, and aggression. . . . Had the Loving Divine willed, He would have made you all into one nation, yet he allows those who choose to stray to go their way, and guides those who desire to be guided. . . .

Consume all that which is healthy and good, and be grateful for the many favors of the Loving Divine, if you are truly devoted to Him. Indeed, He has forbidden you from consuming carrion, blood, the flesh of swine, and anything slaughtered upon the altars of idols. Yet, anyone who partakes in these out of intense necessity, neither driven by desire nor exceeding their immediate need, then let them know that the Loving Divine is ever so forgiving and understanding. And don't invent lies against the Loving Divine by saying: "This is permissible and this is forbidden. . . ." And for the Jews, We have forbidden upon them what We have related to you. . . .

Remember, your Divine Mentor is so forgiving to those who commit wrong out of ignorance yet acknowledge their mistakes and seek to make amends afterward. Indeed, your Divine Mentor is ever so forgiving and understanding. . . . Tenderly guide others to the verdant path of your Cosmic Mentor by using judicious wisdom and calm poise, always engaging in an appealing manner. . . .

Persevere and trust in the Loving Divine, and do not feel sad for them [the Meccans], and do not feel a tightening anxiety due to their malicious schemes.

Indeed, the Loving Divine will always be present with those who seek action-based hope and do beautifying works of kindness.

Inspired by the practical cooperation and resilience of a beehive, the chapter prepared the Qur'an's Meccan followers mentally for the physical transition to Yathrib, encouraging them to release past trauma to focus on a better future. Their movement would no longer be repressed, but instead function openly amidst a dynamic city whose leaders had adopted (at least in theory) core values of interconnected individual and civic repair. In their new home, the Qur'an's followers would need to coexist alongside Jews, with their own particular religious laws, while adopting their own more specific guidelines as Muslims living openly in a broader community. The surah introduced for the first time practical laws (e.g., dietary restrictions) while simultaneously urging gentleness and compassion in enforcing them, recognizing the natural human propensity to fall short of commitments.

Surah An-Nahl was revealed gradually over the course of four months as the Qur'an's followers stealthily departed in small groups. 'Umar jumpstarted the exodus right after hearing the revelation about *Hijrah,* thereby giving a name to the migration. Muhammad insisted on remaining until the last moment, with the surah's final verse emerging only days before he fled the assassins massed outside his home and began a perilous three-week journey to Yathrib pursued by bounty hunters.

Upon arriving in his new home, Muhammad would discover a community committed to the Qur'an in theory but still struggling in practice. The Yathribites remained consumed by ego: riven by rivalries, abused by selfish leaders, and still passively placing utopian hope in external redemption. No new revelations emerged during the first few months of resettlement in Yathrib, which first had to repair civic fractures and forge a renewed identity. The city adopted the name "Medina"—literally, a new place of flowing change founded atop an ancient foundation—a moniker that evoked the concepts of both *Yusra* (flow) and *Sajdah* (grounding).

Under Muhammad's direction, Medina's once-feuding clans came together to draft and refine a constitution guaranteeing equal opportunity under the law—a groundbreaking agreement founded on the principle of mutual support and altruistic pleasure in others' success. The Constitution of Medina was read publicly throughout the city to establish widespread appreciation of the Qur'an's new social order—a public transparency and openness physically reflected in the gate-free masjid constructed in southern Medina with open entrances on three sides.

Like Joseph emerging from jail to lead foresighted civic growth, the Qur'an was finally ready to direct action out in the open, no longer simply proposing values and behavior but guiding implementation from a position of authority. As with the looming famine Joseph faced, the Qur'an anticipated troubles ahead—and would have to move quickly. Muslims could not afford to sit around passively and needed strategic focus to survive the looming turmoil.

6

BAQARAH: THE QUR'AN DIRECTING LASTING IMPACT

THE SHARP WOODEN PLOW THRUST DEEP INTO THE REDDISH-BROWN earth, leaving a visible trace of upturned soft soil as a large cow propelled it forward through the field. A farmer followed, balancing the plow's center of gravity while adjusting the cow's reins to maintain straight and parallel lines of fresh topsoil. During the recent September harvest, crops of wheat, barley, and squash had been cut above the root, leaving a few inches of plant for livestock to graze on. The animals' dung provided a natural fertilizer, which the plow now mixed into the ground. Young boys rushed behind the farmer, scattering seeds along the plow path before covering them with soil.

A sense of urgency drove this age-old replanting ritual. The seeds needed to be embedded in the ground before the onset of the coming rainy season, heralded by a sudden downpour that provided a unique soaking opportunity to spark the emergence of seed roots. While these roots expanded below the surface, the intense planting rush would yield no immediate visible signs of progress, with crops harvested only many months later. The farmer's planting signaled faith in the future, a long-term investment with deferred but bountiful returns. In contrast to barren and transactional Mecca, the vast verdant fields throughout Medina shaped the city around agricultural rhythms and values.

Despite maintaining ancient customs, this year's harvest and planting season in Medina occurred against the backdrop of several striking innovations. A significant percentage of the crop yield had been carefully stored in massive silos recently constructed throughout the city at Muhammad's direction as a prescient hedge against famine or siege. Traversing the fields between palm trees, a network of wooden water conduits (each called *Rasul*) had also sprung up to collect the impending rainwaters and direct them to storage cisterns, from which additional channels would redirect water efficiently to fields during the dry season.

The fall harvest in Medina paralleled the Jewish high holiday season, celebrated by the vast majority of the city's residents. The Rosh Hashanah new year commemoration had preceded the signing of Medina's new constitution, followed shortly thereafter by the Yom Kippur fast day and the Sukkot harvest holiday. During this weeklong celebration, Jews dined and slept outdoors in temporary huts to relive the Israelites' wandering the wilderness and receiving the Torah at Mount Sinai.

The Sukkot festivities culminated in the boisterous ceremony of Simhat Torah, marking the annual conclusion of reading the entire Torah and restarting again with the first lines of Genesis—an echo of the circular process of harvesting and replanting. The word Torah itself derived from the Semitic term for the intense first downpour of the rainy season (*Yoreh*). The resulting temporary streams carved smooth paths through the wilderness, a metaphor for how the Torah offered guidance through an often uncertain world.

On October 5, 622, the Jews of Medina spent Simhat Torah dancing in the streets with their Torah scrolls in a public display of joyous affection. Meanwhile, the Qur'an remained silent. Muhammad had arrived in Medina three months earlier and immediately dazzled the locals, whom he called *Ansar*—literally, "people who provide fertile land ready for planting." The moniker respected the Medinians as loyal supporters while also challenging them to initiate the planting process.

As they observed the transformation of their city, the people of Medina also waited in suspense for the Qur'an to break its silence. When would they hear from it directly—and what would it reveal especially for them, rather than simply repeating passages previously revealed in Mecca?

❦

At dusk, the farmers paused the plowing for the evening as the call to prayer echoed across the fields summoning people to the masjid. As the sun set, the moon began to ascend and starlight poked through the darkening firmament. Several hundred people thronged into the mosque courtyard via open gateways on three sides and organized themselves in straight parallel rows beneath an open canopy of palm fronds held up by a latticework of support ropes. Small lanterns lit by olive oil adorned the center's pillars providing a subtle warm glow.

Twelve and a half years earlier Muhammad had stood before Mecca's midday market to publicly declaim the *Iqra* call to blossom, only to be laughed off the stage. On this evening, he ascended the pulpit at the front of the mosque and for the first time in over a dozen years chanted a new revelation before a mass audience—this time a receptive one that had been waiting months for this highly anticipated moment.

> *Alif Lam Mim.* Given all that has come before, the book [*al-Kitab*] shall have no confusion [*Rayb*], for its purpose is to provide guidance for people who seek action-based hope. These people recognize unseen potential [*Ghayb*]; vigilantly repair frayed connections; and share with others a portion of what they have been given. They acknowledge and believe in what has previously been revealed through you and what was revealed before you, and they remain certain of the long-term impact of their hard work. Such people are guided by their rejuvenating Divine Mentor [*Rabb*] on the path to fulfillment, and it is they who embody action-based hope.

The revelation featured no command or critique, but rather acknowledged the progress already achieved by its audience while also preparing them for major tasks ahead. No longer soothing pain or addressing doubts, the Qur'an spoke in the voice of a praising mentor, reaffirming its audiences' proven talents and urging them to keep striving toward even greater results.

Specifically, the Qur'an praised its audience's ability to implement effective action. The term *Rayb* described dizziness caused by spinning in the same place: a mobilized yet stagnant state of wasted energy without progress. Breaking out of a torpid whirlwind, the audience now saw potential in all things and thus worked hard to repair and elevate one another, driven by a confidence in the deferred harvest. That trust in the future enabled hope and inspired action to transcend the present—just as a *Rabb* gently nurtured the growth of fledgling plants.

Continuing the agricultural motif, Muhammad revealed the new surah's name: *Al-Baqarah*—literally, "leaving a visible trace by plowing a field with a cow." The title conveyed grand action producing a deep and long-lasting impact and spoke directly to the popular desire to be remembered by leaving a profound positive legacy.

These five verses merely marked the beginning of *Al-Baqarah*, as the surah would be revealed in a serialized format over the next nine years. In fact, it would only be completed with the revelation of the Qur'an's last-ever verse. In the meantime, as it emerged in batches, *Al-Baqarah* kept its audiences captivated, maintaining a distinctive style and rhythm even as other new chapters emerged at the same time. It would ultimately become the Qur'an's largest and grandest chapter, embodying the message of its title: extensive and intense work generating magnificent long-term impact.

Though the opening of a new Qur'anic chapter, the passage began in the middle of a process and twice acknowledged what had come before. Just as fresh seeds come from existing plants, the Qur'an positioned itself as a seed of the Torah ("what was revealed before you"), the great original Abrahamic book that had just been paraded through the streets on Simhat Torah. In fact, the surah would go on to repeatedly invoke the word *al-Kitab*, every time as a clear reference to the Torah. "The book [*al-Kitab*] shall have no confusion" thus referred ambiguously to both the Torah and its new seed, the Qur'an, which was not yet a complete formal book.

A second installment of *Al-Baqarah* soon evoked how a single heavenly source of rain yields many kinds of produce, a metaphor for the dynamic implementation of Divine inspiration:

> Oh people, model yourself on the qualities of your Divine Mentor, who created you and those who preceded you so that you may attain a state of action-based hope. It is He who fashioned the earth as a comfortable place of living and the cosmos as an invigorating place of contemplation and inspiration; and it is He who causes revitalizing and rejuvenating rains to descend from the sky, sparking the growth of diverse fruits as a source of sustenance for you. . . .

A few days later, the serialization of *Al-Baqarah* began in earnest, with an evocative summary of the Torah. Mirroring the Jewish calendar's restarting of the Torah reading, it began by recounting the creation of the world and humanity, as well as the travails of Adam and Eve in the Garden of Eden, before continuing on to briefly recount the Israelites' journey out of bondage in Egypt and even expanding to David slaying Goliath and Ezra rebuilding Jerusalem after the Babylonian exile. This compact retelling focused on extracting key values and lessons.

Three new installments directly and affectionately addressed the surah's immediate audience: "Oh, Children of Israel!" The plural "you" mentioned throughout the chapter was clearly the Jews, not pagan Arabs. *Al-Baqarah* aimed to reassure the Jews of Medina that the Qur'an upheld their ancient tradition. In fact, the surah argued that Jews needed to draw on the best of their past in order to build a brighter future, calling out to Arabian Jews— some descended from King David—who had lived in exile for centuries passively awaiting a return to Jerusalem.

> Oh Children of Israel, remember well My many bountiful favors, which I lovingly bestowed upon you, Keep your covenant with Me and I shall keep My covenant with you, and stand in awe of Me. Recognize what I have revealed, affirming the Torah [al-Kitab] that you hold with you. . . . Oh Children of Israel, remember well My many bountiful favors which I lovingly bestowed upon you, and I have chosen you over all people. . . . Recall how We saved you from the people of Pharaoh who were killing your sons. . . . Recall how We split the sea, saving you and drowning the people of Pharaoh as you watched. And recall when We called Moses to meet Us for forty nights [to receive the Torah] while you worshipped the calf as an act of ungrateful transgression. Yet We forgave you all of that and blessed you with many bounties so that you may act in gratitude. And recall how We gave Moses the Torah [Al-Kitab] and the Oral Torah [Al-Furqan] so that you may be guided.

The Qur'an then introduced a new story—drawing on Jewish oral tradition about a red cow heralding the Messianic era—to emphasize the need to stop waiting and start working proactively. The vignette spotlighted newly liberated Israelites, still reeling from the trauma of centuries of slavery in Egypt, procrastinating to avoid entering the Holy Land promised to them—a transformation that would entail taking personal responsibility for their actions and security.

Recall when Moses said to his people: "The Loving Divine asks you to sacrifice a heifer [to enter the Holy Land]." So they responded: "Are you mocking us?" Then Moses said: "I'm not one of the stagnant holding you back with my teachings." So now the people demanded: "Ask your Divine Mentor to tell us what kind of cow this is." Moses answered: "It is a cow neither too old nor too young, so do what you are told without procrastinating." Then they said: "Ask your Divine Mentor what color the cow is." He replied: "She is a red heifer whose color is bright and beautiful to the sight." Then they said: "Ask your Divine Mentor to tell us more about what it looks like, as all cows look alike to us. *In-sha'-Allah,* once we know all this we will follow the direction." Moses explained: "It is a cow that does not till the earth, work in the fields, has not been put to labor, nor has distinct markings." They responded: "This sounds like something we can do." So they grudgingly did what they were told. Then after that your [ancestors'] hearts became hardened, like stones, or I would even say harder than stones. But even then, remember that it is even out of stones that life-giving rivers flow. And even the hardest of stones can split open to bring out life-giving refreshing water.

The Israelites' reluctance revealed their lack of readiness to be accountable. Indeed, the Qur'an invokes the expression *In-sha'-Allah* ("If God wills it") only in situations where people do not actually want to do something, instead shifting the onus onto the Divine. Muhammad's first scribe 'Ali would later explicate this passage by pointing out how persecuted people who have not healed their trauma can themselves easily become persecutors when they attain power. As the Israelites fail the initial test of responsibility, they must wander for forty years in the desert until a new generation emerges without a victimhood mentality.

Al-Baqarah, with its emphasis on generating lasting impact, seeks to empower people to overcome paralyzing fears and heal from trauma in order to progress. The solution, the surah insists, is a shift in mindset. Human beings can definitely change—if they want to. With even just a small opening, life-nourishing waters can emerge from the hardest stone, like a traumatized heart. But achieving such an opening requires acknowledging the underlying cause of pain and recognizing how clinging to trauma harms the survivor most of all.

In its tour of Jewish history highlights, the Qur'an then picks up the Hanukkah story by exploring the example of Hellenized Jews, during the time of the Maccabees, who sold out their tradition and betrayed their people to Greek imperialists. These arrogant Hellenized Jews certainly did not stagnate; their mistake was to engage in toxic oppressive action: erecting idols in the temple, making pig sacrifices, and forcing their ideas on others by persecuting fellow Jews who upheld the Torah. In this Jewish civil war, the Maccabees championing Abrahamic tradition ultimately triumphed, revealing the Hellenization project as a failed shortcut to progress. The Hellenized Jews assumed they had become civilized, but betraying a divine covenant instead left them resembling apes—animals that can from afar appear human yet lack discernment:

> You know very well the story of those among you who maliciously violated the Sabbath. And We said: "You are no better than uncivilized apes." We made that incident an everlasting example for everyone at that time and everyone who followed as an illuminating parable for anyone seeking enduring action-based hope. Indeed, those who were given the Torah [*Al-Kitab*] recite it sincerely and apply its spirit, for they truly believe in it. Indeed, anyone who rejects the Torah is squandering a precious resource. Oh Children of Israel, remember well my many bountiful favors that I lovingly bestowed upon you and I have chosen you over all people. . . .

Jews had suffered from both external and internal persecution (e.g., both Pharaoh and Hellenized fellow Jews), yet the Qur'an repeatedly cites how each time they emerge from trauma greater than before. Redemption came not simply from reading and rejoicing with the Torah, but rather by internalizing and enacting its mindset. In the Qur'an's insistence, the Torah's value is not as a talisman to be venerated but a dynamic guide to action.

Al-Baqarah repeatedly delivers an intense coaching session: Stop wallowing and wasting time—get up and get working. The surah celebrates a young David stepping up to confront Goliath as a mere shepherd with no military training while the great warriors of Israel stand paralyzed in fear of the Philistine giant. Had David not taken action he would never have become King of Israel, established Jerusalem, written the Psalms, or raised Solomon, the builder of the Holy Temple. The chapter also celebrates Ezra's ability to recover from the total annihilation of Jerusalem and the Torah scrolls. "Can this truly be restored after such immense destruction," Ezra wonders in the Qur'an's telling, before getting down to work transcribing the Torah from memory and rebuilding Jerusalem atop its "destroyed foundations."

Via *Al-Baqarah*, the Qur'an firmly grafts itself onto the Torah as a fresh restart grounded in tradition. It also aims to fuse its particular new audience (Arabian Jews in exile) with its veteran audience (former pagan Arabs and Christians from Mecca), declaring: "Thus We have formed you into a balanced community [*Ummataw-Wasata*] in order to be experts modeling exemplary behavior for all people, and in order for the *Rasul* to be an exemplary role model for you." The word *Wasata* conveyed a dynamic mix of balance, moderation, and centralization—and the word *Rasul* (water channel) here made its first-ever Qur'anic appearance as a reference to Muhammad, a leader with family roots in both Mecca and Medina. The two Abrahamic branches of Ishmael and Isaac thus reunited around a shared heritage after centuries of division.

But the chapter's vignettes suggested that the past matters only as much as it empowers present and long-term impact. *Al-Baqarah* evokes the massive return on investment of just a single well-executed action via an agricultural metaphor: "A lasting deed is like one fertile grain planted in lush soil that in turn yields seven large shoots, each with a hundred grains."

❧❦❧

As the Qur'an reemerged in Medina, so did Meccan harassment. The Meccan elite, furious that the Qur'an had managed to escape destruction, remained determined to undermine its positive impact, all the more as Medina flourished under its guidance. Marauders sponsored by the Meccans launched nocturnal raids on the outskirts of Medina, poaching flocks and destroying crops. The raids spooked the people of Medina, who had enjoyed neutrality for centuries and never before faced targeted harassment. At Muhammad's direction, volunteer guards took shifts protecting the periphery of Medina while the city slept.

The frightened people of Medina needed inspiration and reassurance. *Al-Baqarah*'s ongoing review of Jewish history thus highlighted brave individuals who did not let overwhelming opposition faze them. Young David refused to allow his people to be annihilated; Ezra refused to allow the Torah to be lost; and Abraham risked death rather than bow before a tyrannical king demanding worship as a deity. In such defining moments, none of these iconic leaders simply relied on *In-sha'-Allah* but instead boldly acted as others cowered—with world-changing impact.

Amidst these vignettes of brave leaders seizing opportunities despite great uncertainty, the Qur'an delivered a verse that Muhammad declared its greatest passage. The verse contained no action command and described no historical figure, but simply observed the Divine in action: perpetually standing guard and always ready to empower human beings who dared to act. The verse began with two new names for the Divine—*al-Hayy-ul-Qayyum*—which according to Muhammad, combined to form God's greatest name. They described God providing a warm breath of life (*Hayy* invoking heat and action) and constant vigilance (*Qayyum,* evoking a night watchman standing upright with a lantern, peering into the darkness for any looming threats). Together, the words evoked steadfast and purposeful action capable of enduring challenges and producing outstanding results.

The Jews of Medina instantly recognized the phrase from their own tradition. The expression *Hayy v'Qayyam* appeared only once in the Hebrew bible (Daniel 6:27) where the Persian king Kurush (Cyrus the Great) described God as the savior of Daniel in the lion's den, protecting him from dangers as he slept and supporting him as an outstanding visionary advisor to the king. Several hundred years before the Qur'an's revelation, the phrase had been popularized by Talmudic rabbis—such as Yahuda haNasi, circa 200 CE—to inspire Jews living in exile not to feel hopeless. They inserted the term along with a reference to King David beside the blessing for the new full moon—connecting the moon's reemergence from darkness to the return of the House of David. The chant became iconic: *"David, Melekh Yisrael, Hayy v'Qayyam"* (David, King of Israel, Alive and Abiding!). For the Medina audience, the phrase thus naturally evoked the possibility of redemption from exile and the inspiring example of David the poet, prophet, and political maestro. (Shortly after this verse's revelation, the people of Medina began to refer to Muhammad as *Al-Badru Laylat at-Tamam*—"the moon at its fullest.")

As a full moon rose over Medina, Muhammad stood in the masjid and chanted the following verse:

The Loving Divine, there is certainly no comforter but He,
  the Divine Warm Breath of Life standing watch day and night
  [al-Hayy-ul-Qayyum];
Neither fatigue nor sleep overcome Him;
All that exists in the cosmos and on earth are in His tender care;

Nothing occurs in the universe but via His calculated divine plan;
He knows the past and the future of all beings;
His knowledge, like a vast ocean, encompasses all yet itself remains
uncontainable;
Only what He inspires to be known can be comprehended;
The accessible threshold of His unlimited impact [Kursi] *exceeds the*
cosmos and the earth;
Without depreciating His own power, He nurtures all beings to pursue
their full potential;
He as the Highest One elevates all and as the Source of Strength
strengthens all.

After finishing, Muhammad explained the verse had a distinctive name: *Ayat-ul-Kursi*: "the verse of the royal footstool." The image of a king's footstool conveyed multiple concepts. In Semitic cultures, the royal footstool signified the king's powerful dominion, with the furniture piece typically decorated with icons of the empire. The *Kursi* also conveyed direct access to something that seems distant, as subjects could approach only as close as the royal footstool when appealing for the king's assistance. In a related sense, the footstool also demarcated an opening with incredible potential, as the king sat on the throne only when giving an audience. The opportunity to appear before the king could be transformative.

The verse encouraged a Medinian audience, understandably concerned about an uncertain future, to continue the bold action they had taken in providing refuge to the Qur'an despite its intense persecution in Mecca. Just as the King of the Universe had protected Daniel as he slept in the lion's den, the Divine would protect the people of Medina—provided they could overcome feelings of helplessness to act. The verse addressed the need for a comforter and the worry of being battered by the universe's many unpredictable forces. Its soothing and self-assured tone reflected the Divine's own reassuring and empowering role. Muhammad would advise that the verse be recited before going to bed to address nocturnal vulnerability and inspire hope for what could be achieved the next day.

For the past several centuries, ascendant Christians had insisted that God had forsaken the Jews for the New Israel of Christianity. With the trauma of destruction and exile, many Jews surely wondered if God had indeed abandoned them. Yet *Ayat-ul-Kursi* implied God had not, an echo of *Al-Baqarah*'s repeated insistence on the special status of the Children of Israel. The Divine stood waiting for all people to pursue their potential.

The verse's tender observations provoked reflection, forcing audiences to decipher its implications on their own. *Ayat-ul-Kursi* pointedly does not say what to do, hoping that internally driven action will be more powerful and lasting than external command. The verse places a fascinating dilemma before its audience. If God is all-knowing and all-caring, what will you as a human being do: remain overwhelmed and passive before the vast universe—or be inspired to seize opportunities to shape your destiny? If humans lack divine foresight, they have no excuse to let their past or present circumstances determine their future.

Just in case audiences missed the non-compulsory tone of *Ayat-ul-Kursi*, the subsequent verse made the point explicit with a blunt declaration: "There can be no manner of coercion (*Ikrah*) in matters of conscience (*Din*)." The term *Ikrah* described a specific form of discomfort: the wincing face of someone suffering from uncomfortable bowels caused by being forced to consume something unhealthy. Often translated as "religion," *Din* originally referred to an uncharted wilderness path, one developed by a traveler in response to changing terrain and conditions. (Other related Arabic terms include: *Shari'ah*, a path leading uphill to a freshwater source; *Torah*, a consistent downhill path forged by flowing rainwater; and *Sabil*, a multi-branched path forged by dry streams.) By its nature something that each individual chooses, *Din* encompasses mindset, faith, law, and overall life approach.

An ideal community, the Qur'an insisted, never forces people to believe, as both respect for rules and desire for self-improvement are most powerful and lasting when they emerge from within. Compulsion and coercion too often lead to repulsion. Indeed, Abraham, as the Qur'an's great progenitor, rejected forced idolatry as a matter of conscience and revived monotheism for the masses. *Al-Baqarah* pointedly depicts Abraham seeking clarity even from the Divine:

> "My Divine Mentor, show me how you revive the dormant?" God replied: "Do you not have confidence in me?" Abraham responded: "Certainly I believe—but I need logical proof so that my heart can be at peace."

Abraham's nuanced reply reveals that one can trust a mentor without following blindly. Asking questions to better understand reasoning improves action and the chances for long-term impact.

Coercion, of course, is primarily a matter of how human beings treat one another—a pressing challenge in Medina's rapidly evolving social order. The masjid where Muhammad delivered revelations served not only as a place of worship and study, but also a community center hosting celebrations such as weddings and social services: operating a soup kitchen for the needy and a hostel for out-of-town visitors and the homeless. In its additional role as a kind of city hall, the masjid also convened civic leaders for open community discussions of major political decisions. Under the Qur'an's guidance, Medina was for the first time in Arabia forging new ways to coexist outside of tribal structures.

Just outside the eastern gateway of the masjid, a new centralized marketplace hosted merchants of all backgrounds, including—for the first time—female entrepreneurs. Whereas Yathrib had previously been splintered into small markets controlled by individual clans, Medina's new central market was open to all to conduct commerce, attracting many non-Medinians and fledgling merchants. The thriving new commercial center quickly became a regional hub, requiring guidelines for how to do business with non-relatives. The Qur'an's longest verse—known as *Ayat-ud-Dayn* ("The Transaction Verse")—revealed in this context, advises that all business transactions and agreements be written down. Each agreement should be witnessed by two experts, or at least one expert and two non-experts, and any verbal agreement should be backed by some asset as collateral. The verse both sought to make sure Medina's many new merchants had the savvy to avoid scams and to uphold clear standards of commerce to avoid acrimonious disputes.

The city's booming commerce coupled with its vast granaries enabled it to flourish even as a terrible famine hit Arabia. After the initial late-fall downpours, no rain followed during the winter. Scorching sandstorms swept the region, battering communities. Farmers across Arabia watched in horror as their crops withered, wells dried up, and livestock began dying of starvation. People suffering from intense hunger literally crawled through the streets to forage whatever weeds and thornbushes they could find.

Yet Medina, like ancient Egypt under Joseph, had prepared: water from cisterns was efficiently directed via each individual *Rasul* to water fields while stored grain was released to make bread and feed livestock. The city enjoyed enough excess resources that in early summer Muhammad directed emergency aid to be dispatched to his hometown of Mecca to resuscitate a community on the verge of disaster in the blistering heat. To those in Medina who wondered why the city's precious resources should be shared with antagonists in Mecca who had spent months trying to damage the same fields that now fed them, the Qur'an observed:

> The good deed is not equal to the harmful deed; therefore, push away aggression with kindness and understanding; for if you do a seeming antagonist can be transformed into the dearest and most loyal of friends. Yet be aware that only those with maturity and foresight can transform animosity into friendship— and know that anyone who can achieve such a difficult task is truly fortunate and successful!

Although the Meccan elders did not respond positively to the relief caravan— being aided by the Qur'an's followers only further incensed them—the altruistic charity showed that the Medinians had successfully translated ideas into action. In honor of their accomplishment, the Qur'an introduced a new surah on the first anniversary of the *Hijrah* (Muhammad's arrival in Medina). Indeed, whereas in the Meccan period, the Qur'an marked anniversaries from its first mountaintop revelation, now the establishment of a new community served as a key annual spark for new ideas. The chapter, called *Aal 'Imran* ("The Family of Amram"), mirrored *Al-Baqarah* with its verses unfolding over several years, serialized in parallel but with its own distinctive rhythm and rhyme. The surah early on made a point of saluting the Medinians' mature generosity:

> Certainly, the people who have the best claim to Abraham's legacy are those who actually uphold it, including this prophet [*Nabi*] and those who seek serenity under his guidance—and the Loving Divine is the guardian of all who seek serenity.

Though the Meccans nominally served as custodians of the Abraham-built Ka'bah shrine, they had squandered his values—and would surely have let Medina suffer had the situation been reversed (after all, they nearly starved Muhammad's clan to death during the boycott). Upholding Abraham's legacy by sharing food with those in desperate need, the people of Medina had earned the right to a prophet. For the first time ever, the Qur'an recognized Muhammad (albeit not by name) as a *Nabi*—and the first Arabic prophet. After thirteen years of expounding theory, he had finally directed a community to successfully apply it via impactful action and thus secured the mantle of Abraham's mindset.

Two weeks later, the Qur'an explicitly mentioned Muhammad's name for the first time, as if to specify beyond a doubt who "this prophet" was. The verse emphasized that to uphold Abraham's legacy required translating the mindset into action: "People who appreciate the value of what has been revealed over time via Muhammad—a clear path from the Divine Mentor—have internalized the teachings and implemented their convictions via constructive action." The Qur'an at last had a prophet worthy of being named and disciples carrying out its principles.

๛

After *Al-Baqarah* had purposely reassured its Jewish audience that the Qur'an was upholding the legacy of the Torah, the formal declaration of Muhammad as a prophet now pushed at the bounds of accepted Jewish tradition. Whereas *Al-Baqarah* challenged Jews to overcome centuries of passivity, Aal 'Imran exhorted them to share the transcendent wisdom of the Torah with a universal audience. The surah's title referred to the biblical Amram's descendants: Moses, Aaron, Miriam, and the Levites—including the priestly class of Kohanim who served as select scholars and custodians of the Torah. By invoking this elite, the surah indirectly asked who could serve as instrumental guides for the new order in Medina. Its opening echoed the beginning of *Al-Baqarah* as well as its iconic verse *Ayat-ul-Kursi,* but with a pointed shift:

> Alif Lam Mim. Allah there is no Divine but He, the Living and Sustainer of all [*al-Hayy-ul-Qayyum*]. He gradually revealed the book [*Al-Kitab*] to you as a source of clarifying truth, affirming what has been revealed before it. He also previously revealed the Torah and the Gospels as guidance for all people and revealed the *Furqan* [Jewish oral tradition explicating the Torah].

Al-Kitab here clearly referred to the Qur'an and not the Torah, adjusting the formulation of *Al-Baqarah*'s opening sentences. The invocation of the "living"

aspect of the Divine emphasized how tradition necessarily evolves to avoid stagnation. In that spirit, the passage invoked the Gospels, surely a surprise to Jewish
audiences. *Al-Baqarah* had made no mention of Jesus, Mary, or the Christian
tradition. Yet the surah still aimed to reassure its primary audience:

> The Loving Divine has certainly chosen and elevated Adam, Noah, the descen-
> dants of Abraham, and the descendants of Amram [*Aal 'Imran*] over all, gener-
> ations to generation, each inheriting the legacy from the other. . . .

A descendant was not necessarily one of bloodline but of mindset. The
Levites stood out as scholars tasked with educating and uplifting their people,
achieving lasting recognition because of their mission and effort. What made
them valuable was not pedigree or advanced degrees, but acumen and conduct. Similarly, Muhammad's now explicit prophethood came not from inheritance but merit. The surah marked a key transition from a Jewish-centric
approach to a universal one, albeit casting the broadening as a continuation
of the Levitic spirit.

To illustrate the message of transcending artificial boundaries to outstanding pursuit of knowledge and service, the surah recounted the story of Mary's
childhood. Named in honor of Moses' sister Miriam—the daughter of Amram and a prophet in her own right—Mary offered further proof that there
was no reason to exclude women from privileged roles. Mary's mother, Hannah, had suffered a difficult pregnancy and pledged her fetus to service in the
Temple in Jerusalem. When a girl rather than the expected boy emerged, God
reassures a despairing Hannah: "The male does not possess the fine qualities
of a female." Hannah then names her daughter in the spirit of a fellow strong
female Levite, and Mary manages to serve in the Temple via a clever work-
around where her feet never directly touch the sacred ground (she was carried
into the temple and remained in a raised hut specially constructed for her).

The vignette clearly pushed back against chauvinistic boundaries demonstrating that women could serve in key leadership positions. The surah's argument against narrow-minded and parochial restrictions stemmed from an
insistence that they harmed the person who applied them above all:

> There are those among the People of the Book that if you entrust him with a
> massive amount he will guard it and return it to you faithfully, while there are

some among them even if you were to entrust him with a single dinar he would not return it to you unless you continuously pester him. That is because such people have alleged: "We don't need to be faithful to other peoples." They speak falsehood against the Loving Divine and they truly do not know the scriptures. Rather, anyone who upholds his trust faithfully then let them know the Loving Divine will multiply the bounties of those who maintain action-based hope. Certainly, those who sell the pledges they make before the Loving Divine and break their oaths for a meager sum are like empty shells and in the end they will be at a loss, for the Loving Divine will neither speak to such people nor look at them nor elevate them, and for such it will be a disgraceful end.

Merchants across Arabia were notorious for cheating non-tribesmen in business transactions. Yet the passage argued that dishonest merchants actually undermine themselves by damaging their reputations. Long-term success in business and in life required honest interactions with all people, regardless of background. Similarly, the surah argued against hoarding valuable knowledge and denying all people access to it:

Remember when the Loving Divine made a covenant with those entrusted to safeguard the Torah [Al-Kitab]: that you shall make clear the teachings of the scriptures for all people and not conceal it for yourselves. But some among them tossed the covenant behind their backs and sold out the teachings for a meager sum.

If Torah wisdom remains the domain of an artificially limited elite, only a few people can benefit from it—impeding the larger community's potential to flourish. The wisdom carefully preserved by the Levites for close to two millennia was now available to all, and thus anyone could become a spiritual descendant of Amram.

The Qur'an's desire to unify an increasingly diverse community in Medina was not simply principled, but also strategic. The seething Meccans were no longer content to merely harass the city but to annihilate it. The Meccans spread a rumor that the Qur'an's followers intended to raid the annual caravan from Damascus and prepared an attack force of over one thousand warriors to plunder Medina. For fourteen years, the Qur'an had advocated alternatives to violence, using the intellect and nuanced psychological engagement to redirect hostility into productivity. But with an army set to imminently destroy it, the Qur'an reluctantly evolved to condone self-defense, albeit in a remarkable passive declaration: "Permission is granted to those who are attacked, because they have been greatly oppressed."

Despite being outnumbered more than three to one, the Medinians won a decisive victory by heading out to preemptively confront the Meccan attack force by the wells of Badr. For the untrained farmers of Medina who had never taken up arms in their lives, the victory over aggressors felt miraculous, although it derived from superior tactics driven by quick entrepreneurial innovation in battlefield techniques. Rather than play up this astounding success, the Qur'an focused instead on the plight of the defeated: "Remember that in the same way that you feel pain, they also feel pain, so be compassionate." Prisoners of war could earn their freedom simply by teaching people in Medina how to read and write, fulfilling Al-Baqarah's earlier declaration that "a seeming antagonist can be transformed into the dearest and most loyal of friends." More than half of the released POWs remarkably chose to settle with their families in Medina, giving up the hometown they had just fought for to become followers of the Qur'an.

Such setbacks further infuriated the Meccans, who resolved to return a year later with three thousand men supported by a strong cavalry of outstanding knights. Determined to stack the odds in their favor, the Meccan force planned to attack on Saturday morning, assuming Medina's Jewish majority would be immobilized by Sabbath observance. Yet a prominent rabbi named Mukhairiq, himself a Levite, refused to stand by passively. Inspired by the Jewish injunction "anyone who saves a life is as if he saved an entire world," Rabbi Mukhairiq led his congregants from the synagogue to the frontlines on Saturday morning. He would soon give up his life on the battlefield, as fierce fighting nearly claimed Muhammad's own life—with the prophet only saved by a group of nurses who leapt to his defense when male fighters panicked.

The Meccans ultimately retreated, leaving the Medinians to mourn their losses while feeling relived that their city was saved. The Qur'an commemorated the turbulent events first by recognizing the Levite rabbi who was martyred:

> Remember the many rabbis [Ribbiyyun] who fought and died alongside prophets; they neither wavered in the face of overwhelming odds on the path toward the Divine nor showed signs of weakness nor allowed themselves to feel victimized.

It then addressed Muhammad's near death:

> Muhammad was merely a *Rasul* [channeling guide of divine energy] before whom came many *Rusul* [channeling guides]. If he were to die or be killed, would you then revert to your old ways and undo the good work you have achieved?

During the Battle of Uhud, the Medinian fighters had fled simply on a rumor that Muhammad had been killed—a disturbing development that spoke to a lack of self-confidence and a concern about the long-term durability of the Qur'an's message. Yes, Medina's dynamic success had been facilitated by Muhammad's guidance, yet the verse reminded Medinians that the work had been their own. The *Rasul* channeled energy efficiently and for maximum impact, but was merely a guide and not the water itself. Generation after generation had carried on the message of Abraham and Moses long after their deaths. People needed to recognize their own potential and accomplishments and channel their own energy forward.

Medina was going through a kind of adolescence where insecurity was not the only challenge. As the Meccan raids ceased for two years following the Battle of Uhud, internal social differences surfaced. A sudden burst of five brief surahs—in contrast to the epic *Al-Baqarah* and *Aal 'Imran*—emerged in rapid succession over five weeks. Known as the collective *Al-Musabbihat* ("The Forces of Grounding amidst Turbulent Waters"), the chapters sought to channel positive energy out of group tensions. Each surah began with the concept of *Sabbaha*: to prostrate to the ground amidst chaos to praise the Divine as a unique source of stabilization. The surahs also introduced a flurry of new names for God, recognizing that the people of Medina needed dynamic inspiration separate from Muhammad to help them uphold and advance the Qur'an's message. Put another way, people needed to appreciate in vivid ways the true and everlasting force behind the Qur'an.

Al-Hadid ("Iron-Willed"), the first surah, encouraged audiences to be determined visionaries bent on achieving their goals. It began by introducing three pairs of contrasting divine names as a dialogue of creative tension.

> Prostrates in adulation to the Loving Divine all that is in the cosmos and on earth, for He is the Wise Guiding Coach. To him belongs the dominion of the cosmos and the earth. He is the One who Revives the Dormant [*Al-Muhyi*] yet

Induces Repose [*Al-Mumit*]—and He is the one with authority over all. He is the Pioneering First [*Al-Awwal*] yet Last One Remaining [*Al-Akhir*], the One Who Stands Out [*Ath-Thahir*] yet remains Internally Driven [*Al-Batin*]—and He has deep nuanced knowledge of all things.

The surah presented God as an exemplary who constantly fuses tension into progress. That spirit took on particular importance in a rapidly evolving Medina, where returning exiles from Abyssinia joined an increasingly diverse population living in rapidly expanding new mixed neighborhoods no longer organized by clan. The second surah, *Al-Hashr* ("The Ingathering"), spoke directly to these changing demographics:

> These people of receptive hearts actively seek to elevate themselves. They love those who sought refuge with them and bear no resentment in their hearts for all that they have selflessly donated. They sacrifice to aid others, even when it causes them great distress. Indeed, when individuals overcome their personal egotistical inclinations, then the larger community truly succeeds! . . . Oh, you who seek serenity, have action-based hope in the Loving Divine and let each soul reflect on what they have previously established that will endure far into the future.

Al-Hashr's final three verses hosted twelve names of God, each providing a motivational example of how the Divine helps enable potential in people for lasting impact.

- *Al-Malik*: the Reenergizer (used figuratively for "king")
- *Al-Quddus*: the Uplifter to special status (used figuratively for "holy")
- *As-Salam*: the Restorer of Wholeness (literally, "repairer of cracks")
- *Al-Mu'min*: the Security Provider (literally, "builder of strong defensive walls")
- *Al-Muhaimin*: the Clarifier of the Obscure
- *Al-'Aziz*: the Coach (literally, "the builder of strength")
- *Al-Jabbar*: the Healer of Fractures (literally, "the cast maker")
- *Al-Mutakabbir*: the One who Raises Higher (literally, "constructor of additional levels")
- *Al-Khaliq*: the Maker of New Forms from preexisting material
- *Al-Bari*: the Re-fashioner who transforms discarded elements

* *Al-Musawwir*: the Expert Designer refining raw elements into precious objects
* *Al-Hakim*: the Wise (literally, "fuser of weak fragments into one strong unit")

Beyond emulating the divine example on an individual level; achieving synchronization on a communal level marked the greater challenge in Medina. The third surah *As-Saff* ("Organized Straight Row") evoked focused group collaboration for greater impact. Achieving harmony required that each person fulfill their individual obligations, including backing their words with action:

> Oh you who seek serenity, why do you say what you do not do? It is highly undesirable in the eyes of the Loving Divine to say what you do not do. Certainly the Loving Divine raises those who strive together in straight organized lines as if they are a strongly constructed building of well-fitted stones that complement each other despite differences in size.

The metaphor of different-sized rocks organized into a larger beautiful mosaic evoked how even one individual's responsibility—regardless of how small it might seem—had a significant impact on the larger community. It also signified a disparate group organizing into something greater than the sum of its individual parts.

The fourth surah, *Al-Jumu'ah* ("The Inclusion"), further insisted that individual efforts required external support and designated a special time every week when the community should gather to restabilize as a collective: "Oh seekers of serenity, when the call to prayer on the day of Jumu'ah is proclaimed and diligently brings together different people to be uplifted and reminded by the example of the Loving Divine." From this point on, every Friday in the early afternoon, the people of Medina would congregate at the masjid to hear a short sermon featuring a quick revitalizing reminder to inspire people for the week ahead. *Al-Jumu'ah* thus came to signify a designated prayer time and became the new name for Friday.

An organized collective sounded nice in theory, but human beings naturally had a selfish impulse that could easily spark discord. The concluding surah, *At-Taghabun* ("Self-Sabotage"), took its name from someone digging a hole to trap others yet inadvertently falling into it themselves. Malicious damage, the chapter argued, ultimately created lose-lose situations—the opposite of lasting impact.

> Seek action-based hope in the Loving Divine to the best of your ability and remain cognizant and aware. Spend selflessly out of the goodness of your heart. Remember that by taming the darker side of the ego, one can truly attain lasting success.

In warning about how the desire for self-sufficiency can spiral out of control to become self-sabotage, the surah introduced two new names for the Divine:

- *Al-Ghani*: the Self-Sufficient who does not need to harm others to survive and in fact can help sustain others in need
- *Al-Hamid*: the Most Outstanding Role Model of healthy self-confidence

The surah urged audiences to transform natural yet unhealthy ego impulses into constructive self-sufficiency.

In Arabian society, one of the most pervasive forms of self-sabotage was the purposeful and widespread disempowerment of women. In a patriarchal society organized by tribe, women existed as assets that belonged to their male relatives, even inherited as part of an estate like chattels. Women were guaranteed no rights of their own, depending solely on the whims of their male relatives for whatever freedoms they might enjoy. Even wealthy women could not openly conduct business, no matter their status, and orphaned women were particularly vulnerable with no immediate male relative to defend them. Many orphaned females were sold in slavery or trafficked into prostitution.

The Qur'an had previously hailed examples of strong independent women like Mary, but otherwise not directly addressed the status of women in society aside from stridently condemning the infanticide of daughters. But the failure to empower women echoed in all the critiques of the *Musabbihat* surahs that sought to stabilize and strengthen society in turbulent times. It was time for the Qur'an to leave no doubt about the central role women played in a society that sought to make a lasting impact.

On the fourth anniversary of the *Hijrah,* a massive new surah emerged, one that would be serialized over three years and ultimately become the second-longest chapter in the Qur'an. Its name signaled its core message: *An-Nisa* was a particular name for females that translated as "The Uplifting Women." (*Nasa* meant to lift up one's eyes in respectful adoration.) The surah's title reminded everyone that uplifting women uplifts society. The Constitution of Medina, which established equality among all the city's residents, had been signed four years earlier only by male tribal leaders. *An-Nisa* now came as a kind of women's constitution, recognizing the changes that had already emerged in recent years to give women a formal code to uphold their individual rights. It began with a bold declaration of harmonizing equality:

> Oh people, have action-based hope in your Divine Mentor, who created you from one source and from the same source formed its complementary and completing partner, and from them He dispersed many men and women. Therefore, remain mindful of the Loving Divine—in whose name you appeal to one another— and honor the wombs [*Arham*, plural of *Rahim*] that bore you.

The chapter proceeded to specify in great detail how to honor the wombs that had nurtured all human beings, covering a broad range of topics never discussed in public, including: menstruation, menopause, childbirth, and breastfeeding. Verse after verse set down clear legal standards for the rights of women, some of them revolutionary: "Just as men have a right to inheritance, so do women, an equal share." In fact, the Qur'an's detailed discussion of inheritance rights comes only in the context of guaranteeing women's right to inherit in many different circumstances. Notably, the Qur'an first emphasizes the inheritance rights of orphaned girls.

The surah also insisted on respecting the psychological needs of women. Rather than transact a marriage negotiation solely with a bride's parents, a groom must provide his traditional wedding gift to his new wife with physical assets backed by emotional affection: "Give women their bridal gifts with love." In this short phrase, the Qur'an commanded husbands to provide intimate fulfillment to their wives far beyond material gifts. The Qur'an further insisted that a wife's property remained her own and could not be unilaterally confiscated by her husband. The chapter recognized that marriages faced rocky periods that could deeply strain ties between husband and wife—and proposed a nuanced and healthy way to resolve them:

When a toxic atmosphere [*Nushuz*—literally, "flaring fangs secreting venom"] arises in your relationship, communicate your concern gently and clearly. If the situation remains unchanged, cease intimacy yet continue to share a bed. If the stress becomes unbearable, release them to enable healing via temporary separation. . . . If any woman fears rising toxicity [*Nushuz*] or neglect from her husband, then let her seek mediation and reconciliation, for reconciliation is always healthier. Be aware that human egos are naturally disposed to selfishness, therefore if you seek to express altruistic kindness and graciousness and foster action-based hope, then know that the Loving Divine is aware of your sincere sacrifices and will reward you in kind. You will not be able to maintain emotional justice among multiple wives, no matter how hard you may try. Therefore, don't leave a woman hanging by keeping her attached to you in wedlock, while your heart is inclined away from her. . . .

As *An-Nisa* was being serialized, a stand-alone surah emerged to highlight its themes via a particular incident when a neglected wife insisted on her right to sexual intimacy and fulfillment. Her impassioned plea to Muhammad for help sparked the *Surah Al-Mujadilah* ("The Righteous Female Debater") and one of the Qur'an's rare bursts of righteous indignation:

The Loving Divine has surely heard the grievances expressed by the woman righteously debating you concerning her husband's refusal to be intimate. She calls out in distress to the Loving Divine, and the Loving Divine hears your discussion. . . . Those among you [men] who deny intimacy to their wives, comparing them to their mothers, should know that their wives are not their mothers, for their mothers are they that gave birth to them. What they say is detestable and perjurious!

The Qur'an revealed it had been listening to the woman's pleas and fully agreed with her right to sexual gratification as an independent human being and an equal partner in a relationship, who deserved to enjoy sensual intimacy beyond mere procreation. The passage not only recognized the hurt feelings of the wife, but implied that unsatisfied women would hold back society, whereas a happy home bolstered a society creating lasting impact.

After two years of relative quiet, the Meccans returned en masse to destroy the Qur'an once and for all. The Meccan elders assembled a confederation of twelve thousand men from numerous Arabian tribes to annihilate Medina and enslave its inhabitants. With only a few weeks to prepare for the army's assault, the citizens of Medina rushed to dig a massive trench blocking the only entrance to the city, which was otherwise surrounded by a natural defense of impassible volcanic formations. With every man needed on the frontlines, a woman was left in charge as the mayor of Medina and a force of female defenders donned men's armor to bolster the army. Amazingly, the trench gambit succeeded, as none of the Meccan forces were able to traverse it. After weeks of stagnation outside the trench, the confederation crumbled, with successive tribes slinking home under the cover of darkness until no fighters remained.

The Qur'an, which had remained silent during the siege, returned with its third passage mentioning Muhammad by name: "Muhammad was never a father to any of you but rather he is the channeling guide of the Loving Divine and the one who has come to fulfill the legacy of the prophets." (33:40) The Meccans could not eradicate the message of the Qur'an by murdering Muhammad and the Medinians, for they served as channels of a message that transcended time and place. The Qur'an's legacy was transmitted not via a bloodline but by the impact of ideas.

Despite the Meccans' genocidal intent, the Qur'an remained committed to "pushing away aggression with kindness" and "transforming animosity into friendship." Repurposing the injunction of "peace and reconciliation are always best" from the Qur'an's discussion of reconciling strained marriages, Muhammad led a peaceful march on Mecca with over one thousand of his unarmed followers dressed in white (as a sign of nonaggression). The stunned Meccans ultimately agreed to a ten-year peace treaty that featured very generous terms for their side. Preaching the Qur'an was banned from Mecca; the Qur'an's followers were banned from trading in Meccan-controlled markets; and no Meccans were allowed to join the Qur'an's followers in Medina (anyone who tried had to be repatriated). When signing the treaty, the Meccans insisted Muhammad's name not be accompanied by this title of *Rasulullah,* which Muhammad acceded to by smudging out the honorific with his thumb.

The Medinians were shocked by such capitulation. To address their concerns, the Qur'an presented a surah celebrating what it cast as a great success. Titled *Al-Fath* ("The Great Unlocking"), it echoed the iconic early surah of *Al-Fatihah*—expanding the original personal unlocking to a larger civic unlocking—and suggested that the treaty had actually opened up a world of opportunity. For the last time, the Qur'an invoked Muhammad by name: "Muhammad, the challenging guide of the Loving Divine, and his allies are firm and steadfast in the face of those who seek to eliminate them, remaining compassionate and tender amongst themselves." Whereas Muhammad's title had been wiped away in the treaty text, the Qur'an reasserted and immortalized it—while reminding its followers not to confuse compassion with weakness.

Indeed, Medina was now liberated from external threat for the first time. A flood of new and old followers flowed into the city, including Abu Tharr returning with his once-barbaric tribe converted to Qur'anic disciples, as well as many of the original followers who had fled to Abyssinia. As Medina's society experienced a rapid evolution into a cosmopolitan city where people of diverse origins intermingled for the first time in Arabia, the Qur'an provided growing guidelines for a communal code of conduct, in part to help alleviate growing tensions. New laws regulating civic interactions were inserted into serialized mega-chapters like *An-Nisa*:

> Oh you who seek serenity, stand firm in justice bearing witnesses to the truth even if it be against your own selves or your parents or your relatives. . . . Beware of following your prejudices by deviating from justice and acting unjustly. If you willfully distort or falsify a testimony, the Loving Divine is ever aware of what you do and will hold you to account. . . . The Loving Divine does not like negative thoughts to be publicized, except by those who have been treated unjustly. . . . Whether you reveal or conceal a good deed or pardon harm that befell you, the Loving Divine is ever so forgiving to all and able to heal the hearts.

Discontent was occasionally directed at Muhammad himself, sometimes even by his closest followers. One particularly dramatic moment occurred inside the masjid itself. Muhammad had leveraged the period of quiet following the treaty signing to engage in international diplomacy with Arabia's surrounding empires. In particular, he wrote to the ruler of Abyssinia to thank him for hospitably welcoming the Qur'an's followers and proposed a free-trade agreement with Medina. The ruler did not simply write back, but sent a grand delegation of several dozen men bearing gifts to ceremonially establish the alliance. The Abyssinian delegation arrived dressed in their finest—feathers,

animal skins, jewelry, and colorful parasols—and enjoyed several days of festivities to mark the agreement's establishment, even conducting a Christian
prayer service in the masjid on Sunday morning.

That evening, the delegation requested to present a special ceremony of
gratitude, its content mysteriously unspecified. While outsiders had never formally guest-lectured inside the masjid, Muhammad kindly assented to the
Abyssinians' performance. As dusk fell, the Abyssinians lit several dozen African lanterns they had brought as gifts inside the masjid. The hall, normally lit
only by small lights, had never glowed brighter. The aura in the darkening sky
attracted audiences from afar—including 'Umar, the goliath of the Qur'an's
followers, who burst into the masjid shocked by what he beheld . . . and heard.

Abyssinian musicians played drums and African flutes as others sang in
Ethiopic and danced acrobatically with javelins and shields. Beneath a canopy
of starlight, light from the lanterns glinted off the armor and jewelry. Music, let
alone ritualistic dancing, had never before been performed inside the masjid, a
place of holy worship. 'Umar was furious and rushed over to Muhammad to challenge his teacher's refusal to stop the profane performance. Muhammad deftly
drew 'Umar aside, calming him in hushed tones before both returned to watch
the rest of the performance and warmly congratulate the performers at the end.

The next day, Muhammad delivered a fresh Qur'anic revelation that drew
inspiration from the folk-dance performance—which Africans employed as an
educational tool—to ruminate upon the many ways in which knowledge can
be shared and expressed. What Arabs might perceive as mere frivolous enter-
tainment was actually a profound interactive experience to transmit ancient
wisdom. With the Abyssinian delegation about to depart, the revelation—
dubbed *Ayat-un-Nur* ("The Verse of Evening Light")—pointedly included two
terms in Ethiopic (*Mishkah* for the African lanterns and *Zujajah* for crystal
glass) and mentioned olive trees, a species native to the Abyssinian highlands:

> The Loving Divine is the source of illumination for the cosmos and earth: His il-
> lumination is like a lantern, inside it is a lamp, suspended inside a crystal ball, re-
> sembling a brilliantly pulsating star, fueled by a special blessed tree—an olive tree,
> neither from the east nor the west, its oil so luminous it emits light without burning.

The remarkable verse painted a vivid and complex picture, requiring audiences to unravel the source of uniquely refined light. It described a very bright

African lantern illuminating the evening darkness, powered inside by an Asian lamp surrounded by a ball of the finest translucent crystal that diffused the light in all directions. That internal lantern was itself fueled by the product of an ancient olive tree that transcended time and place. This tree's refined oil was so pure that it illuminated the darkness even without an external spark.

The verse used the metaphor of light to explore the complex multidimensional nature of knowledge. The example set by the Loving Divine should inspire one to seek layered knowledge everywhere and to constantly refine knowledge further and further to extract fresh layers of nuance. Because God embeds knowledge everywhere, a seemingly simple African folk dance could be the bearer of transcendent truths.

The verse offered a brilliant methodology for how the Qur'an contains multiple dimensions of meaning rather than merely one simple surface message. A beautiful bright lantern can suffice to inspire people, but a curious knowledge seeker goes deeper, seeking to understand what powers the lamp from within, even looking inside to peel back multiple layers to appreciate how the impressive phenomenon works. The never-ending quest for knowledge entails a process of constant refinement: breaking down elements, searching for deeper insights, drawing on diverse sources, and above all remaining humble and open-minded.

❦

During periods of conflict, the Qur'an attracted few new followers. But in the year and a half of peace following the treaty, the Qur'an's followers more than quadrupled. Recognizing that the treaty had completely failed to curtail the Qur'an, the Meccans began to feel surrounded, as Muhammad secured positive relations with the empires surrounding Arabia. Cornered and flailing, the Meccans lashed out—directing a nighttime massacre of Medina's unarmed pagan allies, a blatant violation of the peace treaty. One lone survivor stumbled across the desert for two weeks before arriving in Medina and collapsing outside the masjid. The shocking murder of dozens of civilians and the shattering of the peaceful relations prompted the Qur'an's harshest surah, ironically titled *At-Tawbah* ("The Reconciliation"). Notably, it was the only surah to begin without invoking the name of God, as it explored the painful dynamics of how to handle human betrayal and hold aggressors accountable in a principled way.

The surah recognized righteous anger—which in Arabia drove an unending cycle of bloody vendettas—yet sought to channel it toward a positive outcome: to stand up to those who massacre innocents without replicating their behavior. An effective response required remaining open to reconciliation (as reflected in the surah's name) yet insisting that atonement required concrete actions. The surah addressed the Meccans directly, offering a vague warning of consequences in four months (giving the annual Meccan caravan plenty of time to return from Damascus) and encouraging acts of repentance to avoid an escalation. Its firm tone balanced outrage and clemency:

The Loving Divine and his Rasul are released from their commitment to the pledge made with the polytheists [in Mecca and their allies]. Therefore, travel in safety throughout the land for four months and remember there is no escaping the Loving Divine's accountability, as the Loving Divine will dishonor those who spread darkness. . . .

Therefore, if you repent and reconcile, it will be advantageous to you. However, if you turn your backs in haughty scorn, then be aware that you cannot escape the Loving Divine's accountability. Warn the warriors of darkness of their impending unpleasant end—except for those among the polytheists who never broke the pledges made with you in the peace treaty and did not assist those who publicly defiled it. . . .

When the months of amnesty expire, then kill the polytheists wherever they are, take them prisoner, detain them, and utilize every available strategy to neutralize them—however, if they repent, atone, reconcile, repair the connections they have severed [i.e., orphaned children cut off from their murdered parents], and make amends by elevating the surviving families of those they wounded, then let them go free, for the Loving Divine is full of forgiveness and compassion. . . .

Do you not see how they publicly defiled the treaty against you, caring neither about chivalrous valor nor the shielding rights enshrined in a pact [*Thimmah*]? They tried to beguile you with their mouths while their obstinate hearts rejected peace, and most are agitators. . . . The aggressors in no way uphold the rights of a person protected by a treaty [*Mu'min*], caring neither about chivalrous valor nor the shielding rights enshrined in a pact [*Thimmah*]. However, if they repent, atone, reconcile, repair the connections they have severed, and make amends by elevating the surviving families of those they wounded—then they are in effect your brothers.

However, should they renege after making strong pledges of peace and instead backstab your reconciling approach, then fight to stop them for they are inverted guides toward concealing darkness. As there can be no trusting sense of safety with them, the only way to keep them from continuing their aggression is to fight to stop them. Thus, fight the guides of darkness who hold no safety of others in their hearts—in the hope that they might cease. Will you not stand up to a people who repeatedly break their pledges of peace and maliciously conspire to exile the Rasul, even as they initiated all this aggression unprovoked? Do not allow their intense aggression to intimidate you, for—if you are truly seekers of serenity—the Loving Divine is more worthy of being revered and held in awe.

Fight them, for the Loving Divine will hold them accountable via your rectifying hands; He will dishonor them; He will give you victory over them; He will heal the heavy hearts of a people of serenity; He will soothe their righteous anger and remove the resentment in their hearts; the Loving Divine will forgive and reconcile with whoever seeks forgiveness. The Loving Divine knows all and is a source of profound wisdom.

The firm warning of *At-Tawbah* was clear: Fight to stop them but not to replicate their actions. Despite its shock over the massacre of pagan allies *(Mu'min)* who had been protected by the treaty *(Thimmah)*, the Qur'an still held out hope that mass murderers might change. Verses repeatedly acknowledged shock and anger, but kept offering escape clauses. If God encouraged transformation of animosity into friendship, perhaps divine foresight could envision the Meccans as future allies of the Medinians.

The chapter provided a codified methodology and etiquette for how to deal with betrayal and aggression: rather than react impulsively, allow time to cool tensions by openly insisting on consequences while providing opportunities for reconciliation based on specific principled repentance. In essence, the surah exemplified how to stay focused on what really matters: justice trumped vengeance driven by a wounded ego. Unchecked retaliation risked undermining all the accomplishments secured by years of hard work. To have a lasting impact required maintaining ethical guidelines for handling inevitable human betrayal.

Part of the Meccans' gambit in attacking Medina's pagan allies was an attempt at plausible deniability. Via a whisper campaign, they had sown discord and provoked murder without physically bloodying their own hands, enabling them to feign ignorance if confronted despite serving as the behind-the-scenes masterminds of a massacre. In so doing, they proved even more dangerous than the killers. While *At-Tawbah* put the Meccan elders on notice that their mind games had failed, a short new surah called *An-Nas* (a double entendre meaning both "humanity" and "seen out in the open") cautioned the Qur'an's followers to learn an important lesson from how the Meccans had manipulated the treaty:

> *Publicly proclaim: "I seek serenity in the Divine Mentor of all people-*
> *The Divine Rejuvenator of all people,*
> *The Divine Comforter of all people-*
> *From the wily whisperer of confusion and chaos, the slinking stirrer of*
> *   discord and disarray.*
> *The one abusing trust to hiss harmful ideas into the unsuspecting minds*
> *   of all people.*
> *Doing so both surreptitiously and visibly."*

The first three verses offered uplifting inspiration for all people, only to be sharply countered by a darkly sober take on the human propensity to mislead others for personal gain. Each line of the surah ended with an Arabic rhyming refrain of "ssss," evoking a snake-hiss whisper and the delirium, confusion, and chaos caused by snakebite venom. The surah drew on the tension between the impulse to embrace the universality of "all people" and the hard-nosed reality that human beings often try to exploit one another. Whereas the first-ever revelation of *Iqra* recognized that all people have the God-given potential to blossom, *An-Nas* reminded audiences that not everyone wants to—and that some may employ hypocrisy to degrade others rather than to elevate one another symbiotically. Reality required a mix of optimism and sobriety.

Within hours of the surah's revelation, Muhammad left Medina with a force of several thousand men to confront Mecca. Two weeks later, the Meccan elders discovered a formidable force of ten thousand warriors on the outskirts of their city—and promptly surrendered without a fight. As the conquerors strode toward the Ka'bah, they chanted a new Qur'anic revelation that declared a formal end to deception-induced stagnation:

> The era of liberating truth has ascended, while the age of deceptive delusions has vanished. Like a shadow, deception always fades away leaving no trace!

The Qur'an, for the first time in two decades, faced no direct opposition. Despite all the obstacles, its message had triumphed. Its followers had consistently applied the Qur'an's methodology and values and emerged ascendant over powerful entrenched forces without compromising. Still, the Qur'an had long worried that once-oppressed people can themselves become oppressors as soon as they gain the upper hand. Precisely because Muhammad had been severely oppressed yet suddenly enjoyed unchecked authority, the Qur'an delivered a cautionary rather than triumphant new surah. Called *An-Nasr* ("The Ultimate Assistance" or "The Victory"), the chapter undermined its own title by emphasizing humility and pointedly addressed its audience in the singular:

> When the ultimate assistance of the Loving Divine has been fulfilled and the great unlocking [conquest of Mecca] has been fulfilled, at that moment you [singular] saw the multitudes of people entering into the path of the Loving Divine in great numbers—therefore, glorify your Divine Mentor for His exemplary role in inspiring you with His tutelage and keep yourself humbled, as the Divine Mentor is constantly renewing people's state.

One of the Qur'an's shortest chapters, *An-Nasr* contained just three verses but pointed to a range of potential challenges in the era of dominance including: vengeance, failure to achieve genuine reconciliation, unchecked authority, superiority, zealousness, judgmentalism, sectarianism, reverting to old ways of stagnation, superstition, disorientation amidst rapid change, fear of an uncertain future, and other negative human impulses. The Qur'an's remaining challenge was thus not to consolidate power but to ensure its core messages persevered in the turbulent era.

※

For the final two years of its existence, the Qur'an added only one new chapter and a handful of verses. Rather than pontificate from a position of power, the Qur'an focused inward and directed its prophet to undertake a monumental editing process to consolidate its many fragments into a coherent single work that could endure for a universal audience. As new followers from across Arabia and beyond streamed into Medina, Muhammad largely withdrew from governing responsibilities to assemble a group of forty-two select disciples to help advance the Qur'an's compilation—paralleling the biblical role of the Levites, though in this case chosen based on merit rather than lineage or status.

The first step in the compilation process required re-grounding the triumphant Qur'an in its humble and painful roots to ensure the new dominant movement did not get carried away with newfound power. Almost the entire Qur'an had been revealed in periods of weakness, oppression, and loneliness—and its followers should never forget where it came from and what it had overcome. Thirteen new verses were revealed in the early editing period and inserted into thirteen different chapters from the Meccan period, the time of the Qur'an's greatest persecution, each time following a major concept. Called *Sajdah* ("re-grounding"), each verse offered an opportunity to reset emotions and perspective by reconnecting humbly with the earth. For example, a *sajdah* was added to *Surah Bani Israel* as follows:

> Whether or not to accept it is your choice. Remember that past sages possessing profound knowledge went down to the ground with their chins prostrate and were humbled by deep prophetic revelation, recognizing the Loving Divine's inspiration by proclaiming: "We know well that the Divine Mentor organizes the events of the universe."

The verse reminded triumphant new followers not to become zealous or domineering, as even outstanding scholars from the past who possessed deeper knowledge and had achieved far greater results knew that the key to success was humility and broadmindedness. To make sure the thirteen *sajdah* stood out, the emerging Qur'anic text included a specific marker indicating that the reciter should bow to the ground after the passage to meditate on its meaning. Muhammad even added a special blessing to be recited while performing the *sajdah*:

> My face has grounded itself and reconnected with the One who first caused it to emerge like a fragile plant from the earth and unleashed its hearing and sight, giving my senses their faculty of discernment and their ability to understand in order to feel whole. Blessed be the Loving Divine, who created me in the most complete form possible.

The next step of the editing process required putting over 110 chapters in order. Rather than assemble them chronologically as a historical narrative, Muhammad realized the Qur'an should not be frozen in time like an idol, and therefore he prioritized theme over sequence, creating dynamic juxtapositions of style, tone, and content. In its spirit of humility, none of the passages bemoaning suffering or criticizing Muhammad were removed, even as several original passages relating to strict biblical law were removed.

In an orchard outside Medina, Muhammad directed his scribes to lay out the scrolls of each chapter on a tarp and then order the surahs by length. Using counting ropes featuring collections of one hundred olive pits, the scribes painstakingly counted the number of words (and even letters) in each chapter. The essential order of the Qur'an thus became length, with the chapters in the final edited version generally flowing from longest to shortest, with some exceptions.

For the Qur'an's brief introduction, Muhammad chose the iconic *Al-Fatihah,* the first complete surah revealed and itself recited as a prayer seventeen times daily. For the book's concise closing, he selected *An-Nas,* with its warning about human manipulation revealed as the last surah before the conquest of Mecca. The Qur'an was thus framed around rejection, with *Al-Fatihah* originating in the days after Muhammad was laughed off the stage in Mecca and *An-Nas* capturing the last moment before the Qur'an became dominant.

Then, Muhammad divided the book into quarters, placing a surah beginning with *Alhamdullilah* at the start of each fourth: *Al-Fatihah* began the book; *An-Naam* started the second section; *Al-Kahf* marked the middle; *Saba* and *Fatir* combined to commence the final quarter. Within each quarter, Muhammad adjusted chapter order slightly, sometimes based on themes. For example, surahs about celestial bodies were all grouped together (chapters 85–93), as were surahs inspired by the lives of persecuted prophets (chapters 10–15). Other times, Muhammad positioned particular chapters based on their numerological significance. *Yusuf* appeared as chapter twelve, representing the twelve sons of Israel, and *Maryam* became chapter nineteen, reflecting the nineteen mentions of Mary in the Gospels.

After the refashioned Qur'an was nearly complete, one final new surah emerged. *Al-Hajj* ("The Illuminating Beacon") welcomed a universal audience to attend a great convention in Mecca to exchange wisdom and strengthen solidarity: "Invite all people up to the hajj." Two *sajdah* would be inserted into *Al-Hajj* as a sober reminder to remain even more grounded, particularly during times of prosperity. With the Qur'an's final surah already revealed, Muhammad stood before a throng of 120,000 people in the wilderness on the outskirts of Mecca to deliver a speech that functioned as the first public analytical interpretation of the Qur'an, the originating hallmark of the field of *Tafsir* (Qur'anic exegesis). This "Farewell Sermon" aimed to clarify the Qur'an's core messages in order to preserve them in perpetuity:

> It is possible I may not be here with you after this year, nonetheless, I expect you to be convening here again. I am handing you a bright torch and a guided path so that you can bring light to the world, liberating people from the darkness of ignorance and stagnation.
>
> Oh people, your blood, wealth, and individual hopes are all uniquely sacred— just like the uniqueness you witness today as we stand together united in this sacred space. All blood spilled before is forgiven. Let there be no more vendettas. Blood money due to us by whoever killed members of my clan is forgiven. . . . Do not transgress upon the rights of others or allow yourselves to suffer transgression.
>
> Oh people, women inherently enjoy the right to be supported on all levels, so uphold their rights. You have a duty to ensure their rights are upheld the same way that you have the right to expect their support. Elevate yourselves by empowering women!
>
> Oh people, do not revert after my death into discord, rivalry, and killing one another. I am leaving you with a sustainable system with the Qur'an, the Loving Divine as your exemplar, and the *Sunnah* [formula] I have outlined for you in my teachings—a method that, if you uphold it, will safeguard you from falling into the ravines of confusion.
>
> Oh people, know that your God is one, unique, and the God of all people. Likewise, you all descend from one common ancestor and as such are equal before God.
>
> Oh people, you all emerged from a thin surface layer of earth, so remain grounded and remember who you are. You are all brothers and sisters before the Divine, emerging from the same source. None has an advantage over another through blood or lineage; neither does an Arab have privileges over a non-Arab. It is only by merit and accomplishments that you can rise one above the other. In a society of equal opportunity, the weakest among you is equal to the strongest.

Seek your own elevation by empowering minorities among you, for they are protected by the sacred covenant of God. The most elevated among you before God
are those with the purest spiritual core.

With these parting words, a visibly weakened Muhammad largely retreated
to the orchard editing sessions with his forty-two disciples. Like a fine carpenter, he spent his final days whittling and refining the book into a masterpiece:
combining verses from different periods, reworking the order of verses, and
transporting verses from one chapter to another. Fifteen days before he died,
Muhammad experienced one final revelation:

Prepare yourself with action-filled hope for a day when you are reunited with the
Loving Divine. Each soul will then receive full recompense for all it has earned,
and none will be treated unjustly.

The verse reemphasized the Qur'an's message that reward derives from merit
and actions—so therefore live each day with purpose and awareness of long-
term goals. It was as if the verse had emerged just in time to fill one last gap in
the Qur'an. Muhammad had it inserted before the Qur'an's longest verse—
Ayat-ud-Dayn—toward the end of *Al-Baqarah,* the grand chapter that had
inaugurated the Medina period of transformative civic impact and only now
nine years later had come to a conclusion.

By placing the last verse where he did, Muhammad ensured that the exact
middle word of *Al-Baqarah* would be *Wasata* ("middle" or "balanced") and
the entire Qur'an's middle word would be *Fal-yatalattaf* ("let him be gentle,"
like someone cradling a newborn). The Qur'an's middle letter: *Lam*—with
its symbolic meaning of "education." Having emerged out of the darkness of
stagnation at the dawn of a new day twenty-two years earlier, the Qur'an remained a fragile being that sought to educate and inspire while requiring a
balanced community to support it with tender care.

Right before he died, Muhammad entrusted the sole complete manuscript of the Qur'an to a woman. He soon drew his last breath—and then the
Qur'an belonged to the ages.

PART III

THE
QUR'AN'S
LEGACY

7

THE STRUGGLE FOR CUSTODIANSHIP

THE SNIPERS IN GREEN CAMOUFLAGED THEMSELVES AMIDST THE PALM branches, tightly gripping poison-tipped arrows as they spied their marks marching below. Each of the forty-two snipers had spent over a year preparing for this moment. They had infiltrated Medina disguised as students eager to learn from Qur'anic masters, meticulously observing the personal habits of each of Muhammad's forty-two top disciples during scholarly discussions of Qur'anic passages. Their mission, however, was not to explore the Qur'an's deep knowledge but to obscure it—by assassinating all the elite young men tasked by Muhammad with preserving the Qur'an as a living force for future generations.

Each sniper had been assigned to eliminate one particular Qur'anic expert, with the assassination unit together intending to wipe out the Qur'an's main guardians in one fell swoop. Secured by palm-fiber ropes to the treetops, each assassin patiently awaited the arrival of their target, with bows pulled back ready to release their deadly arrows. Then, one by one they fired, and one by one the irreplaceable guardians of the Qur'an fell dead, the unique knowledge painstakingly preserved in their minds wiped out for eternity.

The snipers' barrage of arrows sent the Medinian forces fleeing in disarray. Muhammad had died just six months earlier, and suddenly it seemed all the experts he had personally selected to preserve the Qur'an's wisdom had been cut down. Because the sole written manuscript seemed useless without these specialists to help decipher it, the Qur'an's future hung in the balance.

As the retreating forces limped back to camp, the Medinians took stock of their losses. Three hundred and sixty men and women who had committed the Qur'an to memory lay dead on the battlefield, among them forty of Muhammad's top disciples. By a small miracle, two of the experts had fallen ill and remained in their tents recuperating while the battle raged. These two young men were the only remaining living links left to the Qur'an's oral tradition of advanced exegesis: just two fragile strands of expert knowledge to bridge the *Rasul's* oral teachings to future generations.

The Qur'an had survived over two decades of antagonism without strong military protection and attracted hundreds of thousands of followers across Arabia. Those followers assumed the Qur'an was invincible, misunderstanding a verse that declared: "We inspired the Qur'an's elevating power, and it is We who will preserve and safeguard it." Divine protection still required human initiative. In fact, the Qur'an's remarkable success in unifying the diverse tribes of Arabia for the first time in history made it appear both threatening to external empires (like the Byzantines) and appealing to internal forces opportunistically seeking power.

Within a few months of Muhammad's death, the Byzantine empire began preparing an unprecedented invasion of Arabia to quickly quell the nascent unified Arab force. Muhammad's longtime confidant Abu Bakr had been selected as his successor, but he lacked any advanced military experience. He dispatched a volunteer force northward to stop the Byzantines—only to discover an imminent internal threat emerging from eastern Arabia. A charismatic tribal leader named Musailimah had observed the Qur'an's dramatic rise to dominate Arabia in less than two years and sought to commandeer it for his own ambition. He astutely discerned that Muhammad's forty-two expert scholars were the Qur'an's weak link and devised a sophisticated assassination plot to eliminate them. Killing these scholarly caretakers would enable Musailimah to deviously reinterpret the Qur'an unchecked. He and his sniper team even joined the great pilgrimage to Mecca to spend time with the experts as part of their surreptitious preparation.

Envious of the Qur'an's mellifluous Arabic without appreciating its depth, Musailimah tried to fashion himself as a copycat prophet who would inherit the Qur'an's mantle, even producing his own poor imitation verses. One example of his hollow Qur'anic mimicry mused inanely about an amphibian:

Froggy, daughter of Mr. and Mrs. Frog,
Trilling and croaking in a bog,
Half your time is spent in water, the other on a muddy log.

As Muhammad lay dying, Musailimah emerged publicly claiming to be the new *Nabi,* part of a trend of ten pretender prophets across Arabia seeking power. Three days before Muhammad's death, a veiled horseman appeared outside the masjid in Medina with a terse letter from Musailimah demanding power:

From Musailimah, the Rasul of the Loving Divine, to Muhammad, the Rasul of the Loving Divine: I have been entrusted with the custodianship of the Qur'an after you. In terms of inheritance, my tribe, Rabi'ah, will take half of Arabia. We are willing to share the other half with your tribe, Quraish, even though Quraish has a tendency to overreach.

Muhammad, frail and on death's door, refused to name a successor. Instead, he had the letter flipped over and dictated a response to be written on its reverse side as a sign of rejection:

To Musailimah, the manipulative liar: Peace shall be the state of those who genuinely follow the guidance [of the Qur'an], which says: "The earth belongs to the Loving Divine, who allots it to whomever He wills; yet the most lasting legacy will be the enduring impact of those who have action-based hope."

The letter quoted Moses' response in the Qur'an to Pharaoh boasting of God-like power, with the Israelite prophet insisting that what truly lasts is not wealth or domination but the impact of ideas and values. Muhammad's brief reply exposed Musailimah as a fraud who failed to comprehend that the Qur'an's true legacy was not ephemeral resources like land or power, but a timeless and irrepressible message.

Musailimah sought to corrupt the role of *Rasul* to channel other people's wealth into his pocket, rather than channeling transformative divine energy to inspire blossoming. Manipulating the Qur'an as a force of domination inverted its purpose as an uplifting source of guidance and healing. Those maintaining such a misguided attitude, Muhammad's letter implied, would not achieve a "state of peace." Indeed, Musailimah soon launched a bloody insurgency in which thousands of men would die before it sputtered.

Revealed almost entirely amidst rejection and pain, the Qur'an had now became a coveted political prize for legitimizing the same power-hungry men who had once tried to silence it. While this marked a perversion of the Qur'an's message of healing and unleashing potential in all human beings, the Qur'an from its inception was the product of a battle to shape human consciousness. It emerged amidst great tension, rarely enjoying any extended calm and instead exploring how to transform conflict and suffering into opportunities for growth and greatness. During the Qur'an's formative twenty-two years of revelation, its future always remained precarious—and so too would its legacy upon completion.

The Qur'an had collected and amplified intense divine energy into a compact form. Once its channeling prophet died, that energy had no single guardian to guide its flow. Instead, energy radiated in all directions as individuals struggled to harness its powerful force. Like electricity—which can kill if not handled with great care, yet can also light up the world—the Qur'an contained powerful latent energy whose effective use depended on imperfect human beings. The Qur'an itself accepted the world's untidy complexity, acknowledging early on that "the Loving Divine created both the chaos of darkness and the order of light." Directing and redirecting the Qur'an's energy would be a constant struggle for its competing custodians.

A key challenge for the inheritors of the Qur'an was how it presented an unfulfilled legacy, specifically describing what it hoped to look like physically (a mass-distributed beautiful paper book) and intellectually (supported by a sophisticated scholarly system elucidating how to apply its nuanced message). At the time of the Qur'an's completion, neither of these existed. The Qur'an circulated primarily as an oral experience, chanted at prayers (especially *Al-Fatihah*) and in public gatherings. Its only formal complete written copy was privately held and existed in rough Arabic script written on raw animal hides.

Moreover, following the battle with Musailimah's forces, its scholarly support system consisted of only two experts. In this stunted form, the Qur'an could hardly fulfill its desired role to inspire blossoming on a mass scale.

Despite the lack of libraries in Arabia, the Qur'an adores books, constantly describing how the Divine documents everything in the universe and in each person's life via a massive library. The calling of humanity to emulate the Divine clearly required aspiring to collect vast amounts of knowledge in books. The Qur'an repeatedly refers to itself as a bound book (al-Kitab). Early in its existence, in the chapter Al-Qalam ("the Pen"), the Qur'an already began to envision its future physical state, musing on the kind of pen and ink that would be used to transcribe it. The script should be beautifully composed (Mutahharah), in parallel straight lines (Mastur), written on fine paper (Qirtas), illuminated with gold ink (Thahab), and distributed far and wide (Munashsharah).

These each represented physical manifestations of Qur'anic values in the real world. As a living guide, the Qur'an needed to be clean, organized, presentable, and appealing. Becoming a bound book helped translate abstract ruminations into something tangible to be taken seriously, as writing and reading spark intellectual reflection far deeper than memorization. Widespread physical copies would also help propel popular literacy. Yet the Qur'an's initial custodians lacked the technology and resources required to achieve any aspects of this vision and faced the enormous challenge of producing the innovations capable of fulfilling it.

By setting ambitious goals without providing a specific roadmap, the Qur'an prompted its followers to do the hard work of blossoming on their own and thus take pride in their eventual accomplishments. The approach also allowed for visionaries to develop their own solutions, encouraging diverse forms of blossoming. The challenge engaged healthy manifestations of the ego—the desire to achieve and leave a lasting legacy—as an incentive to transcend stagnation.

In the immediate term, everything depended on the two young expert disciples of Muhammad who had survived Musailimah's massacre. Upon their shoulders rested the responsibility to create the system of scholarship the Qur'an had envisioned for itself, where people "extensively analyze and deeply study the Qur'an." The Qur'an's second main chapter (Aal-'Imran) had been named in honor of the Kohanim (Israelite priestly class) for their role as elite scholarly custodians of the Torah who made its wisdom accessible to the masses. Inspired by this vision of "nuanced knowledge passed from generation to generation," the Qur'an repeatedly describes itself surrounded by "outstanding people of knowledge" (*Ulul-'Ilm, Ahlath-Thikr, Al-'Ulama*). And four times it insists: "The process of studying the Qur'an offers a means for achieving success—so are there any willing to take up the challenge?"

Yet the Arabs had no scholarly tradition to launch such a culture of scholarship. Muhammad had invested the last years of his life training a small cadre of expert guides to access the Qur'an's deeper layers of wisdom, yet without a formal system for passing knowledge from "generation to generation." And suddenly just two of these trainees remained, causing a major crisis for Abu Bakr—the man selected as Muhammad's successor after the prophet's death. Given the title *Khalifatu-Rasulillah* ("the custodian of the legacy of channeling divine energy"), Abu Bakr felt a great responsibility to protect these two young experts. He decreed that they would work as the first-ever full-time Qur'an scholars, supported by a salary.

Both young men were from the same Banu Najjar tribe as Muhammad's mother and had been trained in their youth in the Jewish scholarly tradition, whose insular structure they would adapt and expand to meet the Qur'an's universal focus. These two experts would provide the initial nodes in a chain of transmission from which all traditional Islamic scholarship descends.

The elder of the two was twenty-eight-year-old Ubayy ibnu Ka'b, a brilliant scholar-entrepreneur who had served as Muhammad's closest scribe in Medina, typically the first individual to transcribe new Qur'anic revelations. "I learned the Qur'an fresh [*Ratib*] as it was being revealed," he recalled, likening the new passages to fresh dates, the sweet first product of blossoming. He also deeply experienced the Qur'an as a dynamic life-force, urging students: "Take the Qur'an as your Imam, and allow it to be your discerning and wise mentor." Muhammad once placed his right hand on Ubayy's chest and declared: "You rejoice in the depth of learning, oh Inspirer of Enlightenment!" Known for both his commercial prowess as a farmer-merchant and his intellectual acuity (reading and studying the entire Qur'an every eight days), Ubayy was recognized as a community leader and had the kind of holistic personality needed to initiate a formal Qur'anic scholarly system.

His counterpart, Zaid Ibnu Thabit, was just twenty-two. As an adolescent, he had become one of Muhammad's key scribes, impressing the prophet with his meticulous handwriting. Trained as a carpenter in the Banu Najjar tribal tradition, he evinced both an artistic flair and an amazing capacity for

THE STRUGGLE FOR CUSTODIANSHIP

absorbing details, particularly languages. Fluent in Hebrew and Aramaic, he quickly learned Greek and Coptic—each in one month—at Muhammad's request in order to compose the prophet's diplomatic outreach letters. Muhammad noticed that Zaid's organized mind and careful attention to detail enabled him to absorb complex patterns with ease, earning him the prophet's affectionate moniker *Afradhu-Ummati*—"the most meticulous of my people." *Afradh* described a precise master craftsman who molds raw stones into gems—precisely what Zaid would need to do with raw Qur'anic students of great yet untapped potential.

The two scholars' first task involved stabilizing the systems used to propagate Qur'anic literacy, specifically ensuring accurate pronunciation and comprehension. As most people in Arabia had never seen a book, let alone knew how to read one, the two fields focused on the interactive experience that surrounded reciting and discussing Qur'anic verses. Muhammad had bequeathed two general fields for these purposes, both using terms for transforming raw potential into refined results.

The first was *Tajwid*—literally, "taming a wild stallion"—and aimed to tame the tongue to accurately pronounce Qur'anic words. As written Arabic at the time lacked any vowel markings or punctuation, words were at risk of being misread and misspoken, potentially fundamentally altering their meaning. *Tajwid* both ensured a precise, uniform elocution and directed a particular tone and rhythm for chanting. With its generally somber and melancholic ambiance, *Tajwid* created a dramatic interactive experience for presenting Qur'anic passages in an appealing manner, capturing attention and taming flaring emotions in order to enable deeper reflection.

To help inspire refined analysis of the Qur'an's content, the second field was called *Tafsir*—literally, "separating strands of raw flax and weaving them into a garment." *Tafsir* sought to become an oral tradition for preserving knowledge about how to understand and apply the Qur'an. The field covered the meaning of words (including their Semitic root concepts and the implication of grammatical structures); their context (when it was said, to whom, and why); and their application (initial purpose, lessons for other situations, and distilled wisdom). The field aimed to capture commentary by Muhammad, the historical insights of his companions, and knowledge of preexisting Abrahamic traditions.

Just as Ubayy and Zaid began to refine the raw fields of *Tajwid* and *Tafsir* with a handful of new students in Medina, Abu Bakr died, designating 'Umar as his successor. With no formal political structure to protect the Qur'an and no military leadership experience, 'Umar panicked at the weighty responsibility thrust upon him, fretting to his advisors: "I fear knowledge of the Qur'an may wither and be lost forever." His position of *Khalifah* (or "caliph") was a volunteer one with no palace, budget, or formal guard. Massive surrounding empires were poised to march on Arabia to suppress the Qur'an's followers, who in turn formed a ragtag volunteer army. These ill-equipped desert nomads— mostly barefoot, bare-chested, covered in dust, and lacking armor—were about to confront the world's greatest militaries.

While facing overwhelming odds, 'Umar turned to Qur'anic principles to guide his crisis response, particularly making highly efficient use of limited resources and liberating human potential to flow. He elevated the most talented fighters based on merit and sought strategies to quickly quell threats with as little bloodshed as possible, most notably by meeting the enemy on its own territory and incentivizing local populations by ending external repressive rule and excessive taxation. He directed envoys to declare before each city in their path: "We come to emancipate the masses from the yoke of subjugation to the liberty of the Qur'an's teachings, to liberate their minds from the enslavement of tyrants to the compassion of the Loving Divine."

In these communities beyond Arabia, locals saw 'Umar enter their cities wearing rags and walking barefoot. Rather than act as a rapacious conqueror, he presented an unprecedented model of a humble liberator who encouraged individual blossoming. Pointedly, he refused to describe the "conquest" of new territories, instead invoking an "unlocking" (*Fath*), echoing the iconic introductory chapter of the Qur'an. His armies swelled with enthusiastic peasants formerly enslaved by the Byzantine and Sassanian empires—which soon lost massive territory.

Not by might but by persuasion, the underdog forces of 'Umar channeled the liberating energies of the Qur'an to suddenly administer a vast realm of their own. Within months, followers of the Qur'an controlled land from Egypt to Iraq to Syria. Reflecting his new responsibility as head of growing territory, 'Umar received a new title: *Amir-ul-Muminin*—"the one accountable to the people he protects." The honorific reflected not dominance or glory but responsibility to preserve the liberating rights that had been promised. To fulfill his obligations, 'Umar embarked on transformative civic projects to implement Qur'anic teachings about flow, most notably digging a massive canal connecting the Nile River to the Red Sea, part of a larger grand plan to irrigate the desert throughout the growing realm.

Eager to safeguard the Qur'an's future amidst these rapid changes, 'Umar resolved to provide Ubayy and Zaid with more than just a paid position: each would oversee a brand-new scholarly city as dean of a formidable academic institution. He selected southern Iraq for these competing new scholarly cities: Kufah ("the Abode of Learning") would be run by Ubayy, with his more conservative methodical approach, while its creative rival Basrah ("the Abode of Reason") would be run by Zaid, with his more liberal humanistic approach. To preserve the scholars' independence, 'Umar created the concept of a *Waqf*, an endowment providing ongoing financial support for academic institutions and scholars.

'Umar served as the master planner for both cities, establishing an urban model he would soon replicate throughout the expanding territory. The Qur'an comprised the spiritual heart of the city via a central mosque—which served as a school, medical clinic, and community center—surrounded by a bustling market. The city's leader was not a politician or a warrior, but rather an imam, a man of scholarship.

The choice of southern Iraq was not coincidental, as 'Umar deliberately set the academies beside Judaism's own legendary Talmudic academy in Sura, just a dozen miles from Kufah. The Jewish scholarly center provided a model to emulate and expand upon for systematically perpetuating spiritual knowledge despite constant threats. In turning to the Jewish scholastic tradition for inspiration, 'Umar was following the Qur'anic injunction to "seek knowledge from the people of knowledge"—a clear reference to Jewish sages, which the Qur'an calls *'Ulama Bani Israel* and *Ahlath-Thikr*. Indeed, the Qur'an initially invokes the term *'ulama* as a reference to Jewish scholars and *imam* as a reference to the Torah.

Ubayy and Zaid further leveraged Talmudic concepts as they created the new infrastructure of Qur'anic scholarship. To create an Arabic name for these new academic institutions, they borrowed the Hebrew term *Beit Midrash* to form *Madrasah*. A student in the madrasah became a *Tilmith* (adopted *Talmid*), with more advanced experts known as *Hibr* (from the Hebrew *Haver* used to describe outstanding rabbinic students in Babylon). The physical arrangements of the classroom sessions adopted the circles of scholars discussing scriptural passages, analyzing a text, and debating how to apply it in real life. One notable difference, however, was the large cohort of female students (roughly one-third), who were mostly absent from the Jewish academies.

Christians flowed into the new cities as experts in script development. Syriac scribes joined the academies to help develop new refined forms of Arabic writing, helping to fulfill the Qur'an's vision of being presented in beautiful calligraphy. The Kufic script they developed would soon set the standard for Arabic writing throughout the growing empire and helped launch a nascent publishing industry, staffed in part by expert Jewish transcribers who could quickly duplicate manuscripts. Within just a few years, Kufah saw the opening of its first synagogue and basilica cathedral to accommodate the local Jews and Christians. Kufah's intellectual swirl also produced the Arabic language's first named book (after the Qur'an): *Nahjul-Balaghah* ("The Methodology of Eloquence"), a guide to Arabian wisdom. The dedicated room where academies stored this text alongside ancient ones required a new Arabic term: *Maktabah*—"library."

❦❦❦

As Ubayy and Zaid refined a formal Qur'anic education system and trained teachers to serve as scholastic leaders across the region, 'Umar found himself administering rapidly growing territories. While the Qur'an provides ethical guidelines for a healthy society, describing etiquette for a vibrant community, it pointedly abstains from promoting a specific governmental structure. Instead, it repeatedly cautions against dominating others and denying free choice, warning that theological doctrine and political power are often manipulated to persecute those with opposing views. The result of such corruption inhibits, rather than enables, blossoming. With no clear political blueprint, 'Umar had to determine how to apply Qur'anic values to an unexpectedly vast realm that required a political system to function.

The first principle he upheld was personal accountability. "If a camel sprains her ankle because of an uneven road in rural Iraq, I would feel personally responsible," he confided in his advisors. "The Loving Divine will hold me accountable, asking me: 'Oh 'Umar, why didn't you mend the road for her?" In each city that welcomed his forces, 'Umar made a point of never confiscating personal or communal property. After the gates of Damascus opened to his forces, 'Umar refused to displace any locals or take over the city's great symbol of power: the Cathedral of St. John the Baptist. Instead, he rented half of the cathedral to use as a mosque and academy.

By applying Qur'anic principles to political leadership, 'Umar quickly became the Qur'an's best advocate, impressing the public with his sincere example. In fact, so many Sassanian conscripts began defecting in battle that their commanders had to chain fighters together so they would not flee across the frontlines.

The steady expansion of territory soon enabled 'Umar to fulfill another Qur'anic vision. *Surah Bani Israel*'s had presented a divine promise to Jews exiled from Jerusalem for over five hundred years: "Once you have invested your full effort will We gather you from far and wide." Sure enough, principled action paved the way for realizing that dream. As he approached the Holy City to accept its surrender, 'Umar invited hundreds of long-displaced Jews to join him.

Throughout the journey toward Jerusalem, he upheld another Qur'anic injunction calling for "compassion to all creation" by giving his camel and his servant breaks, during which he would walk on foot guiding the camel. When his delegation approached Jerusalem, his servant was sitting atop his camel as 'Umar held the reins while dressed in rags. The Christian leaders of Jerusalem assumed the well-dressed camel rider must be the caliph and were shocked to discover the grand ruler was actually the barefoot man loping before the camel and guiding his own servant. To reassure the locals, 'Umar issued a new Constitution of Jerusalem, guaranteeing freedom and safety for all:

> This is the covenant which 'Umar, the servant of the Loving Divine, protector of those guaranteed safety, grants to the people of Jerusalem. To all, whether sick or sound, he grants security for their lives, their possessions, their churches, their crosses, their religious icons, and for all that concerns the complete practice of their religion. Their churches shall not be changed into dwelling places, nor destroyed, neither shall they nor their accessories be in any way diminished, nor the crosses of the inhabitants nor any of their possessions, nor shall any constraint be placed upon them in the matter of their faith or conscience, nor shall any one of them be harmed or treated unjustly.

After inspecting several cities that came under his jurisdiction, 'Umar would return to his modest home in Medina to re-ground himself. He could count on local governors (each chosen based on merit) to uphold the new order with justice, but just in case he also created an internal inspection service to clandestinely monitor local leaders for signs of corruption. In Medina, he lived without any protective guard and preferred to spend his time interacting with common people.

One evening, he volunteered to lead prayers and began reciting *Surah Taha,* the very Qur'anic chapter that decades earlier had transformed his life from an angry brute into a sensitive soul. As he stood reciting: "We did not reveal the Qur'an to weigh you down, but rather to help liberate and elevate for a lasting legacy anyone willing to listen," a disgruntled former Sassanian soldier stabbed him multiple times in the abdomen. The caliph collapsed in a pool of blood. As he lay dying, 'Umar ordered a popular election to select his successor, identifying seven early followers of the Qur'an as candidates.

'Umar's murder and rushed succession process created an unsteady template for the next 120 years of politics surrounding the Qur'an, with violence and uncertainty chaotically injected in the struggle for custodianship. The election process 'Umar launched faced allegations of fraud, but ultimately resulted in 'Uthman (an early follower of Muhammad) emerging as caliph. Unlike his predecessor, 'Uthman largely withdrew from public affairs, delegating rather than exercising power. He requested the one extant copy of the Qur'an be delivered to his home, and he spent his days poring over the manuscript. His focus on personal piety stunted his civic application of Qur'anic principles.

Most notably, 'Uthman replaced meritocracy in governance with family patronage, placing his own cousins as governors as part of the old tribal mentality that relatives are more likely to remain loyal. That approach yielded ironic results, as key relatives included some of the Qur'an's one-time fiercest opponents. Egypt's governor, for example, was 'Amr ibn Al-'As, the Meccan envoy sent years earlier to chase down the Qur'an's followers who had fled to Abyssinia—and whose mission in Africa specifically required him to denounce the Qur'an.

In Damascus, 'Uthman's cousin Mu'awiyah stepped in as the new governor. His own father had led the persecution of Muhammad, only to lose power in disgrace and have key family members killed in battles over the Qur'an. The Umayyad clan—from which 'Uthman and his cousins hailed—faced an awkward adjustment, as they had once been the Qur'an's main antagonists yet now ruled in its name. Still, just as 'Umar had transformed from violent persecutor to brave Qur'anic upholder, Mu'awiyah was afforded a fresh start.

Unlike the early caliphs who had no political experience, Mu'awiyah had been raised to rule, trained at an early age in the arts of politics and diplomacy. While his ancestors had feared that any Arabian political ambition would mark their society for annihilation, Mu'awiyah realized that the growing political realm under the Qur'an's banner offered a far superior method for burnishing the eternal memory of the Umayyad clan. Instead of merely serving as merchants transporting goods from Sana'a to Damascus, the Umayyad clan could rule from Yemen to Syria, not to mention Egypt and Persia. With the right political ambition and vision, the Umayyads, Mu'awiyah realized, could leverage the Qur'an to recreate the Roman empire.

Shrewd and ambitious, Mu'awiyah carefully plotted his rise to power. In 649, the death of Ubayy, the Qur'anic expert, emboldened Mu'awiyah to present the Qur'an in politically expedient new ways. As governor of Damascus, he demanded the privilege of delivering the main Friday sermon to burnish his authority. With growing boldness, he focused on recasting the Qur'an's iconic *Al-Fatihah* chapter, recited seventeen times a day, particularly its concluding verse. While the line originally asked for divine guidance to "a path unconstrained by a stagnant reality of willful manipulation and blind acceptance," Mu'awiyah began insinuating that willful manipulation was a Jewish trait, while blind acceptance described heretical Christians. This reworking aimed to curry favor with Damascus's majority Christian population, which had longstanding biases: blaming the Jews for the death of Jesus and heretical Christians for questioning the nature of his divinity. As a cunning politician looking to enhance popular support, Mu'awiyah was testing the potential to repurpose the Qur'an for political gain.

Watching from the sidelines in Damascus was Abu Tharr, one of Muhammad's early students who had brought the message of the Qur'an to Arabia's fiercest tribes. As Muhammad once observed about his star pupil: "Neither sky above nor earth below have witnessed a man more pure in his dedication to seeking and speaking the truth than Abu Tharr." Unable to sit silently as Mu'awiyah sought to modify an iconic Qur'anic verse, Abu Tharr challenged the Damascus governor to a public debate in the city's mosque. Dressed in his finest robes, the handsome Mu'awiyah argued his case with eloquence, a sharp contrast to the ascetic Abu Tharr dressed in rags ranting with raw passion. Abu

Tharr insisted that as an early student of Muhammad's he knew firsthand the core message of *Al-Fatihah*, yet Mu'awiyah countered that as Muhammad's brother-in-law and native Meccan he better understood passages revealed in his hometown's Arabic dialect.

The debate publicly raised the issue of who had a better claim to eluci-date the Qur'an's content. Threatened by Abu Tharr's grassroots credibility, Mu'awiyah requested his cousin 'Uthman recall the scholar to Medina for sparking civic unrest. Abu Tharr appeared before the caliph and maintained his *Hanif* stance: challenging abuses of interpretation as well as governance by nepotism. Rather than engage his critic, 'Uthman had Abu Tharr exiled to the barren wilderness (just as had once been done to Abraham and Mu-hammad), where he soon died in isolation.

Such repression sparked a popular backlash against 'Uthman for failing to embrace open dialogue and blossoming. To burnish his political image, 'Uthman commissioned a definitive edition of the Qur'an. He tasked Zaid Ibnu Thabit with creating a refined copy of the single original manuscript. Using the new Kufic script, Zaid produced five meticulous copies, each with straight lines, clear writing, and uniform structure—precisely what scribes would need to propagate the Qur'an en masse. As these five editions were sent to academic centers for reproduction, all other extant versions of the Qur'an were confiscated and publicly burned.

Generating a definitive edition of the Qur'an, however, did little to ad-dress popular discontent. Simply agreeing on words did not prevent intense debate over their meaning and application. The beginnings of mass produc-tion of the Qur'an, ironically, coincided with a mass uprising, with hundreds of dissidents protesting outside the caliph's unprotected home in Medina. One evening in the year 656, three assassins stealthily breached the residence and stabbed 'Uthman to death as he read the original Qur'anic manuscript, his blood splattering its pages. For the first time, a follower of the Qur'an had been murdered by a fellow follower—destroying forever any universal con-sensus over the Qur'an's custodianship.

Rivers of blood would soon flow in civil wars. Enticed by Mu'awiyah, Mu-hammad's widow 'Aishah led an army to attack the new caliph, 'Ali, whom she held accountable for not avenging the murder of 'Uthman (despite reports that her own brother was among the assassins). At the Battle of the Camel fought outside Basrah, thirteen hundred followers of the Qur'an died before

'Ali emerged victorious, magnanimously forgiving 'Aishah and sending her back to Medina with dignity. Yet a terrible new precedent had been set: followers of the Qur'an could instigate violent vendettas if aggrieved.

Eight months later, Mu'awiyah organized his own attack, seeking to crush 'Ali and assume custodianship of the Qur'an. On the battlefield of Siffin in northern Syria, over 230,000 followers of the Qur'an clashed, resulting in 70,000 deaths—including leading Qur'anic scholars of the day. (Among those killed by Mu'awiyah's forces was 'Ammar Ibnu Yasir, whose parents, Sumayyah and Yasir, were the Qur'an's first martyrs.)

As the forces of Mu'awiyah retreated amidst the carnage, they launched a desperate ploy to halt an imminent defeat. Affixing Qur'anic manuscripts to their lances, the frontline soldiers of Mu'awiyah began to shout: "Let the Qur'an judge between us." Unwilling to desecrate the Qur'an, 'Ali ordered his men to suspend their attack—and reluctantly agreed to a scholarly debate to resolve the battle.

The next morning, over 150,000 soldiers surrounded an elevated platform where a leather-bound copy of the Qur'an sat atop a wooden table. Two men stepped forward to debate, taking turns flipping through the manuscript and pointing to passages, chanting them in a duel of words to bolster their claims. Instead of fighting with arms, they clashed with words, citing Qur'anic passages to justify their side as the rightful inheritors of its legacy. Though surrounded by carnage, the Qur'an had nonetheless realized part of its vision as a refined physical book with mass appeal as an authority promoting humanitarian ideals and their nonviolent application.

Debating for Mu'awiyah's side was his relative 'Amr Ibn al-'As, the same suave diplomat once sent to Abyssinia to condemn the Qur'an before the local king (a debate he lost). His father had decades earlier publicly debated Muhammad over the Qur'an's use of the obscure Arabic word *Kubbara* (a debate also lost). There would not be a third debate loss. The finely dressed master orator 'Amr found himself up against Abu Musa, the simple and cerebral dean of the Basrah academy. 'Amr derided Abu Musa's roots in Yemen, arguing he lacked a Meccan familiarity with the Qur'an's original dialect. Abu Musa found himself repeatedly on the defensive and mostly offered esoteric academic arguments.

After two days of debate in the hot sun, 'Amr approached Abu Musa offstage before the start of the third day's session. "In order to achieve peace, let us both concede our mistakes," suggested 'Amr. "Out of respect for your venerable seniority, please commence and lead the conference." Abu Musa mounted the stage and offered the first concession: that 'Ali was in the wrong and should not be caliph. He then turned to 'Amr to offer a parallel concession about his side's conduct, only to hear the sly debater declare: "That settles it—Abu Musa has resolved the debate and acknowledged that his side is the aggressor!"

The resulting stalemate left divided territories: 'Ali governed Iraq, Persia, and Arabia, while Mu'awiyah ruled the Levant with his ally 'Amr serving as regent in Egypt. The debate's shocking conclusion sparked an angry commotion among 'Ali's followers and sparked a schism that echoes until today. Half of 'Ali's forces continued to support his custodianship of the Qur'an—forming the *Shi'atu-'Ali* (literally, "'Ali's faction") or *Ash-Shi'ah* ("the faction")—and the other half furiously denounced what they perceived as a humiliating leadership failure. These rebels quit the battlefield in a huff, earning the moniker *Kharijites* ("those who exited" or "the dissenters"), and denounced 'Ali and his followers as apostates and traitors to the Qur'an. The Kharijites began attacking caravans, raiding towns, and killing at will to impose their rigid interpretations, which recast the Qur'an as an advocate of intolerance in a polarized clash of sanctimonious virtue against despicable evil.

One of the Qur'an's final chapters, *Al-Bayyinah* ("The Transparent Clarity"), warned about precisely such an outcome by citing how once-united persecuted Christian sects began massacring one another over interpretive disputes after achieving political power:

> Alas, it was only after order and clarity were established among the People of the Book that they descended into bitter animosity and discord. . . . It is those who seek serenity and exert their efforts in works of reparation who are the most outstanding among the creation. (98:4,7)

The chapter lamented how intra-Christian persecution far exceeded the movement's initial opposition as a caution for the future, echoing Muhammad's own farewell sermon:

> Do not revert after my death into discord, rivalry, and killing one another. I am leaving you with a sustainable system with the Qur'an, the Loving Di-

vine as your exemplar, and the *Sunnah* [formula] I have outlined for you in my teachings—a method that, if you uphold it, will safeguard you from falling into the ravines of confusion.

By emphasizing the potential for repair, the Qur'an insisted that dismaying calamity nonetheless held seeds of rejuvenation—and that competition should not concern who has the better doctrine but rather who is better able to repair the world for lasting impact.

The Qur'an also cited an example of Jewish internal strife from the period of Hellenic influence driven by manipulation of the Torah's language. *"Yuharrifunal-Kalima 'An Mawadhi'ihi,"* warned *Surah An-Nisa*: "They systematically shift the words from their original meaning." (4:46) Hellenized Jews could not change the words of the long-established Torah, so they resorted to reinterpreting them to legitimize their political agenda. Likewise, simply claiming to be a supporter of the Qur'an was not sufficient to make you a responsible custodian. The battlefield debate over the Qur'an revealed how 'Amr had transformed from assailing the Qur'an's words in Abyssinia for political ends to disingenuously embracing Qur'anic verses by systematically shifting their meaning. Moreover, the Kharijites advanced a radical rereading of the Qur'an's Arabic that completely distorted its nonviolent message.

With so many original followers of Muhammad dying in battle or of old age, the academic centers in Kufah and Basrah launched an urgent effort to set definitive Qur'anic scholarship standards. 'Ali assigned 'Abdullah Ibnu 'Abbas (whose mother, Lubabah, was at the first Qur'anic study session with Muhammad) to lead the effort. Ibnu 'Abbas—a prominent student of Ubayy—was highly motivated to establish accurate standards, particularly after one incident where he heard a zealous student insist Muhammad had been so holy he should never have touched the ground. Seeing a mortal who insisted on never being idolized transformed into a quasi-divine icon, Ibnu 'Abbas insisted on setting the record straight by creating the first book of *Sirah* (literally, "retracing footsteps"), and establishing the field of authentic prophetic biography to counter the emerging mythology.

Establishing the credibility of people claiming details about Muhammad's life and Qur'anic interpretations needed a formal test. The academies thus introduced the concept of *Isnad* (literally, "to lean back on for support") to delineate human chains of transmission linking back directly to Muhammad.

The distinction between a genuine scholar and a pseudo-scholar inventing traditions was his ability to trace his knowledge back to Muhammad via a chain of credible teachers. The Kharijites, notably, lacked any *Isnad,* whereas the leaders of the traditional academies all traced their expertise back through Muhammad's top students.

Just as the concept of *Isnad* became formalized, one of the key first links in its chain, Zaid Ibnu Thabit, died, marking the end of an era. One of only two surviving hand-picked experts and the definitive compiler of the Qur'an, Zaid left behind a wealth of knowledge and a cohort of disciples who would have to carefully guard traditional knowledge over the next century of chaos. Indeed, the harbinger of the next wave of civil strife soon came when 'Ali (the Qur'an's first scribe) was stabbed to death while reciting Qur'anic passages at the mosque in Kufah. With no formal process for selecting the next caliph, 'Ali's allies (the *Shi'ah*) swore in his son Al-Hasan as the caliph—only to see him concede to Mu'awiyah to avoid bloodshed and end a period of constant turmoil. This abdication provided a temporary relief from political violence, yet resolved none of the interpretive strife roiling the divided followers of the Qur'an.

As Mu'awiyah consolidated his power as the new caliph amidst chaos, he immediately recognized the urgency of securing his own successor. In one of his first formal acts, he compelled key Arabian elders to swear allegiance to his son Yazid as heir—establishing hereditary rule in place of 'Umar's vision of popular elections. The same clan that once fiercely opposed the Qur'an now co-opted it to secure a grand dynasty. Under Mu'awiyah, the territory—which had remained a nameless domain under the guardianship of the Qur'an—became a formal empire, under the new Arabic term *Dawlah* ("victorious powerhouse"). The Umayyads had not initiated their own empire, but rather appropriated the unprecedented popular impact of the Qur'an, which had captured the hearts and minds of millions, even driving hardened warriors to tears by its moving rhythm and powerful message.

For the first time in history, the Arabs were not merely an insignificant sidenote overshadowed by great empires. Mu'awiyah boldly sought to establish the dominance of Arabic language and culture to forge an Arab-aligned ruling elite throughout the new empire. While he suppressed several local languages (for example, banning the use of Persian in public), his empire also forged a new universal language—the language of the Qur'an—that allowed for a dynamic exchange of ideas among many diverse ethnic groups. The Umayyads advanced 'Ali's work to standardize Arabic writing, including developing a written vowel system, and promoted widespread adult literacy via government-run Arabic schools. In the new Umayyad capital of Damascus, Christian bookbinders produced hundreds of written copies of the Qur'an, part of a nascent Arabic publishing industry. Bureaucrats created the first-ever Arabic governmental records, and key officials began writing personal memoirs.

In a sense, Mu'awiyah applied aspects of the Qur'an's transformative vision, like the *Iqra* call to blossom and the *Al-'Asr* enjoinder to squeeze the most out of every opportunity in order to achieve lasting impact. Yet his driving purpose was not elevating all people with action-based hope to achieve their potential, but a self-interested drive for glory, power, and riches. He lived in a grand palace, protected by a pretorian guard of elite soldiers, and hosted sumptuous feasts with a royal court dressed in the finest linens.

To legitimize such personal expediency, Mu'awiyah justified his actions in the name of the Qur'an. Whereas 'Umar had created financial trusts to ensure the independence of Qur'anic scholars, Mu'awiyah established a new class of scholars dependent on government salaries, dismissed by traditional scholars as *'Ulama-us-Sultan* ("the ruler's scholars") or *'Ulama-ul-Bilat* ("court scholars"). Their sermons were dictated by Umayyad officials, who included both pro-government propaganda and the requirement to pray for the caliph and formally curse his late nemesis 'Ali every Friday.

With hundreds of copies of the Qur'an in circulation, the Umayyads could not change its words. Instead, they began to redefine their meaning and fabricate a corpus of traditions (*Hadith*) falsely attributed to Muhammad. Propagandists on the Umayyad payroll claimed to recall Muhammad somehow predicting: "Oh Mu'awiyah, when you rule, apply the [Qur'anic] concept of *Ihsan*." To insinuate that opposition to the caliph meant disobeying the Divine, an invented *Hadith* alleged: "The sultan is God's shadow on earth." In the new narrative, anyone who rebelled faced a fate of "hellfire" and eternal torture—driven by an avenging deity with little resemblance to the Loving Divine and Divine Mentor.

Eager to enrich the royal treasury and conquer the domains of the former

Roman empire, the Umayyads initiated wars of expansion. To recruit volunteer soldiers, their pseudo-scholars created the lure of a heavenly reward for fighting, arguing that the Qur'anic concept of *Jihad* ("intense exertion of effort" to repair the world) actually signified "holy war" to advance the Qur'an's message. Warriors were also lured with the concocted prophetic sayings claiming that martyrs enjoyed lavish heavenly rewards. Regime clerics would even hijack the *Isnad* system of chains of transmission by falsely citing traditional scholars as the source of vivid fake *Hadith* extolling martyrs' blissful afterlife. In a classic incident, a famous independent scholar visiting a mosque in Damascus was shocked to hear his name invoked as the source of such an invented fable by a government preacher whom he had never met before.

These forced propaganda efforts, however, failed to fully overcome the Qur'an's clear message and instead provoked a popular backlash. Protests throughout the Umayyad empire were met with an often brutal response, and many traditional scholars who tried to confront interpretive abuses were driven underground—a throwback to the early days of the Qur'an with clandestine nocturnal meetings in Dar-ul-Arqam. The Qur'an had to watch in silence as its divine content was manipulated by mortals with competing partisan agendas. In this turbulent phase, the Umayyads besieged Mecca itself, catapulting fire at the city (which had for the first time been forced to erect defensive walls) and burning down the Ka'bah. Just forty years after the Qur'an's completion, its own followers had managed to destroy the very shrine toward which their daily prayers were directed.

Amidst a full-blown civil war among the Qur'an's feuding followers, an unanticipated caliph emerged in 685. 'Abdul-Malik Ibn Marwan had not been born into the usual line of succession, but an uncle's sudden demise switched the empire's inheritance to his family. In his pre-political youth, the ruler had studied with traditional scholars in Medina and realized that allowing them to teach openly rather than underground had the potential to quell uprisings. In fact, the thirty-eight-year-old sovereign made a public display of humility by regularly attending the classes of a traditional female Islamic scholar, Umm Ad-Darda As-Sughra, studying at her feet.

Despite such gestures, rebellion raged and caravans to the annual Hajj pilgrimage could no longer travel safely to Mecca. Losing control of the sacred shrine posed a crisis of legitimacy for 'Abdul-Malik, who in turn decided to define himself against the rebels as the definitive upholder of the Qur'an. He immediately rerouted the pilgrimage focus to Jerusalem, building a monument next to 'Umar's modest shrine on the Temple Mount. The edifice, known as the Dome of the Rock, marked the first-ever structure in a distinctive Qur'anic architectural style, displaying a fresh fusion of Byzantine and Sassanian styles and featuring Qur'anic verses on a building for the first time, inscribed via intricate mosaics. The Dome of the Rock's pioneering success inspired the regime's expanded development of a distinctive Qur'anic cultural style: a formal flag featuring Qur'anic verses set atop a green background; royal robes embroidered with Qur'anic verses on the sleeves; and even royal turbans highlighting an excerpt from *Al-Fatihah* as the royal motto.

'Abdul-Malik's masterstroke, however, fit in the palm of one's hand: the first-ever Qur'anic coin. Until then, the Umayyad empire had simply reminted Sassanian coins featuring two Zoroastrian fire priests. 'Abdul-Malik's first coin, issued in 691, depicted the caliph himself, and on the reverse side Qur'anic verses encircling a scale. Two years later, he refined the coin by removing his image and replacing it with the brief *Surah Al-Ikhlas* that proclaimed the oneness and dominion of God. The Qur'an had long desired mass distribution *(Munasharah)*, and via these coins, written Qur'anic verses spread over thousands of miles and changed hands among millions of people.

With Qur'anic verses featured on royal clothing, government buildings, official flags, and ubiquitous gold and silver coins, 'Abdul-Malik's authority as custodian of the Qur'an triumphed and the rebellion slowly crumbled. When the caliph retook control of the Ka'bah, he removed the traditional white covering of 'Umar and replaced it with a large tapestry featuring embroidered Qur'anic verses in golden thread over green silk: the empire's new official color. The empire's new postal system, called *Al-Barid* ("expedited service"), spurred the flow of knowledge as never before, spreading thousands of Qur'ans to reinforce the regime's legitimacy.

Under 'Abdul-Malik's political program, "Islam" for the first time became consolidated as a distinct doctrinal state religion. What had begun as a civic reform movement renewing a universal Abrahamic spirit was remodeled as the religion of a distinct empire. Its rivals responded in kind, with the Byzantine Christian empire adding a Jesus icon to its coins and the Khazar Jewish kingdom minting coins featuring Arabic script that declared: "Moses is the Rasul of the Loving Divine." In the spirit of the age, political powers flaunted religious creeds to distinguish themselves from competitors. In this polarized environment, followers of the Qur'an for the first time became "Muslims" in formal contrast to Jews and Christians, whereas previously there had been a fluidity of identity where someone born Jewish or Christian could be a follower of the Qur'an without feeling they had converted to a new religion.

To compete with the illuminated Bibles of other faiths, Muslim scribes began adorning Qur'ans with floral and geometric decorations and experimenting with gold ink and calligraphy. The new visual life of the Qur'an flourished in a wave of creativity that transformed a rustic rudimentary text into a work of art. Yet the artisans still lacked *Qirtas*—the refined paper upon which the Qur'an had envisioned itself inscribed. Leveraging the empire's access to the Silk Road, travelers discovered advanced Chinese papermaking and imported expert artisans from the Far East to Damascus. Local entrepreneurs in turn applied the Chinese techniques to develop technology for mass-producing high-quality paper via large mills. The new paper medium was cheaper and quicker to manufacture than animal skins; easier to mold into standardized sizes; and enabled scribes to practice on disposable surfaces. The Qur'an finally had the tools needed to fulfill its physical ambitions—even if the fulfillment of its teachings remained fractured.

Over several decades, the Umayyad empire began to ossify as discontent over nepotism and the marginalization of non-Arabs simmered. Grassroots grumbling sought a "return to the spirit of *'Arafah*"—evoking the universalist spirit of Muhammad's farewell sermon delivered from Mount 'Arafah outside Mecca. Muhammad's chaperone at that first Hajj—who amplified the prophet's weak voice in front of 120,000 people—was his uncle Al-'Abbas. One hundred and twenty years later, his descendants subsisted as marginalized independent scholars on the peripheries of the Umayyad empire. One of them, Al-Mansur, was an ambitious visionary who saw an opportunity to harness the growing wave of popular agitation to rise to power and reclaim the family's glory.

Dressed in black scholarly garb, Al-Mansur and his brothers cast themselves as the Qur'an's rightful custodians by invoking their *Isnad* chain back to their great-grandfather, Ibnu 'Abbas, an expert praised by Muhammad as "possessing profound understanding of the Qur'an." With no existing mass support for their clan, the Abbasids aligned themselves with the descendants of ʿAli and their *Shiʿah* supporters, uniting two sidelined lineages. A military genius named Abu Muslim joined this alliance; he mobilized a network of disgruntled fighters from Persian warrior clans. The growing movement launched a propaganda campaign demanding meritocracy and denouncing the Umayyads for usurping the Qurʾan.

After four years of clandestine preparation, the alliance suddenly swept in from Afghanistan with black banners (the same color Muhammad's forces carried) and quickly routed the overwhelmed Umayyad armies. In 750, Al-Mansur's older brother As-Saffah ("Blood-Spiller") became the first Abbasid caliph and ruthlessly lived up to his moniker by decimating the Umayyad family, killing thirty thousand. One man, twenty-one-year-old ʿAbdur-Rahman, managed to evade the massacre. Escaping through the city's sewers he fled to Spain, where he would establish a reformed and progressive Umayyad empire—this time based on Qurʾanic principles.

The Abbasids promptly shifted the new empire's capital to the academic city of Kufah to bolster their claim as scholars ruling in the name of the Qurʾan. As-Saffah removed potential internal threats by assassinating Abu Muslim and cynically cutting off ʿAli's descendants from any political power despite their supposed alliance. To justify this betrayal, the Abbasids issued an injunction reinterpreting Qurʾanic inheritance laws in *Surah An-Nisa*. Whereas the Qurʾan established gender equality in inheritance, the Abbasids—who descended from Muhammad's uncle—insisted that males had more right to inheritance than females, thus negating any claims by ʿAli's heirs who descended from Muhammad's daughter. Clerics who refused to acquiesce to the new decree were persecuted, some even beaten to death.

Amidst the chaos, most traditional Qurʾanic scholars sought to remain apolitical. Their concern was that ordinary people lacked time and expertise to extract healthy guidance from the Qurʾan. One Beirut-based scholar named Al-Awzaʿi invented a novel solution, creating a standardized rubric for living that explained how Muslims could apply the Qurʾan's teachings to all aspects of living. He dubbed the streamlined approach a *Mathhab* ("navigation method"), with expert scholars responsible for distilling Qurʾanic wisdom and providing practical guidance customized to the needs of each person. These interpretive schools of thought blossomed and quickly gained popular support, with individuals seeking out particular approaches that matched their unique circumstances. A female sage, Rabi'ah Al-'Adawiyyah, developed a spirituality-infused *Mathhab* centered on the doctrine of divine love (her philosophy would later inspire thinkers like Rumi and Thomas Aquinas). The rationalistic expert Abu Hanifah developed an advanced *Mathhab* based on logic that attracted hundreds of thousands of devotees. Within a few decades, hundreds of new schools of thought flowered.

After assuming the position of caliph from his late brother, Al-Mansur watched the *Mathhab* phenomenon with great interest, wondering how he might harness it to enhance his political capital. He summoned the field's visionary Al-Awza'i from Beirut to Kufah for an interrogation:

AL-MANSUR: What do you think about our massacre of the Umayyads?

AL-AWZA'I: The Qur'an forbade the spilling of innocent blood—their blood was unlawful for you to spill.

AL-MANSUR: What do you say of the caliphate?

AL-AWZA'I: The prophet never assigned a successor.

AL-MANSUR: The caliphate is a divine right the Umayyads stole from us—and thus they deserved to be killed!

AL-AWZA'I: Not at all, the prophet never assigned a successor. The Qur'an's message was never about a political empire. You had no right to massacre them.

AL-MANSUR: What do you say of our confiscation of the wealth of the Umayyads?

AL-AWZA'I: Had they gained it via lawful means, it would definitely be unlawful for you to seize it. And had they acquired it via unlawful means, it would be even more unlawful to seize it.

The elderly sage then took control of the debate, boldly admonishing the fuming caliph: "Remember that your relation to the prophet does not make you privileged, but rather places a burden of responsibility upon you to uphold the highest etiquette and do good in the world."

"Get out of my face!" shouted Al-Mansur. The old man shuffled out of the royal court and began his journey by horseback to Beirut. A soldier overtook him on the way, and the scholar dropped to the ground to perform his last prayer before being executed. Yet instead of swinging his sword, the cavalryman remarkably announced: "The caliph respects you for attempting to set him right. Had you told him what you assumed he wanted to hear, he would have had you imprisoned. Instead, even though you angered him, he was proud of you for standing your ground as a true scholar and defending the Qur'an's principles. In recognition of your integrity, he sent you this pouch of gold coins."

Al-Mansur's peculiar response established a lasting precedent for how political rulers claiming the Qur'anic mantle would relate to traditional apolitical scholars: on the one hand resenting their presence, on the other craving their approval, and simultaneously admiring their principled independence. The debate transformed Al-Mansur, prompting him to reclaim his own scholarly roots and fulfill the campaign slogans he had exclaimed during the Abbasid uprising. He would become a kind of enlightened despot, patronizing the arts and scholarship—including the rights of traditional scholars to challenge political abuse, even by the caliph.

Eager to promote literacy as a means of spreading knowledge, Al-Mansur issues a decree that every child in the empire—both male and female—had to learn to read and write in Arabic by age six. Compulsory education through age ten was enforced with legal action against parents for truancy. Government-funded elementary schools throughout the empire featured supplies of paper, ink, and reusable writing tablets. The impact of Al-Mansur's literacy drive was felt particularly strongly in the periphery and countryside, where peasant children for the first time gained the ability to read the Qur'an and the thousands of books of scholarly commentary that now surrounded it. In 762, to symbolize and propel the new order, Al-Mansur decided to build the grand new capital of Baghdad as a massive round city. The caliph assembled an elite team of the empire's top engineers, architects, and visionaries—notably including Zoroastrians, Christians, and Jews, such as Mashallah Ibnul-Athari.

Meanwhile, the surviving Umayyad outpost in Spain had developed its own thriving capital in Córdoba. Unable to challenge the Abbasids on the battlefield, the revived Umayyad empire in the West—under the rule of visionary caliph 'Abdur-Rahman—instead sought to outshine their rivals via blossoming. The once-desolate Andalusian landscape saw scores of new aqueducts, highways, and vibrant orchards of olives, oranges, lemons, and dates. Top scholars from across Muslim lands were lured to lead start-up academies in a meritocratic open society directed by a constitution guaranteeing the full freedom of religion and thought. Rather than focus on brutally maintaining political control, the neo-Umayyad approach secured power by upholding Qur'anic principles that produced flourishing results.

Competition between Córdoba and Baghdad centered around innovation and accomplishment, rather than military force or invented religious propaganda. Superior scholarship, architecture, and civic beauty became the hallmarks of this vigorous rivalry, which sought to harness the Qur'an's mindset of blossoming to demonstrate real-world results rather than mere rhetoric. True strength came from empowering the Qur'an to fulfill its destiny, with legitimacy secured via tangible success rather than manipulating verses.

As the Qur'an itself had quoted Moses to declare (and as Muhammad had cited in his final letter to the assassin Musailimah): "The earth belongs to the Loving Divine, who allots it to whomever He wills; yet the most lasting legacy will be the enduring impact of those who have action-based hope." Tellingly, when Al-Mansur inaugurated his new capital, the cornerstone of Baghdad featured that very verse etched for all to see.

8

THE RACE TO UNLOCK THE QUR'AN'S VISION OF BLOSSOMING

AS NIGHT DESCENDED, A SIX-YEAR-OLD BOY STOOD GAZING AT THE stars in a remote village along a tributary of the Aral Sea in rural Uzbekistan. Above his head, millions of stars formed a sparkling canopy silhouetted against the black sky—a dazzling display mirrored in shimmering patterns beneath his feet on the surface of the inky waters outside his home.

The boy—who was named Muhammad and had recently memorized the Qur'an revealed through his namesake 154 years earlier—turned over in his mind its many passages ruminating on celestial bodies. "Stare deeply at the Cosmos and reflect—can you detect any flaws?" the Qur'an challenged. "You will be dazzled, exhausted, and still find nothing out of alignment."

The Qur'an had pointedly named its chapters *"Surah"* after constellations and its individual verses *"Ayah"* after the brightest star in them. Many chapters derived their titles from celestial phenomena, which served as compelling clues to an intricate divine order for humans to emulate. As one verse declared: "In the creation of the universe is embedded the power of calculation and arithmetic so human beings can decipher and harness it."

Surveying the stars every evening, young Muhammad noticed precise patterns in their journey, as the Qur'an noted: "The heavenly bodies flow in a calculated orbit with specific ordered patterns." What hidden code drove their distinctive movements, and how might it be leveraged by mortals? The universe's opaque and sometimes harsh forces had already scarred the young boy's life, as he had lost his father to a mysterious illness while only an infant. Still, the young boy could take inspiration from the Qur'an's insistence that "everything that grows on earth is calculated and measured."

Hoping to secure her orphaned son's future, Muhammad's mother turned to the Qur'an as a guiding mentor to help him transcend obstacles. She had enrolled him in the local public school—recently opened at the direction of the Abbasid empire—where a Qur'anic instructor trained in the Kufah academy taught children Arabic and Qur'anic memorization techniques. Reflecting the era's proliferation of paper books, the rural school had several physical copies of the Qur'an that young Muhammad cradled as he pored over their content. One vivid passage from *Surah Aal-'Imran* captured his imagination:

> In the underlying workings of the cosmos's creation and in the transformation from day to night are guiding signs [*Ayat*] for those who deeply contemplate. These thinkers ponder the Loving Divine's wisdom and the universe's inner workings at all times, standing, sitting, and lying down. They critically observe everything in creation and analyze it. Their conclusion: "Our Divine Mentor, You did not create all this arbitrarily or chaotically!" (3:190–191)

Inspired by the stars above and the Qur'anic challenge in his hands, young Muhammad discovered he could intuitively decipher complex patterns and draw connections between disparate forces. The local Qur'anic teacher recognized the young Uzbek's brilliance and suggested he study with experts in the regional center of Samarkand. A charitable *Waqf* would sponsor him, with an extra stipend for orphans provided by the *Zakah* system.

A hub on the Silk Road merchant trail linking Europe to China, Samarkand rose out of the desolate desert landscape as a sparkling oasis. Its shimmering tiled buildings dazzled the young Muhammad, who gaped at the large passing caravans that included Indians, Chinese, and other ethnic groups he had never encountered before. Qur'anic academies representing diverse schools of Islamic thought vied to attract the best students. Muhammad studied alongside some of the most brilliant minds in the region, immersing himself in Arabic grammar and Qur'anic exegesis in the hopes of unlocking more clues to the divine cosmic code.

Muhammad soon discovered that even Samarkand's top Qur'anic experts lacked the tools to pinpoint the precise direction toward Mecca for daily prayers. They also struggled to calculate complex inheritance laws outlined in *Surah An-Nisa* that guided equitable distribution of estates. The hidden mathematical code embedded in the stars above, Muhammad reasoned, could potentially unlock complex calculations on earth.

Because Arabic lacked numerals, letters were employed as numeric stand-ins, with *Alif* representing one, *Bayt* representing two, and so on. Muhammad quickly discovered that calculating equations with letters—especially without a representation of zero—was arduous and highly inefficient. From passing caravans, however, he learned that Indian astronomers had invented numerals for calculation. Intrigued, he decided to explore firsthand the Hindustani system. "Travel the earth and discover the profound workings of creation," (29:20) the Qur'an urged him.

So teenage Muhammad joined a caravan to northern India, clutching a pouch of coins provided by the Samarkand *Waqf* as a research stipend. Within two months in Southeast Asia he had become fluent in Sanskrit and began studying with master mathematicians. The Indians' scientific insights were compelling, yet complicated by an infusion of ancient mythology. Recognizing how superstition and myth hindered the Indians' ability to apply their insights, Muhammad (acting as a classic *Hanif*) decided that science must be driven by methodical observations backed by rational and verifiable experimentation.

After two years critically absorbing knowledge in India, he returned along the Silk Road to Samarkand to process his findings and begin his teaching career. Students hungered to study with him to glean new techniques for unlocking the universe's hidden heavenly code. His findings even attracted interest from local rabbis, who sought guidance on how to improve precision in timing the start of Jewish festivals—thus launching a lifelong intellectual exchange that would result in Muhammad transforming the Jewish calendar.

The wunderkind of Samarkand also attracted the attention of visiting merchants from the empire's capital in Baghdad. As they traded goods, these men also transported scholarly texts between academies and scouted for outstanding local talent. The merchants encouraged sixteen-year-old Muhammad to join Baghdad's new premier institution: Bayt-ul-Hikmah—"The House of Wisdom." This start-up intellectual center aimed to collect wisdom from around the world and support brilliant minds in translating that knowledge into innovative applications. Could Bayt-ul-Hikmah help Muhammad decipher the cosmic code? He decided to find out.

Armed with letters of introduction from his teachers in Samarkand, Muhammad set out for Baghdad. After several weeks' travel through the deserts of Persia, the grand glittering capital at last appeared on the horizon. It was the largest city in the world, a perfectly round metropolis irrigated by an intricate canal network and surrounded by verdant suburbs dotted with extravagant mansions. The city's massive wooden gates had been transported from Egypt's ancient Temple of Amun. They opened to forty-foot-wide boulevards that converged around a grand central mosque—itself featuring the ancient doors of the Temple of Solomon, which had been confiscated by the Babylonians over one thousand years earlier.

As he approached Baghdad, Muhammad could see from afar the green dome of Bayt-ul-Hikmah and atop it a golden depiction of a horseman messenger—symbolizing the empire's vast postal service that brought knowledge from afar to the capital. The blowing wind rotated the horseman, signifying how Bayt-ul-Hikmah's scholars sought wisdom from all sources. Their research mission was embodied in the Qur'anic exhortation: "If you seek to beautify and repair via action-based hope, then know that the Loving Divine is aware of your extensive efforts." (4:128)

The men of Bayt-ul-Hikmah approached their work with urgency, as a competing center in the Andalusian capital of Córdoba similarly sought to attract the era's outstanding visionaries. Both centers strove to realize the Qur'an's vision to "beautify and repair the world via action-based hope"—achieving dynamic innovation via research and creativity rather than raw power via manipulation and domination. "True success is realized through self-improvement while seeking a state of higher consciousness!" (87:14) declared the Qur'an. "In pursuit of such wondrous inspiration—and for lasting impact—let competitors compete!" (83:26)

The young Muhammad plunged into the heart of this race to decode the secrets of the universe in order to beautify, heal, and blossom. Indeed, the Qur'an not only envisioned its future as a mass-distributed beautiful book supported by a system of scholarship—but also as a force inspiring human beings to harness the universe's powers to positively transform society. Books and scholarship were merely tools for this larger transcendent pursuit. The Qur'an did not reveal the cosmic code, but declared it existed and offered tantalizing clues for how to unlock its secrets, inviting its audience to observe, explore, and experiment.

By setting out this larger mission, the Qur'an sustained a dynamic relationship with humans long after its final revelation—and the great innovators who took up its challenge saw themselves creating direct continuations of the Qur'anic spirit. In so doing, they would ultimately launch modernity: developing the first camera, pioneering advanced surgery, inventing the concept of seconds and minutes, and even creating the very Arabic numerals used on this page. In fact, Muhammad the Uzbek—who became known as Al-Khawarizmi after his native region of Khawarizm—would see his own moniker adopted for the term "algorithm," defining the concept of complex calculation that underpins modern technology. In a dizzying burst of innovation, Al-Khawarizmi and his peers would develop Qur'an-inspired inventions that transformed the world.

❦❦❦

Upon arriving in Baghdad, Al-Khawarizmi discovered avenues paved with refined, inlaid stones—an unimaginable luxury compared to Samarkand, let alone his native village. The streets were spotless, thanks to a massive municipal crew that scrubbed the city clean twice a day. Rosebushes and palm trees lined the boulevards, hosting chattering birds, as Baghdad's residents paraded in their finest garb. Fountains and canals saturated the city with fresh water.

Al-Khawarizmi passed by Bayt-ul-Hikmah but could not enter the domed edifice. Unlike the city's public libraries, the center was an elite institution with restricted access. Only outstanding scholars who passed a series of rigorous tests gained entrance. Over the main gate, a Qur'anic verse etched in stone provided a cryptic hint as to the activities conducted inside: "Proclaim, 'Oh, My Divine Mentor, increase me in nuanced knowledge!'"

In contrast, the grand mosque at Baghdad's center opened its doors to all. As Al-Khawarizmi entered, melodious Qur'anic recitations echoed from all corners of the courtyard. Hundreds of students buzzed through the building, as dozens of teachers led learning circles analyzing Qur'anic passages. A large fountain flowed with the soothing sound of bubbling water, and white silks draped across the courtyard's archways fluttered in the cool breeze. Dangling incense burners infused the air with the sweet scent of frankincense, their undulating wafts of smoke setting a calming ambience above the scholastic hubbub.

Inside the main hall, a venerable scholar with a white beard, black turban, and kind face perched atop an elevated pulpit, an olive-branch staff in his right hand. On the floor surrounding him sat the academy's top students, engaged in an intense discussion. The teenager from Uzbekistan stood patiently outside the circle until the teacher—Imam Al-Kisa'i, one of the greatest living Islamic scholars—invited him to sit by his right hand. An impromptu admission test began, with the imam requesting recitation of random Qur'anic passages to evaluate articulation and intonation, then interrupting with questions about the meaning of particular verses and words.

Though Al-Khawarizmi had only been in the metropolis of Baghdad for a few hours, he was determined not to waste time. As a devoted Qur'anic student, he had been trained to be prepared for any scholarly encounter and to squeeze the most out of every moment. His performance greatly impressed Imam Al-Kisa'i, who promptly admitted Al-Khawarizmi as a disciple. The adolescent from a remote Uzbek village suddenly had a teacher who was just three links removed in the chain of transmission from the prophet Muhammad himself.

For the next decade, Al-Khawarizmi immersed himself in Baghdad's unique scholastic scene. Thanks to his teacher's short chain of transmission, he gained access to little-known insights on Qur'anic verses that Muhammad had shared with his closest scribes. His teacher was also a master of the Arabic language, sharing advanced techniques for analyzing Semitic roots and subtle grammatical forms. Some afternoons Al-Khawarizmi would walk across the city to the Jewish Talmudic academy, which had moved from Sura to Baghdad. He spent hours learning Hebrew and Aramaic, studying with top rabbis and advancing his work on refining the Jewish calendar to better harmonize its lunar cycle with solar years.

Although he had yet to gain access to Bayt-ul-Hikmah, Al-Khawarizmi made a point of engaging its top scholars, many of them friends of his master teacher. At first, he simply observed their discussions, but with time began to inject his own ideas. The scholars recognized a keen mind. Thanks to a formal recommendation by Imam Al-Kisa'i, the Uzbek was at last invited to apply for admission to Bayt-ul-Hikmah as a junior researcher.

Entering Bayt-ul-Hikmah, Al-Khawarizmi passed beneath its gateway motto—"Increase me in nuanced knowledge!"—and entered a pleasant court-yard that offered a quiet refuge from the bustling Baghdad streets. As the center's wooden front doors clanged shut, he encountered a semicircle of nineteen men in refined linens awaiting him. Silence permeated the intense scene, punctuated only by the bubbling courtyard fountain and swallows chirping overhead.

His test began suddenly with a barrage of questions. Each inquisitor de-livered a rapid-fire stream of information, a jumble of facts and fiction that the young scholar needed to parse in real time. Once the nineteen completed their drill, Al-Khawarizmi calmly addressed them one by one, repeating the information each had mentioned while analyzing its veracity. Before he con-cluded, he offered his personal insights on the material.

The stoic scholars stood expressionless before retreating to a seminar room to privately evaluate the candidate, who remained in the courtyard. The admis-sions committee eventually returned. Its chair stepped before Al-Khawarizmi, placing upon his head a fine black turban embroidered with a Qur'an-inspired phrase: *Wa Bihi Nasta'in* ("We seek the Divine's guidance in all we do").

The committee members warmly embraced their new colleague and wel-comed him for a tour of the facilities. The institution, they explained, had been the brainchild of caliph Al-Mansur as he designed Baghdad. Originally called *Khizanatu Kutub-il-Hikmah* ("The Storehouse of Books of Wisdom"), it collected Arabic books from libraries across the Abbasid empire. One prized possession was the original manuscript of the Qur'an, still stained by 'Uth-man's blood.

When Al-Mansur's pious grandson Harun Ar-Rashid became caliph in 786, he decided to transform the storehouse into the world's premier reposi-tory of human knowledge. Formally rebranded as Bayt-ul-Hikmah, the center aimed to collect wisdom from around the world as an unparalleled resource to drive expert discussion. To confidently demonstrate no idea was taboo, the caliph even collected books that criticized Islam and promoted atheism—just as the Qur'an quotes its critics rather than anxiously suppressing their con-demnations.

As Al-Khawarizmi's tour passed through the center's main discussion hall, he noticed a Qur'anic verse etched beneath the high ceiling: "With wisdom and beautiful eloquence, warmly invite people to explore the methodology of your Divine Mentor—and when you debate, do so in the most beautiful manner." (16:125) Qur'anic experts knew well that the prophet Muhammad had explicated this verse as a call for open inquiry: "Wisdom is the objective of the Qur'an's followers, so seek wisdom from anyone and anywhere." Bayt-ul-Hikmah had been created to fulfill this injunction. *Hikmah* literally described weaving together individual palm fibers into a strong unified rope capable of restraining a formidable beast. In the Semitic mindset, wisdom was not simply information, but insights based on experience that provide vital foresight.

In the discussion hall, Al-Khawarizmi joined a circle of experts, each grasping a book. While the scene echoed the learning circles of Baghdad's central mosque, the topic was not theological but mathematical, debating ways to calculate elements of the universe's cosmic code. The Uzbek scholar shared his own insights gleaned from studying in India, revealing that mathematical books in Sanskrit already possessed advanced techniques unknown in Baghdad. Indian wisdom, he realized, needed to be translated so experts in Baghdad could harness it.

Al-Khawarizmi's first major project thus became translating into Arabic the epic Sanskrit treatise *Brahmasphutasiddhanta*, a compendium of Indian mathematics from 628. For the first time, Bayt-ul-Hikmah was not merely collecting international works of wisdom but also making them accessible to its experts. Publication of the Arabic translation established Al-Khawarizmi's renown and inspired him to pursue a larger vision: translating all the great ancient works of wisdom into Arabic. While he lacked the authority and financing to realize such a grand project, his own research amalgamated insights from ancient Greeks, Romans, and Egyptians.

In 813, Al-Khawarizmi fused these diverse strands to produce his first original book: *Al-Mukhtasar fi Hisab-il-Jabri-wal-Muqabalah* ("Essentials of Calculation by Mending and Balancing Numbers"). The title played on one of the Qur'an's names for the Divine: *Al-Jabbar,* "the one who heals broken fractures." Inspired by the Qur'an's call to mend brokenness and repair the world, the book saw mathematical fractions as fragmented entities that could be reconciled and made whole via precise equations. With the book's publication, Al-Khawarizmi invented the field of algebra (derived from *al-Jabr*), which unlocked essential elements of the universe's mathematical code.

Rather than rely on unwieldly Roman numerals or alphabetical stand-ins, Al-Khawarizmi's book also invented Arabic numerals that presented digits based on the number of angles they contained. His symbol for two, for example, contained two angles, resembling a *Z*. To represent zero, he offered a round circle devoid of angles, in the process creating another indispensable element of advanced computation.

Algebra did not simply ease how numbers were depicted or calculated, but fundamentally revolutionized how to operate efficiently. Inspired by the message of *Surah Al-'Asr,* it aimed to squeeze the most out of every situation, calculating the minimum input required for maximum output. For example, where massive pillars were once required to support buildings, algebra enabled advanced calculations of force to design slimmer columns capable of supporting far larger rooms. Buildings could be constructed faster and with fewer materials, sparking the development of a sophisticated Qur'anic-inspired style of architecture.

In essence, the algebra mindset transformed broken situations into dynamic opportunities for lasting impact. And it did so with elegant equations, precise numerals, and dynamic efficiency. The world would never be the same.

In the short term, the book's publication sealed Al-Khawarizmi's future. Just after its publication, a new caliph ascended the throne and appointed the Uzbek scholar as dean of Bayt-ul-Hikmah. Only thirty-three years old, Al-Khawarizmi suddenly had the opportunity to create the world's greatest intellectual hub. He benefited from the new caliph's support; who declared his own commitment to free inquiry: "Proclaim whatever you please and present your evidence. We are an open society, so do not fear persecution." In Baghdad's main market, he even constructed a dedicated free-speech podium with no restrictions—aside from sedition against the caliph.

To seize the moment, Al-Khawarizmi realized his center needed a massive team of visionary scholars, as well as philanthropists to finance their work. Enter the Banu Musa brothers. Unlike most of Baghdad's elite who hailed from generations of established wealth, the brothers had been born into poverty in rural Afghanistan. Hardly an aristocrat, their father robbed travelers on the Silk Road. One victim was an unarmed Qur'anic scholar, who handed over his meager coins along with an invaluable insight: "*Zakah* funds were established to elevate people in difficult circumstances." The scholar recognized the bandit had acted out of desperation to feed his children and offered to provide funding and introductions so the man could start a legitimate business.

The onetime outlaw soon became a millionaire merchant, and his three sons further parlayed their father's success to become billionaires. They relocated their headquarters to Baghdad, taking advantage of the city's experts to expand their construction business. Evincing a curiosity for translating novel ideas into practical innovations, the Banu Musa brothers made excellent partners for Al-Khawarizmi. The young dean recruited the billionaires to serve as active philanthropists within Bayt-ul-Hikmah. They both underwrote a massive new translation project and ran their own experimental team of over one hundred scholars, some supported by salaries of 500 dinars per month (more than $100,000 per person in today's money).

Rather than rely solely on government sponsorship or religious trusts, Bayt-ul-Hikmah cultivated mega-philanthropists like the Banu Musa brothers to rapidly scale the center into a nucleus of knowledge. From Constantinople to China, emissaries were sent far and wide to acquire books for translation in Baghdad by a team of polyglots. As these linguists spoke aloud translations into Arabic, a team of scribes furiously recorded the content, enabling each translator to process over two hundred books each year.

As they revived ancient wisdom from pagan cultures, the center's expert scholars were able to explore non-monotheistic ideas without feeling threatened. Still, Al-Khawarizmi emphasized the importance of interrogating and expanding upon preexisting ideas. For example, one research effort sought to calculate the circumference of the earth by refining ancient Greek estimates with advanced algebraic calculations. Al-Khawarizmi, backed by a team of seventy scholars including the Banu Musa brothers, led a field expedition in the Syrian wilderness to determine the earth's curvature. After spending weeks painstakingly measuring a mile-long segment of land, the scholars then extrapolated the globe's full expanse—producing a projection off by just 1 percent from modern computer measurements.

At Al-Khawarizmi's direction, researchers were recruited solely on merit. The halls of Bayt-ul-Hikmah became filled with women (comprising one-third of all staff) and non-Muslims, including a priest named Yusuf Al-Khuri who served as a top aide to Al-Khawarizmi. At the center's ecumenical chapel, Muslims, Christians, Jews, and others could be found engaged in spiritual introspection.

The staff pioneered all sorts of innovations, including calculating the solar year precisely to 365 days and six hours; dividing the day into minutes and seconds; inventing programmable robots; creating the first music sequencer;

developing new models of water flow in urban design; and naming thousands of new stars. The translation efforts driving such advances also succeeded in preserving classical Greek and Roman knowledge, which had been abandoned in Europe after the destruction of Rome. Had it not been for Bayt-ul-Hikmah's systematic translation program, these works of antiquity might have been lost forever.

᪥

To reflect Bayt-ul-Hikmah's ambitious mission, Al-Khawarizmi sought to overhaul the center's design with an advanced campus reflecting algebraic values. Part of his inspiration came from Baghdad's central mosque, whose ornate doors had been repurposed from King Solomon's Temple in Jerusalem. Indeed, the Qur'an praises that ancient edifice's architectural splendor as an advanced fusion of art and technology: "Solomon's skilled craftsmen made whatever he desired: magnificent buildings, sophisticated statues, imposing monuments, and gigantic vats." It further recounts the Queen of Sheba's astonishment at its pioneering engineering. "As soon as she entered the grand hall, she thought that its floor was a large pool and so she lifted her skirt, exposing her calves, prompting Solomon to explain: 'It is merely a well-polished crystal floor.'"

Solomon's Jerusalem served as a lost monotheistic model of aesthetic and technical creativity that Muslim artists aspired to revive and exceed. The Qur'an describes such exquisite beauty as *Ihsan*: visual perfection driven by a rare combination of proportionality, intricacy, distinction, efficiency, and enchantment—an echo of the creative brilliance found in the divine cosmic code. "The Loving Divine beautified and perfected everything He created," the Qur'an explains, while challenging its followers to emulate the divine example: "Proclaim the methods of beautification to all people."

Recognizing that scientific advancement required artistic accompaniment, Al-Khawarizmi sought out an emerging master designer to reimagine Bayt-ul-Hikmah's campus. The visionary was a handsome twenty-four-year-old Kurdish polymath who fused music, astronomy, mathematics, architecture, and fashion. His name: Ziryab ("the blackbird"), a moniker derived from his dark complexion and melodious voice. The descendant of enslaved entertainers who had become elite members of the caliph's court, Ziryab as a young boy had emerged as a musical prodigy, designing his own proto-guitar and demonstrating a unique ability to extemporize marvelous odes on command. Known for his vibrant style, he dressed in fine robes he had designed himself and emitted a trademark aroma via self-distilled cologne. More than anyone in Baghdad, Ziryab lived the concept of *Ihsan*. A meticulous perfectionist, he designed entire rooms down to the smallest detail; organized elaborate royal banquets; and conducted his own symphonies—often all in the same week.

Al-Khawarizmi shared his mathematical work with Ziryab and challenged the young artist to create an architectural style for Bayt-ul-Hikmah that would embody algebraic principles. Inspired by algebra's calculated efficiency coupled with intricate balancing, Ziryab invented a revolutionary style of repetitive ceiling molding called *Muqarnas* (replication cornice). The ornamentation evoked a beehive via complex interlocking geometric shapes that spanned heights with hypnotizing grandeur. The sophisticated geometric patterns evolved over the course of an individual span, and each archway featured unique styling tailored to its particular distance.

The beehive motif was no accident, as Ziryab drew inspiration from the Qur'an praising bees for creating adaptable buzzing hubs of cooperation:

> Your Divine Mentor inspired bees with the flexibility to construct their hives in mountains, trees, vineyards, and even cities, saying: "And extract your nourishment from a variety of fruits, and seek diverse paths always adjusting. . . ." (16:68)

Bayt-ul-Hikmah's hexagonal window frames symbolically evoked beehives, and Ziryab's internal layout provided no reserved space for any one scholar—just as their hive forces bees to interact rather than isolate. Ziryab also incorporated advanced laboratories with proper fume ventilation via chimneys and windows carefully positioned to optimize air flow. From Syrian master glassblowers, he commissioned special crystal containers for storing chemicals as well as intricate lamps to enable evening research.

Inside the center's grand dome, Ziryab inscribed in elaborate calligraphy *Ayat-un-Nur,* the Qur'an's iconic verse about unlocking layers of learning to counter the darkness of ignorance.

> The Loving Divine is the source of illumination for the cosmos and earth: His illumination is like a lantern, inside it is a lamp, suspended inside a crystal ball,

resembling a brilliantly pulsating star, fueled by a special blessed tree—an olive tree, neither from the east nor the west, its oil so luminous it emits light without burning.

The verse embodied how Bayt-ul-Hikmah's mission—while secular and led by people of diverse faiths—was quintessentially Qur'anic and served as a dazzling beacon to inspire other visionaries around the world.

For the Abbasid caliph, however, Ziryab proved too brilliant—his flamboyant outfits jarred in a subdued royal court whose official color was black. After completing his redesign of Bayt-ul-Hikmah, Ziryab left Baghdad and was eventually lured to Córdoba, Spain, by the Umayyad caliph to serve as Minister of Culture. Along with an enormous salary, the position afforded Ziryab carte blanche to pursue his artistic vision and help the Umayyads outshine their Abbasid rivals. He unleashed his creativity across all areas of the arts: establishing Andalusian music as a distinctive genre; pioneering aromatherapy (with eighty recipes still used in iconic French perfumes); defining the three-course meal; and even inventing toothpaste alongside new deodorants and shampoos. Following the Qur'anic injunction, Ziryab like no prior innovator brought "methods of beautification" to the masses.

Beyond aesthetic advances, Ziryab employed his scientific background to help a fellow inventor develop methods of human flight. He partnered with 'Abbas Ibnu Firnas to calculate the necessary aerodynamics for prosthetic wings that might enable human flight. After extensive algebraic computations and prototyping, the seventy-six-year-old Ibnu Firnas ascended the towering minaret of Córdoba's grand mosque and made a literal leap of faith. Amazingly, as Ziryab watched, the old man remained airborne for over an hour, soaring with his canvas wings over the city. Of course, the team had forgotten to design a rudder or a landing method, so the first successful test pilot in history improvised a crash landing.

On the other side of the Straits of Gibraltar, the Idrisid empire in Morocco eagerly sought to join the Golden Age of Qur'anic innovation. The breakthrough in the Maghreb came not from the government but via an Amazigh female philanthropist named Fatimah Al-Fihri. Thanks to proper application of Qur'anic inheritance laws, Fatimah received the bulk of her wealthy father's estate and decided to dedicate a major portion of it to establishing the world's first university. She knew that the driving force behind Bayt-ul-Hikmah's early success was a woman: the wife of the caliph Harun Ar-Rashid, who had given her husband the vision of transforming a storehouse into a vibrant creative center and donated a major portion of her personal wealth to accelerate the process.

Though only in her twenties, Fatimah purchased a prime piece of land in the heart of the capital city of Fez and designed a massive complex combining a library, mosque, and center of higher education. She named the university Al-Qarawiyyin ("The Commoners") to reflect its mission as an academic institution for all people, not just elites. Coining a new derivative of the Arabic term for a central mosque, Fatimah called the site a *Jami'ah* (literally, "an inclusive site that gathers all"), as reflecting its mission to make knowledge accessible to the masses. Its students would study a wide range of subjects, including medicine, economics, philosophy, Qur'an, and even Hebrew and the Talmud, recognized as keys to unlocking some obscure Qur'anic concepts.

In a sense, Al-Qarawiyyin fused the structure of religious academies with the secular model of Bayt-ul-Hikmah. Spanish artisans trained by Ziryab were hired to decorate the building in his algebra-infused Andalusian style. Students accessed the complex via a gateway featuring the Qur'anic verse exhorting the Divine to "increase my knowledge" and entered a splendid vast courtyard dotted with fountains. A vast library with a well-lit reading room on one end of the courtyard faced a great hall, used for classes and convocations. Nearby stood a series of *Mukhtabar* ("testing centers"), laboratories where students experimented with chemicals and medical techniques.

The university was divided into specific faculties *(Kulliyyat),* each led by a senior professor who sat on an elevated chair, thus creating the concept of department chairs. Professors also stood out via distinctive academic dress, including robes (inspired by the prophet Muhammad's *Burdah* cloak) and special tasseled hats (named "fezzes" after their city of origin). Once students completed their required courses, a festive graduation ceremony bestowed upon them diplomas (*Ijazah*—literally, "license to practice"). The world's oldest medical degree, in fact, remains in the university's archives. With these systems, Al-Qarawiyyin set the model for future universities and even established Europe's first university via its satellite school of medicine in Salerno, Italy. Prominent Al-Qarawiyyin alumni included a future pope (Sylvester II—who returned to Europe with the Arabic numerals); iconic Jewish philosopher Maimonides; and Ibnu Khaldun, the founder of modern sociology.

At the other end of North Africa, the Fatimid empire in Cairo was keen to outshine its rival Muslim empires. The caliph proposed the invention of a new technology that might give the empire a dramatic academic edge. "We envision the construction of a pen that can write without the need for an ink holder as its ink will be self-contained," he envisioned. "A writer can fill this pen with ink to write without pause and store it anywhere he wishes without fearing leaks or stains. Its ink will flow only when there is an intention to write." When the caliph's shocked advisors insisted such technology seemed impossible, he retorted: "Anything is possible when one puts their trust in the Loving Divine!"

An enterprising Egyptian craftsman took up the caliph's challenge. He fashioned the first-ever fountain pen out of gold. It could be turned about without spilling, with ink emerging only when the tip pressed against paper. Requiring no external inkwell for a constant resupply of ink, it enabled continuous beautiful writing without a mess. The invention dramatically accelerated the speed at which scribes could produce books, leading to an explosion in Arabic publishing with Egypt at its center.

Cairo thus needed its own outstanding academic institution to rival Baghdad, Córdoba, and Fez. In the center of the city, the Fatimid caliph constructed a university double the size of Al-Qarawiyyin. Named Al-Azhar ("The Illuminating"), it too combined an enormous library, mosque, and diverse academic faculties—becoming the second oldest university in the world. To bring its name to life, Al-Azhar's builders stripped white marble from the Great Pyramid at Giza and hauled it nearly twenty miles to serve as the university's brilliant exterior sheen. Under both sunlight and moonlight, Al-Azhar's facade emitted an enchanting glow visible far beyond Cairo.

The Fatimids also created their own research and development think tank to outdo Bayt-ul-Hikmah. The center's 1.6 million books and forty large research rooms dwarfed anything in Baghdad, and the center was open to the public in contrast to its Iraqi rival. Lest anyone miss its competitive purpose, the Cairo institution bore a familiar name: Dar-ul-Hikmah—"The Abode of Wisdom."

❦❦❦

The proliferation of advanced scholarly centers and major private philanthropists throughout Muslim empires spurred the rise of independent innovators: brilliant minds who leveraged institutions as resource centers yet pursued their own breakthroughs. Free from the constraints of organizational bureaucracy, they advanced idiosyncratic projects on their own terms.

For example, Hasan Ibnul-Haytham grew up in a family plagued by inherited ocular diseases. Determined to help cure ailments of the eye—whose interior functioning remained an enigma—he set off from his native Basra to pore over materials in Cairo's Dar-ul-Hikmah library. He discovered that Ibnu Firnas, the elderly pioneer of human flight in Spain, had tried to forge quartz into "seeing crystals" (portable magnifying glasses) to offset his failing eyesight. Ibnul-Haytham realized that any practical solutions required understanding the eye's anatomy.

Without any official approval, he surreptitiously acquired eyes from corpses and began dissecting them. Word of his unsanctioned research reached authorities, and he soon found himself under house arrest. Sitting alone one night, he noticed moonlight pouring into his dark room via a small hole, producing an inverted image of the world outside on the opposite wall. In a eureka moment, Ibnul-Haytham understood that the pupil functioned in precisely the same way: a small aperture focusing light into a reflected image on the cornea, an inverted depiction the brain translated into reality.

On his roof Ibnul-Haytham constructed a small dark room with a tiny hole in the center of one wall. An inverted image of Al-Azhar university opposite his home projected onto the opposite wall. He experimented with chemically refined animal fats to burn the image onto hide canvases. After several weeks he found a suitable combination and recorded the world's first permanent image: a rendition of Al-Azhar's minaret. Combining insights from his camera, dissection, and algebra, Ibnul-Haytham then fashioned a groundbreaking pair of reading glasses that focused blurry images by adjusting the angle of light entering the cornea. (His pioneering lens work served as the precursor for Isaac Newton's telescope.)

Word of Ibnul-Haytham's reading glasses reached the caliph, who not only granted a royal pardon but also sponsored a research stipend at Dar-ul-Hikmah. Employing the newly invented pen, Ibnul-Haytham wrote over two hundred books. In one of these, he codified the modern scientific method: "If learning the truth is the objective, the researcher investigating scientists' writings must be analytically critical of all he reads. . . . This includes his own findings as he performs his critical examination so as to avoid falling into either prejudice or leniency." This declaration of open inquiry elaborated on the Qur'anic reminder that deep thinkers "critically observe everything in creation and analyze it."

Ibnul-Haytham's books arrived in Spain, where a veteran physician named Az-Zahrawi harnessed them to perform the first successful cataract surgeries in history. Az-Zahrawi directed a unique hospital that combined patient care and scientific research, an institution where graduates of Al-Qarawiyyin performed their medical residencies and developed new medicines. Relying on the support of major philanthropists, the hospital provided free care to the poor while conducting daring research. Beautifully designed in Ziryab's Andalusian style, the complex also employed his aromatherapy techniques to pair psychological and physical healing.

A descendant of Muhammad's scribe Ubayy Ibnu Ka'b, Az-Zahrawi achieved a dizzying array of medical breakthroughs. He performed the first-ever tooth reimplantation; introduced catgut for internal stitching; designed a urological instrument to break down kidney stones without surgery; developed a pharmacological headache medication and the forerunner to stick deodorant; discovered the cause of paralysis; performed the first successful spinal neurosurgery; and invented over two hundred surgical instruments still used in hospitals today. He also founded the field of medical ethics, including meticulously documenting each case for recordkeeping, accountability, and educational opportunities—thus establishing the tradition of medical notes.

In one of his many books, Az-Zahrawi summarized the mindset of the Golden Age: "Any of my skills are derived from extensively researching the books of the Ancients with a thirst to understand them and extract the essence of the knowledge they contain. Throughout my life, I have experimented to expand my horizons of understanding. Finally, I simplify my findings so they are accessible for readers and safe from the abyss of wordiness."

While inspired by the ancients, the era's medical pioneers also saw their work as a continuation of the Qur'anic spirit. Their textbooks began with the same invocation of the Loving Divine that opens each surah, and their prose mimicked the Qur'an's literary style. As one book noted in its introduction: "There are two main categories of illness: psychological and physical. Both are clearly outlined in the Qur'an, which declares they can be cured." Like its call to decipher the hidden code of the cosmos, the Qur'an insisted that cures existed yet left it to human visionaries to both diagnose and heal.

Even the laboratory tools they created invoked the Qur'an. The newly invented alembic ("curved container") for distillation included a glass tube to channel liquid flow called *Ar-Rasl*, echoing the Qur'anic moniker for prophets channeling divine inspiration. Mortar and pestle kits used for grinding chemical compounds featured as decoration in Qur'anic passages declaring "healing for what ails the hearts" and "healing for what ails the body."

Indeed, the Qur'an repeatedly links human psychology with physical health. Just as the Torah describes how God "hardened Pharaoh's heart" to explain the Egyptian ruler's unrelenting persecution, the Qur'an repeatedly invokes a range of cardiac abnormalities to diagnose complex mental states. When Joseph is accosted by his master's aroused wife, the Qur'an describes her uncontrollable passion as *Shaghaf* (literally, "the skin layer of the heart"). After the Israelites create the golden calf, they explain their rebellious antagonism as *Qulubuna Ghulf* ("our hearts are encrusted"). Observing how Meccan elders couple generous hospitality for visitors with the capacity to murder their own daughters, the Qur'an labels their intense polarity *Rana 'Ala Qulubihim* (literally, "discolored cardiac tissue").

These cryptic descriptions intrigued Golden Age medical pioneers. Avicenna, an itinerant Persian physician born near Al-Khawarizmi's hometown, diagnosed Qur'anic cardiac concepts as both physical and mental ailments. *Shaghaf* represented both heart-membrane disease and obsessive mania. *Ghulf* marked a heart tumor as well as a layered mind haunted by past trauma, like PTSD. *Rana* signified cardiac muscular degeneration and bipolar mood swings.

A prickly genius who refused to be confined to any scholarly institution or caliph's court, Avicenna maintained his scholarly independence thanks to the generosity of wealthy philanthropists he healed. Known as the "master of medicine," he wrote over 450 books on topics from metaphysics to mental illness to astronomy. His treatise "The Canon of Medicine"—a compendium classifying all known eleventh-century medical knowledge—remained the standard medical textbook in Europe into the 1700s.

❧❦❧

"Everything on earth inevitably withers," (55:26) observes the Qur'an, recognizing that even ages of great progress cannot last forever. Immensely wealthy Muslim empires grew decadent and haughty, convinced of their own invincibility and their rivals' inferiority. As their host capitals basked in unimaginable material and intellectual riches, institutions like Bayt-ul-Hikmah gradually lost their innovative drive. Then came a wave of violent incursions: the Crusades in the Holy Land, the Reconquista in Spain, and the collapse of the Idrisid and Fatimid empires. As much of Islamic Spain fell, Córdoba's legendary institutions were sacked and millions of books burned. While Baghdad remained safe, ascendant Mongol forces ravaging China and India slowly encroached from the East.

Amidst political instability and looming external threats, a researcher from Bayt-ul-Hikmah named Al-Jazari returned to his native Syria to help develop irrigation systems to address an extended drought. Fascinated by gears' ability to translate minimum energy input into maximum output, Al-Jazari loved designing robotic and hydraulic systems that applied algebra to hydrology. He invented the piston as well as many advanced gears still used in electrical generation and transportation vehicles, earning him the moniker "the father of modern engineering and robotics."

In 1206, as he sensed both his impending mortality and the Golden Age's expiration, Al-Jazari constructed one final masterwork: an advanced mechanical clock that calculated time based on celestial movements. Powered by a network of sophisticated gears and water-flow regulators, the timepiece marked each new hour with a clang of mechanized cymbals and announced dawn and dusk with imitation bird chirps generated via gurgling water. Its exterior depicted an elephant carrying a towering assortment of symbols paying homage to diverse cultures whose wisdom had propelled the era. As Al-Jazari explained: "The elephant represents Indian and African cultures; the two dragons represent Chinese culture; the phoenix represents Persian culture; the water work represents Greek culture; and the turban represents Islamic culture."

On the bottom corner of his colorful blueprint for the elephant clock's design, Al-Jazari wrote an enigmatic Qur'anic allusion: *Al-'Asr*. A reference to the surah describing the squeeze of time and the importance of maximizing every ephemeral moment, the word also contained a sad irony. Reciting *Surah Al-'Asr* traditionally marked the end of a session—or in this case, an era. Indeed, the clock was ticking down on the Golden Age, of which Al-Jazari represented the last exceptional inventor.

Just fifty-two years after Al-Jazari's death, Mongol forces burst into Baghdad. Before ransacking the opulent Abbasid capital, soldiers headed straight for Bayt-ul-Hikmah. They burned Al-Khawarizmi's legendary center to the ground, massacred its scholars, and hurled thousands of books into the Tigris River. Ink once painstakingly deployed to preserve priceless wisdom bled somberly into the water. The Mongol warriors then moved on to destroy Baghdad's central mosque—in the process incinerating the ancient doors of Solomon's Temple and symbolically ending an extraordinary era of world-changing Qur'anic innovation.

EPILOGUE

A REBIRTH
OF QUR'ANIC
HEALING

*A seeming antagonist can be transformed
into the dearest and most loyal of friends.*
—*Surah Fussilat (41:34)*

FROM ITS EARLIEST DAYS, THE QUR'AN DISPLAYED A REMARKABLE ABIL-
ity to transform fierce antagonists into devoted followers. An enraged 'Umar
tried to choke off the Qur'an's revelatory flow by murdering Muhammad, only
to stumble upon a scroll of *Surah Taha*—which melted his heart and converted him into a lifelong guardian of the Qur'an. The Umayyad clan spent
decades attacking the Qur'an, including a debilitating two-year boycott that
silenced revelation as well as repeated military assaults on the Qur'an's safe-
haven of Medina. Yet the clan's top political prodigy, Mu'awiyah, later raised
the Qur'an as the driving force of a global empire.

The ferocious Mongol conquerors who decimated Baghdad were not immune to the Qur'an's transformative charm, as their descendants came to
build majestic Qur'anic monuments. Though his ancestors sacked Samarkand, Tamerlane rebuilt the Uzbek capital into an even more glorious Islamic

center, complete with magnificent algebraic mosques and renowned academies. Indeed, even as the Muslim world's Arabian heartland stagnated after the destruction of Baghdad, periphery Muslim communities flourished, like Timbuktu in West Africa's Songhai empire, led by history's wealthiest man, Mansa Musa.

In India, another Mongol descendant named Shah Jahan stewarded the Mughal empire to its own Golden Age, constructing the Taj Mahal as a monumental mausoleum featuring a mosque and Qur'anic academy. Considered one of the world's finest buildings, the Taj Mahal aimed to embody the Qur'anic ideal of *Ihsan*: visual perfection fusing elegance, symmetry, serenity, and allure. Its white marble walls, carefully cut to exude a lucent shimmering effect, appeared to change color as the day progressed: pinkish-yellow hues at dawn, bright white at midday, golden at dusk, and blue by night.

The name Taj Mahal employed an Arabic-infused Persian expression ("Crowning Place") to describe the building's aspiration to be the unsurpassed manifestation of Qur'anic architecture. One of the tallest buildings of its day, the Taj Mahal took twenty-two years to build, the same duration as the Qur'an's revelation. Inspired by the Qur'an's praise for the innovative engineering of Solomon's Jerusalem, Shah Jahan's mausoleum cost a million dollars per week to construct, employing the world's premier artisans and finest materials. Precious jewels like sapphires and emeralds were inlaid in marble in addition to reflective tiles set at angles to create a glittering three-dimensional effect suggesting the building was itself a living being. The vibrant thematic was reinforced by vivid depictions of symbolic flora: the lotus signifying purity, the pomegranate abundance, and the tulip love. Exquisitely carved marble lattices utilized complex algebraic calculations to sculpt intricate geometric patterns that evoked honeycombs.

Lest visitors miss the integral Qur'anic connection, *Surah Yasin* appeared in delicate Arabic calligraphy as a decorative border along the mausoleum's exterior. The chapter recounts the struggles of three eloquent envoys respectfully delivering an important message to a skeptical town, whose hostile residents refuse to listen and instead superstitiously blame the messengers for destabilizing their community. The vignette illustrated that ideas cannot be imposed on obstinate audiences, even via the most compelling presentation:

The messengers replied: ". . . Our task is merely to convey the message clearly and eloquently." To which the townsfolk retorted: "We clearly perceive you as a bad omen! Either you cease advising us or you will be ostracized and harshly punished!"

The Taj Mahal dazzlingly manifested Qur'anic values without making demands, demonstrating rather than preaching. Yet its noble expression of tolerance disturbed Shah Jahan's own son, who adopted a grimmer theological approach. He disdained people who did not embrace the Qur'an and instead sought to subjugate them. Unable to sway his open-minded father who maintained a court of scholars from diverse religious traditions, he instead "ostracized and harshly punished" him—arresting Shah Jahan for the charge of heresy!

The generational conflict between Shah Jahan and his son reflected an ongoing rift among the Qur'an's followers between beautifying open innovation and austere repressive judgmentalism—a stark divide that could even lead a son to suppress his own father. Despite doubling the size of his father's empire and building hundreds of mosques throughout India, Shah Jahan's son earned a notorious reputation for manic and divisive governance—producing nothing like the glorious lasting impact of the Taj Mahal. "The Loving Divine created both the chaos of darkness and the order of light," (6:1) observes the Qur'an.

❈❈❈

Humans process profound trauma in diverse ways: sometimes retreating inward, wearily stagnating to secure a small measure of safety; other times lashing out, frantically reinventing themselves to escape past pain. Rarely is achieving healing and serenity a simple journey.

The reaction of Shah Jahan's son reflected a lingering trauma among the Qur'an's followers sparked by the collapse of the Golden Age in Baghdad and beyond. Falling from glorious heights of unprecedented wealth and ingenuity to defeat at the hands of "savage barbarians" was a profound shock and source of deep disillusionment. (After the Mongols captured Baghdad's last caliph, they wrapped him in his finest Persian carpet and then crushed him beneath their horses' hooves.) Compounding the political degradation was the intellectual annihilation of a generation of expert scholars and their irreplaceable libraries. Thousands of acclaimed Golden Age books no longer exist, known today only via references in other texts. Centuries of wisdom disappeared forever in flames.

The surviving scholars of the traditional *'Ulama* desperately sought to preserve existing knowledge at all costs. They instituted a formal freeze on fresh Qur'anic interpretations to focus instead on canonization of existing methodologies and memorization. The mind, they reasoned, offered a safer storehouse than libraries. Favoring conservation over creative innovation, scholars lamented an idealized lost past of saintly sages and political leaders beyond reproach, part of a desperate bid for unity amidst turmoil. "A thousand days of tyranny are better than one day of chaos," became one of their mantras. As students were discouraged from critical thinking in favor of merely absorbing past systems, traditional scholarship lost its creative edge. Discarding dynamic exegesis to prioritize rote memorization was initially merely a temporary measure implemented by panicked scholars to preserve knowledge, yet the state of emergency became permanent.

In the void left by the *'Ulama*'s stagnation, puritan revivalist movements sought to rally the Qur'an's followers back into action to reclaim the lost Golden Age. The Divine had abandoned Muslims, they insisted, because of their sins, punishing them for straying from the original message and implementing decadent innovations that corrupted the true faith. Appeasing an exasperated God required rooting out sin from within the community and eliminating sacrilege outside it. In this binary worldview, success derived directly from piety and harm from sin—as a stern God penalized entire communities for the behavior of even one individual.

These revivalist approaches provided simple explanations and direct action plans for restoring order. Because Muslim empires had ostensibly succumbed to infidels due to aberrant behavior, eliminating sin was the only way to revive the Golden Age. With a clear scapegoat identified, corrective action required communal uniformity and severe punishment to prevent deviance. A public beating or execution for private behaviors enabled the community to escape God's wrath by carrying out His punishment themselves.

Qur'anic passages were presented to emphasize hellfire as a looming eternal punishment for sins. Other passages were reinterpreted to describe scary unseen forces as supernatural causes of mysterious phenomena like mental illness. To protect from all this danger, the Qur'an was recast not as a guide for healthy living but a protective talisman. Simply carrying an amulet of its passages could purify one. With *Iqra* interpreted literally as "read the Qur'an," revivalists emphasized rote recitation, as if pronouncing words without understanding or applying them sufficed. Questioning any of this dogma became taboo, with ordinary people pressured into conformity with the fear of being ostracized as heretics.

The puritan revivalists had seen Muslims chased out of Spain after centuries of glorious civilization, with millions more forced to convert during the notorious Inquisition. Desperate to preserve identity in perilous conditions, revivalist leaders created a new theological division of the globe between Dar-ul-Islam ("the realm of Islam") and Dar-ul-Harb ("the realm of war"). Only lands ruled by Muslims were deemed safe, and new rules forbade travel to non-Muslim lands. Although the Qur'an encouraged seeking knowledge in all places, a new insularity set in—and as Europe began to progress into the Renaissance, Muslim societies began to lag.

Whereas the Qur'an's opening chapter *Al-Fatihah* directly advocated "unlocking," the new era emphasized locking up and closing inward. Qur'anic verses were recast to take on menacing tones: "Do not consider the Jews and Christians as your friends" and "Whoever desires a religion other than Islam, it will not be accepted from him." The closing phrase of *Al-Fatihah* was reinterpreted as a cautionary reminder about the failings of Jews ("those who deserve God's anger") and Christians ("those who have gone astray"). Even though the word *Sayf* ("sword") never appears in the Qur'an, revivalist leaders rebranded a Qur'anic verse as *Ayat-us-Sayf*, alleging that it abrogated all tolerant and compassionate verses in the Qur'an in favor of intolerance and force. Ironically, the revivalist movement adopted the very repressive aggression of the Mongols, Crusaders, and Spanish Inquisitors from which they sought to differentiate themselves.

Similarly, even as these revivalists concocted a wave of innovations in interpretation, they instilled a popular fear of innovation, claiming that anything but a "pure" faith would lead to disaster. With an invented mythical past, they ironically mimicked the Meccans' blind refusal to be open to fresh ideas. The Qur'an critically quotes this attitude: "We merely worship these idols because our ancestors before us had done so, as we are merely progeny following in their footsteps." (7:173) Aspects of this fear persisted for centuries, with the Ottoman sultan initially rejecting the newly invented printing press as a tool of the devil, and many mosque leaders refusing to introduce electricity to their sanctuaries well into the 1930s. Insular self-preservation led to a defensive and fearful inward focus, otherwise known as stagnation.

Rather than work hard to blossom and unlock potential, the ironically stagnant Muslim attitude sought external salvation. A *Mahdi,* or messianic figure, would soon appear, went the popular trope, to eradicate injustice and restore the Golden Age as a triumphant political leader. The Qur'an of course had admonished the Jews for adopting a similar passivity:

> "Confusion will always be the uncomfortable condition of those who choose to sit passively awaiting external salvation. . . . We declared to the Children of Israel:
>
>> "Live throughout the earth [in exile], and only once you have invested your full effort will We gather you from far and wide."

Yet the Golden Age was not a political or theological order, but a mindset of open inquiry and creative innovation—a place where people regardless of background collaborated to unlock and harness the universe's powerful cosmic code for the betterment of humanity. The trauma of losing that order led some to advocate destructive shortcuts that could, by their inherently repressive nature, never succeed. The deep yet long-unfulfilled desire to resurrect the past without understanding its essence instead spawned superficial substitutes. Declaring a caliphate more often signaled the inversion—and thus repression—of core Qur'anic values rather than their revival. Humans might claim to uphold the banner of the Qur'an while their actions instead degrade it.

❧❧❧

In the Muslim world today, the Qur'an is more widespread than ever in its history. Over a billion print copies circulate. Miniature replicas hang from millions of rearview mirrors. Iconic verses set in gold and silver jewelry adorn the necks of millions. Five times a day, thousands of loudspeakers atop minarets broadcast its passages. The words of the Qur'an are omnipresent—yet its spirit lies dormant. Instead of individuality nurtured in empowering open societies that compete to lead creative innovation, too often suppression and conformity dominate.

The Qur'an's critics argue that the Muslim world's serious challenges are proof of the book's failure. After all, if the Qur'an's devout followers lag behind the rest of the world, then it must be because they uphold flawed values. The critics, however, have it backward: The Qur'an is not the source of the Muslim world's problems, but its untapped solution.

Strikingly, the core condition of the Muslim world today—willful stagnation—mirrors the same paralysis the Qur'an originally emerged to repair. The Arabs of Mecca clung to their ancestors' tradition without questioning, fearing both real and imagined threats to their identity. Their stubborn commitment not to change at all costs ironically led them to betray positive values of generosity and honesty by murdering their own daughters, boycotting independent thinkers, and even physically attacking outsiders who provided aid in times of need. Experts in propaganda and self-deception, the Meccans twisted themselves to justify actions that betrayed their tradition while maintaining a haughty superiority complex despite lagging far behind the outside world.

Meanwhile, the Jews in nearby Yathrib venerated their holy monotheistic scripture yet passively waited in exile for an external savior. They spent their days piously reciting, memorizing, and debating minutiae of rituals while ignoring their tradition's core call to act boldly in pursuing one's own destiny and improving the world. Their monotheistic cousins the Christians had emerged from centuries of persecution only to become violent persecutors themselves, waging bloody sectarian wars over trivial doctrinal differences. Throughout Arabia, tribalism trumped merit, with limited opportunities for social mobility.

Into this stagnant reality, the Qur'an delivered an alien message of daring to blossom. Hardly a scripture of triumphant dominance, the Qur'an spent many lonely years persistently calling on human beings to find the courage to break out of hibernation. When intense persecution forced it into extended silence, the Qur'an demonstrated the resilience to return with renewed vigor. Withdrawing and then finding the motivation to reemerge is embedded in the Qur'an's psyche. In that light, the Qur'an holds the keys to its own re-unlocking.

Its first word inherently recognizes that blossoming is not simplistic poetic flowering but rather an intimidating and painful process that requires courage. *Iqra*—"allow yourself to blossom"—invokes the metaphor of a plant daring to open its petals to the sunlight despite the hazards of the outside world. It also recognizes that emerging from hibernation is a decision that cannot be forced, only encouraged. The Qur'an—which derives its name from *Iqra*—is effectively an extended effort to spark and then sustain the spirit of pursuing fruition:

> Blossom forth, inspired by your rejuvenating Divine Mentor, who revives the dormant to forge empowering connections. Dare to blossom, as your Divine Mentor provides spiritual comfort. The Visionary One, who guides the unlocking of layers of learning, elevates the stagnant to once-inconceivable heights.

Stripping back the man-made debris that can hinder access to the Qur'an's core message, one encounters a dynamic coach committed to guiding long-term change. Blossoming, its second revelation clarifies, is for a noble purpose that transcends personal advancement:

> Oh, you who are covered up and shivering in fear, get up and go out to proclaim the message of self-deliverance! Empower people to rebuild themselves inspired by the Cosmic Mentor, but bring clarity to yourself before you try to change others. Cast off the constellation of obstacles weighing you down! Help others out of sincerity without expecting any personal benefit. Trust in your Cosmic Mentor and persevere through the difficult process ahead.

In the Qur'an's vision, God provides support but human beings must do the hard work. There are no shortcuts, nor scapegoats. Dwelling in victimhood—blaming others for one's own stagnation—only disempowers people from being able to rebuild themselves, cast off obstacles, and remain resilient. The Qur'an's third revelation, which became the iconic prayer *Al-Fatihah* ("The Unlocking"), recited seventeen times each day, summarizes the essential practical steps for how to successfully blossom:

> Emulate the Ultimate Source of Unconditional Love, who gently nourishes growth in all things; Who optimistically empowers even the most fragile and comforts in moments of vulnerability; Who provides fresh energy for each unfolding phase in the journey of life. We strive to reflect the way You rejuvenate and trust in Your support to shield our weaknesses. Guide us to navigate a safe path with flexibility—a path previously forged by the foresighted, who steadily restore brokenness to reach a state of serenity; a path unconstrained by a stagnant reality of willful manipulation and blind acceptance.

The Qur'an is hardly naïve. The "constellation of obstacles" includes flawed human beings, who possess natural impulses to both manipulate others for their own benefit and follow manipulators without questioning. Healthy blossoming fuses optimism, vigilance, and flexibility, and transformative growth ironically requires making constant change a tradition, lest one revert to stagnation.

The Qur'an's first three revelations not only contain the essence of its timeless message, but also recognize that human beings and societies can easily relapse. Blossoming is not a default, and the constellation of obstacles hindering self-deliverance can seem overwhelming. In other words, it is not the Qur'an stuck in protracted stagnation, but rather its followers. An eternal life-force, the Qur'an is always present and dynamic, like electricity waiting to be utilized by anyone able to positively harness its energy.

Rereading the Qur'an in its unfolding original chronology, one discovers a guide that seeks out people regardless of background, one where "Islam" represents a mindset rather than a doctrinal faith. It calls on all people to relentlessly seek wholeness via critical thinking, healing society's fractures, and leaving a lasting impact. Man-made structures have over the centuries surrounded the Qur'an with detailed rituals, formal schools of thought, sectarian traditions, and doctrinal theology. All provide important access points, but none are prerequisites to engage the Qur'an's essence.

The chains of transmission of Qur'anic wisdom flowing back to the prophet Muhammad remain unbroken. You, dear reader—regardless of your particular background or spiritual outlook—can be a new link in that philosophical chain. Anyone can appreciate the unique power of Qur'anic wisdom and apply its ancient insights to our modern lives. Doing so, however, requires relinquishing any preconceptions about the Qur'an, to approach it and one's own life with fresh eyes and an open mind.

The Qur'an has repeatedly emerged from periods of stagnation and manipulation—and will no doubt do so again. Despite a constellation of contemporary obstacles blocking access to the Qur'an, a new generation will eventually muster the determination to unlock its wisdom and harness its latent energy. When that happens, the next Golden Age will far surpass any past splendor. After all, the more difficult the task, the greater the results.

That next chapter, dear reader, can be written by you.

SOURCE
MATERIALS

AS IN MY PREVIOUS BOOK, *MUHAMMAD, THE WORLD-CHANGER*, THE
information in this book primarily derives from the oral tradition of Islamic
scholarship passed down generation by generation via unbroken chains of
transmission. My own training in the Islamic sciences includes links back
to the prophet Muhammad via several diverse chains of transmission (as
an example, I have included one of those chains at the end of this section). I
evaluated numerous raw data-points gathered throughout three decades of
extensive research before refining them into this book's narrative. All the
specifics of this due-diligence process cannot easily be replicated for the
lay reader, all the more so because this specialized field's primary works
are in Arabic. For readability and practicality, not every single fact presented in this book can be documented by a specific footnote in this sourcing section. I endeavor here to provide sufficient details for both scholars
and lay readers to understand the core underlying dynamics of the book's
sourcing process.

Although I am a devotee of the wise cosmic message of the Qur'an, I still
make a point of not simply accepting claims on faith alone and have spent

decades critically examining the Islamic tradition in its many facets. My
work aims to derive conclusions only from extensive research and nuanced
analyses while striving to synthesize a consistent and coherent narrative. As
with all human efforts, this book surely contains flaws. In the words of the
celebrated scholar Ash-Shafi'i, "Our opinion is correct and bears the possibility of error, likewise, our opponent's opinion is incorrect, yet bears the
possibility of accuracy."

The "Source Materials" section in my previous book *Muhammad, the World-
Changer* provides extensive references for much of the material covered in this
book. The most significant new research presented in this book is the chrono-
logical order of Qur'anic revelations. Evidence for the timing of each passage's
revelation is scattered among many sources, and no one clear authoritative
chronology exists. There have been several attempts to configure the order of
Qur'anic revelation, yet for the most part they merely copy each other and
contain imprecisions.

To pinpoint the precise order of Qur'anic chapters, I meticulously mapped
the original revelation of the core initial part of each Surah across the twenty-
two years of the Qur'an's unfolding. Building this timeline required cross-
referencing thousands of Hadith sources, extracting details from eye-witness
accounts, and deciphering clues from the passages themselves. Despite my decades of training, I was shocked to discover a myriad hidden gems when examining the Qur'an chronologically. This humbling process allowed me to
appreciate the Qur'an's genius and thoroughly-structured logic in fresh ways.
Tracking how revelations switch from singular to plural, when specific terms
are invoked for the first time, and instances where iconic revelations coincide
with dramatic events all provided exhilarating moments of discovery.

A few specific notes on my approach to sourcing are as follows. First, I
had to grapple with the fact that divergent Sunni and Shi'ah scholarship
traditions do not always view sources in the same manner, and sometimes
their views even collide. Although my training and chains of transmission
are primarily within the Sunni schools of scholarship, I have considered all
source material on the basis of its historical accuracy and/or credibility, as
opposed to sectarian preferences. Rather than bias one tradition over the
other, I endeavored whenever possible to include material agreed upon by
both. In areas of dispute, I drew on techniques from diverse traditions to try

to synthesize the most likely authentic meaning, always relying on Semitic root words as key guides.

Several traditional scholarly texts on Qur'anic exegesis, from diverse schools of thought, can serve as key references to concepts and points mentioned throughout this book. Due to the onerous task of including the massive number of references to each idea covered in this book, individual citations will not be provided, yet can be examined in the following Arabic books:

- *Tafsir-ul-Qur'an* by At-Tusturi
- *At-Tibyan-ul-Jami'u li 'Ulumil-Qur'an* by At-Tusi
- *Tafsir-ul-Qur'an* by 'Ali Al-Qummi
- *Tafsir-ul-Qur'an* by Ibnu 'Arabi
- *Haqaiq-ut-Tafsir* by As-Sulami
- *Jami'-ul-Bayan Fi Tafsir-il-Qur'an* by At-Tabari
- *Lata'if-ul-Isharat* by Al-Qushairi
- *Ruhul-Bayan fi Tafsir-il-Qur'an* by Haqqi
- *Tafsiru Mujahid by Mujahid* by Al-Makhzumi
- *Tafsiru Kitabillahil-'Aziz* by Al-Hawari
- *Ad-Durr-ul-Masun* by Al-Halabi
- *At-Tashilu li-'Ulumit-Tanzil* by Al-Gharnati
- *At-Tafsir-ul-Kabir* by At-Tabarani
- *At-Tahriru wat-Tanwir* by Ibnu 'Ashur
- *Al-Wajiz* by Al-Wahidi
- *Tafsir-us-San'ani* by As-San'ani
- *Ta'wilatu-Ahlis-Sunnah* by Al-Maturidi
- *Tafsiru-Sufyan-ith-Thawri* by Al-Kufi
- *Gharib-ul-Qur'an* by Zayd Ibnu 'Ali
- *Al-Kashfu wal-Bayan* by Ath-Tha'alibi
- *An-Nahr-ul-Madd* by Al-Andalusi
- *Tafsiru Furat-il-Kufi* by Furat-il-Kufi
- *Al-Kash-shaf* by Az-Zamakhshari
- *Tafsir-ul-A'qam* by Al-A'qam
- *As-Safi fi Tafsiri-Kalamillah-il-Wafi* by Al-Faydh-ul-Kashani
- *Tafsir-ul-Hibri* by Al-Hibri
- *Majma'-ul-Bayan Fi Tafsir-il-Qur'an* by At-Tubrusi

- *Mafatih-ul-Ghayb* by Ar-Razi
- *Al-Jami'u li Ahkam-il-Qur'an* by Al-Qurtubi
- *Anwar-ut-Tanzil wa Asrar-ut-Ta'wil* by Al-Baydhawi
- *Bahr-ul-'Ulum* by As-Samarqandi
- *An-Nukat wal-'Uyun* by Al-Mawardi
- *Al-Bahr-ul-Muhit* by Abu Hayyan
- *Ma'alimut-Tanzil* by Al-Baghawi
- *At-Tafsir* by Ibnu 'Urfah
- *Al-Muharrar-ul-Wajiz* by Ibnu 'Atiyyah
- *Ghara'ib-ul-Qur'an wa Ragha'ib-ul-Furqan* by Al-Qummi An-Naisaburi
- *Zad-ul-Masir fir 'Ulumit-Tafsir* by Ibnul-Jawzi
- *Al-Jawahir-ul-Hisan fi Tafsir-il-Qur'an* by Ath-Tha'alibi
- *Tafsir-ul-Qur'an* by Ibnu 'Abdis-Salam
- *Al-Lubabu Fi 'Ulum-il-Kitab* by Ibnu 'Adil
- *Madarikut-Tanzil wa Haqa'iqut-Ta'wil* by An-Nasafi
- *Nathmud-Durar fi Tanasubil-Ayati was-Suwar* by Al-Biqa'i
- *Lubab-ut-Ta'wil fi Ma'anit-Tanzil* by Al-Khazin
- *Ad-Durr-ul-Manthur fit-Tafsiri bil-Ma'thur* by As-Suyuti

Books are referenced below by citing the author's name along with volume/page or hadith number in parentheses. When a book does not contain volumes, the letter "p." precedes the page number. In situations when the entire book can serve as a reference, I have not included a specific citation. Traditional scholars who collected hadith created a standard order for them in their books, enabling specific hadith to be referenced by an assigned number. For example, "Al-Bukhari (6830)" refers to Imam Al-Bukhari's *Sahih,* hadith number 6830, while "Ibnu Kathir (5/215)" refers to page 215 of the fifth volume of Imam Ibnu Kathir's *Al-Bidayatu Wan-Nihayah.*

Translations of the divine names, Qur'anic passages, and terminologies are based on numerous Arabic etymological and linguistic sources including (but not limited to):

- *Lisan-ul-'Arab* by Ibn Manthur
- *Tahthib-ul-Lughah* by Al-Azhari
- *Al-Kitab* by Sibawayh
- *Al-'Ayn* by Al-Khalil Ibn Ahmad

- *Asas-ul-Balaghah* by Az-Zamakhshari
- *Taj-ul-'Arus* by Az-Zubaidi
- *Tafsir Asma'il-lahil-Husna* by Az-Zajjaj
- *Al-Mughith fi Gharibay-il-Qur'ani wal-Hadith* by Al-Madini
- *Mat-Tafaqa Lafthuhu Wakh-talafa Ma'nahu Fil-Qur'anil-Majid* by Al-Mubarrid
- *Al-Asma'u was-Sifat* by Al-Bayhaqi
- *Al-Maqsad-ul-Asna* by Al-Ghazali
- *At-Tahbir Fit-Tathkir* by Al-Qushairi
- *Al-Luma'u Fil-'Arabiyyah* by Ibn Junni
- *Al-Bayan wat-Tabyin* by Al-Jahith
- *Mabadi'-ul-Lughah* by Al-Iskafi
- *Fawa'id Fi Mushkili-Qur'an* by Al-'Izz Ibn 'Abdis-Salam
- *Dalil-ul-Ayati-Mutashabihatil-Alfath* by Siraj Salih Mala'ikah
- *Mukhtar-us-Sihah* by Ar-Razi
- *Al-Mu'Jam-ul-Kamil fi Lahjatil-Fusha* by Dawud Sallum
- *Mu'jam Maqayis-ul-Lughah* by Ar-Razi
- *Al-Muyassar Fi Takhrijil-Qira'atil-Mutawatirah* by Muhaisin
- *Al-Buduruz-Zahir* by Al-Qadhi
- *Al-Muzhir Fi 'Ulumil-Lughah* by As-Suyuti
- *Al-Mudhish* by Ibnul-Jawzi
- *Al-Ajnas Min Kalamil-'Arab* by Al-Qasim Ibnu Sallam
- *Sharh-Al-Mu'allaqatis-Sab'* by Az-Zawzuni
- *I'rab Amma Ba'd* by Ibn Al-Amin Al-Jaza'iri
- *Tarikh-ul-Adab-il-'Arabi* by Hanna Al-Fakhuri
- *Sharhu Milhatil-I'rab* by Al-Hariri
- *Asrar-ul-Balaghah fi 'Ilmil-Bayan Dala'il-ul-i'jaz fir'ilmil-Ma'ani* by Al-Jurjani

INTRODUCTION

The description of the Qur'an's first revelation derives from numerous sources, including Al-Bukhari (3, 4, 4953, 6982); Muslim (160, 161); As-Suhaili (1/396–411); Al-Qurtubi (10/358–62); Ar-Razi (11/215–19); Ibnu Hibban (33); Al-Haithami (8/259); At-Tabarani (6/287); Ibnul-'Arabi (4/418–23); Az-Zamakhshari (4/781–

85); Al-Baghawi (4/647–50); Al-'Ukbari (392); Al-Ujhuri (785–86); Al-Halabi (1/334–75); Al-Maturidi (10/575–82); Abu Hayyan (10/309–40); Ibnul-Athir (2/48–50).

The first Qur'anic word revealed, *Iqra*, is the imperative form of the root *Q-R-A*, indicating an instruction for action to take place after the time of utterance—in other words, a necessary action required in the immediate or distant future. The root *Q-R-A* though deeply nuanced, simply indicates movement, change, and/or transformation. The ancient Arabs would say:

- *Iqra*: "Stand out!"; "Be distinguished!"; "Be unique!"
- *Iqra*: "Gather diverse parts and fuse them into something outstanding and remarkable!"
- *Istaqri*: "Thoroughly investigate with precision in order to arrive at holistically nuanced conclusions."
- *Aqra'al-Amru*: "The time is drawing near for action to take place."
- *Qara'a lil-Mustaqbali hisaba*: "He prepared for the future, with alertness and foresight."
- *Aqra'a 'Anhu*: "He departed from him wiser than before."
- *Aqra'a minas-safar*: "He returned from travel, having gained new insights."
- *Qarra'a-Shi'ra*: "He eloquently composed elaborately intricate and captivating poetry."
- *Taqarra'a*: "He became well-educated and informed."

The root also carries the connotation of fertility:

- *Qara'at-il-azhar:* "The flowers blossomed."
- *Aqra'al-'Am:* "The rain returned after drought and sparked widespread blossoming."
- *Aqra'at-il-mar'ah:* "The woman menstruated/ended her menstruating cycle."
- *Qara'atil-Mar'ah:* "The woman delivered a healthy birth."
- *Qaryah:* "farming locality"

Even in the root's connotations of reading, reciting, or declaring, it literally describes "the exit of words from the mouth," since words were seen as "the figurative blossoms of the mind." See Ibnu Manthur (7/283–286), Al-Fairuzabadi (47), Al-Azhari (9/208–212).

Despite the efforts of zealous devotees who later attributed hundreds and even "a thousand miracles" to the prophet Muhammad, in an attempt to compete with other religions, the only "miracle" unanimously agreed upon by traditional Islamic scholars is the Qur'an itself. Al-Baqillani (circa 1000 CE) affirms this point in his book *I'jaz-ul-Qur'an*, under the heading, "The Cardinal Miraculous Proof of the Prophethood of the Prophet (Muhammad) is the Qur'an": "What must be understood with considerable care regarding the miraculous nature of the Qur'an is that our prophet's prophethood is chiefly dependent on this miracle. . . ."

CHAPTER 1

The scholar Ar-Razi collected twenty distinctive opinions from prominent scholars regarding the meaning of the opening letters at the start of several Qur'anic chapters. He noted that the Arabs traditionally attributed meaning to Arabic letters, each of which was originally a symbol of a physical object that over time came to signify abstract concepts. He provided an example: "The letter *Nun* depicted an 'inkwell' or a 'fish' and thus came to symbolize knowledge." For discussion of the letters at the beginning of Qur'anic chapters, see: Ar-Razi (1/249–258); Az-Zarkashi (1/213–226); Az-Zamakhshari (1/63–73); As-Suhaili (2/308); Al-Baghawi (1/11–12).

In cases when words have an irregular usage, whereby scholars struggle to make sense of their intended meaning, returning to their roots unveils a clearer and more coherent explanation. For example, similar to its peculiar employment of the word *Kubbara*, when speaking of Moses being instructed by the Divine, the Qur'an says, "*Kallama Allahu Musa Taklima.*" The seemingly incongruous word here is *Taklima*. Scholars struggle with what this word connotes. Some have taken it to mean that the Divine spoke to Moses with physical sounds, basically anthropomorphizing the Divine. If it was indeed about "talking," the sentence should have read as "*Kallama Allahu Musa Kalama,*" which would be more grammatically correct though theologically problematic. However, when *Taklima* is taken back to its root, we are presented with a more consistent explanation and an enhanced translation: "The Loving Divine distinguished Moses with clear defining signs/wisdom."

The term *Nushuz* ("toxicity," referring literally to the flaring fangs of a venomous snake secreting lethal poison) is mentioned only twice in the Qur'an (4:34, 128). Verse 34 refers to a woman initiating *Nushuz*, whereas verse 128 refers to a man initiating it. If *Nushuz* means rebellion or disobedience as some would suggest, then it creates a dilemma for them, since it conflicts with their interpretation that men are superior. If that is truly the case, how then can this alleged superior rebel against/disobey a woman, whom they assume is inferior? Rather, the passages refer to a state of affairs in a strained relationship and offer advice on de-escalation of tensions and recommendations for reconciliation before dire measures such as a petition of divorce can be considered. In fact, verse 35 advises that two mediators, acceptable to both parties, be chosen to seek a resolution if the partners cannot resolve the conflict on their own. Verse 32 mentions that men have strengths that women lack, and likewise women possess strengths that men lack, and that each should complement and support the other, rather than feel threatened by their strengths. Verse 129 warns a man from neglecting his wife and advises him to care for her well-being and, if this is not possible, to part ways in a blameless divorce. Verse 130 concludes by mentioning that if a divorce was inevitable, God will continue to bless both partners and that a divorce is not a mark of shame. For further discussion see: Al-Azhari (11/208–209); Ibnu Manthur (8/555–556); Ar-Razi (4/70–75, 235–237).

For discussion of the psychology of the Arabic language and its employment see the following books: *Al-Muqaddimah*; *Lahajat-ul-Fusha*; *Qasas-ul-'Arab*; *Al-Muzhir*; *Amthal-ul-'Arab*; *'Aja'ibu-'Ulumi-il-Qur'an*; *At-Tibyanu Fi I'rabil-Qur'an*; *Jamal-ul-Qurra wa Kamal-ul-Iqra*; *Taqribun-Nashri Fil-Qira'atil-'Ashr*.

The Qur'an employs several non-Arabic words. Its first foreign word appears very early in its revelation. The word *Sirata*, in *Surah Al-Fatihah*, is derived from the Latin *strada*. It referred to a sophisticated kind of highway, carrying the nuance of a layered and well-organized road, unlike the rugged and hazardous paths found in Arabia. Other examples include *Qistas*, meaning "scale," which appears twice (17:35 and 26:182) and is derived from the Latin *castus*, meaning "pure, clean, innocent, uncorruptible, stainless." *Qirtas*, meaning "refined paper" and mentioned twice (6:7, 91), is derived from the Greek *khartes* ("chart, map"; adopted into Latin as "carta," as in Magna

Carta). *Firdaws*, meaning "elegant garden" or "paradise" via the Hebrew *Pardes* (orchard) is ultimately derived from the ancient Persian *Pairi Daeza*, literally "surrounding wall."

CHAPTER 2

The enigma of the term *Thalik* can be explained by looking at another unique usage of the concept in Surah Al-Hajj, verse 32: "*Thalik wa man ya'ath-thim hurumatillah*," which is traditionally read by pausing at Thalik, and rendered as "Considering all that has passed, remember that whoever honors the wisdom the Loving Divine has inspired, their heart will open to hope and their minds to action." See Abu Hayyan (1/56); Ar-Razi (8/222–224); Al-Baghawi (3/218); Abu Hayyan (7/503–504); Az-Zamakhshari (3/155).

Contrary to common misconception, the Prophet Muhammad was known for his cordial relations with Jews. He visited Jewish neighbors when they were sick, as described in *Al-Fath-ur-Rabbani* (1/524). On several occasions, Jewish neighbors invited Muhammad for the Passover Seder, which he attended. Anas Ibnu Malik recounts: "A Jew invited the prophet for a meal and served him unleavened bread and a spread of diverse foods," as chronicled in *Irwa Al-Ghalil* (35).

When a Jewish funeral passed by as he sat with his disciples, Muhammad stood out of respect and instructed his followers to help carry the bier, via eyewitnesses Jabir ibnu 'Abdillah and Anas ibn Malik. See Al-Bukhari (1311); Muslim (960); Ahmad (8527, 14427, 14591, 14812); Abu Dawud (3174); An-Nasa'i (1922, 1928, 2049); Ibnu Majah (1543), Al-Haythami (30/3); Al-'Aini (7/278); Al-Baghawi (70, 1262); At-Tabarani (6/40).

Muhammad was known to treat the Torah with reverence, as evidenced by the following vignette: "A group of Jews invited the prophet Muhammad to Quff to visit them at their seminary, which he did . . . The Torah was brought to him and he placed it upon a platform saying, 'I believe in you and in Him who revealed you.' Then he said, 'Bring me a learned scholar from among you,' and a young rabbi was brought forth to read it for him." See Abu Dawud (4449) and Al-'Asqalani (12/177).

Muhammad upheld certain teachings of the Torah and added to them, as attested by Salman Al-Farisi, who recalled: "I read in the Torah that the blessing of food is via washing the hands before eating. So I told the prophet what I had read and he said, 'The blessing of food is both to wash before and after eating.'" See Abu Dawud (3761); At-Tirmithi (1846); Ahmad (23732). 'Aishah added: "The prophet strictly forbade the desecration of the Torah." See Ibnu 'Adi (1/283).

Jewish troops were considerable in Muhammad's army, see At-Tirmithi (1558). Due to the cordiality between Muhammad and Medina's Jews, Rabbi Mukhairiq interrupted Sabbath services and encouraged his congregation to join Muhammad's army at Uhud. See: Ibnu Sa'd (1/502); Al-'Asqalani (3/373); Ibnu Rajab (2/485).

Finally, when Muhammad died, he had pawned his armor to a Jewish neighbor. See Ibnu Majah (1992, 2439); An-Nasa'i (4651); Ahmad (2109); At-Tirmithi (1214); Al-'Asqalani (3/994).

These facts reveal the inaccuracy of mythologies alleging that Muhammad massacred and expelled the Jews of Medina, legends created many years after the prophet's death for political purposes. Al-Awza'i (eighth century) greatly objected to the myth of the massacre of Jews, stating, "As far as I know it is not a decree of the Divine to chastise the many for the fault of the few; rather to reprimand the few for the fault of the many." Ibnu Hajar al-'Asqalani called the legend a "deviant tale" in his *Tahthib-ut-Tahthib*, and At-Tabari called the fable an "unsubstantiated allegation!" See: Al-Bukhari (2639, 5792, 5825); *Tafsir Al-Mizan* by Allamah At-Tabtaba'i (9/82); *Tahthib-ut-Tahthib* by Al-'Asqalani (9/40); *Tarikh Tahlil Al-Islam* by Dr. Shahidi (pp. 88–90); *'Uyun Al-Athar* by Ibn Sayyid An-Nas (1/17); *Al-Maghazi An-Nabawiyyah* by Ibn 'Uqbah (pp. 82–83).

CHAPTER 3

Sourcing for details of the context into which the Qur'an was revealed, including particulars about prophet Muhammad and Arabia, is covered extensively in the "Source Materials" section of *Muhammad, the World-Changer*.

For additional sourcing, see Ibnul-Athir (2/41–42); Al-Halabi (1/171–195, 322–34); As-Suhaili (1/242–56); Ibnu Hisham (1/141–42); Ibnul-Mulqin (2/153); Al-'Asqalani (3/1097); Al-Bukhari (379, 4953); Muslim (214); Ibnu Hibban (330); Ibnul-Mulqin (7/325); Al-Haithami (8/89); Ibnu 'Adi (4/59); Ibnu Mundah (969); Abu Na'im (3/318); Ibnul-Qaisarani (3/1690); Ahmad

(24892); Abu Ya'la (4672); At-Tirmithi (708, 3620); Ibnu Taymiyyah (8/540); An-Najjar (p. 100) Al-Khudhari (1/14); Al-Albani (72); As-Suhaili (1/313–18); Ibnul-Athir (2/37); Ath-Thahabi (1/55); Ibnu Kathir (2/264); Al-Bazzar (3096); At-Tabari (11/80); Al-Waqidi (2/33); Al-Qurtubi (10/335–51); Ar-Razi (11/190–209); Ibnul-'Arabi (4/408–13); Az-Zamakhshari (4/770–77); Al-Baghawi (4/631–42); Ibnul-Athir (2/46–47).

Ibnu 'Abbas said: "Khadijah was twenty-eight years old when the prophet married her." See Ibnu Sa'd in *At-Tabaqat-ul-Kubra* (18/13). Ibnu Ishaq said: "Abu Talib and Khadijah Bint Khuwailid died in the same year. This was three years before the emigration of the prophet to Medina. . . . She was twenty-eight years old when the prophet married her." See also Al-Hakim in *Al-Mustadrak* (4837). For a more detailed discussion of Khadijah's age at marriage to Muhammad, see the sourcing section of *Muhammad, the World-Changer*.

CHAPTER 4

The initial *Iqra* revelation that became the first part of *Surah Al-'Alaq*, was revealed in different phases. A telling clue to the distinctive phases is how each segment contains a unique rhyme and rhythm while speaking to a specific context. The style and rhyme of the first five verses is clearly distinct (*Khalaq, 'Alaq, Akram, Qalam, Ya'lam*) from the second segment with its unique rhyming scheme that matches the period of its revelation: *Layatgha, Istaghna, Ar-Ruj'a, Yanha, Salla, Huda, Taqwa, Tawalla, Yara* etc.

Ibnu 'Abbas declared: "The first of the Qur'an to be revealed, at Mecca, was *Iqra*. . . ." which appears in various narrations via several of Muhammad's close followers. These include: "The first of the Qur'an to be revealed was *Iqra* . . . until . . . *Ya'lam*," and "The first Surah revealed was 'Iqra." See Al-Hakim (2/529); At-Tabari (30/252); As-Suyuti (8/561); Ar-Razi (11/215); Az-Zamakhshari (4/781). Al-Baghawi wrote: "The majority are in agreement that this Surah [*Al-'Alaq*] is the first of the Qur'an to be revealed, and the first of it to be revealed are its first five verses until *Ma lam Ya'lam*." See *Ma'alim-ut-Tanzil* (4/647). Al-Qurtubi said: "This Surah is the first to be revealed from the Qur'an, according to the majority . . . it was revealed at Hira. . . ." See *Al-Jami'u Li-Ahkamil-Qur'an* (10/358); Al-Bukhari (3, 4953, 6982); Muslim (160).

Regarding the second phase of this chapter's revelation, which comes in the context of 'Amr Ibnu Hisham's persecution, see At-Tabari (30/254); Ibnu Kathir (4/529); Ar-Razi (11/219–227); Al-Baghawi (4/649); Az-Zamakhshari (4/783); Ibnu Abi Hatim (p. 3450); Al-Qurtubi (10/362); Ibnu 'Abdis-Salam in *Fawa'idun Fi Mushkil-il-Qur'an* (p. 257); As-Suyuti in *Asbab-un-Nuzul* (p. 248); Al-Ujhuri in *Irshadur-Rahman* (p. 785).

At times, Qur'anic passages provide clues as to timing and context. *Surah Al-Qadr*, placed after *Surah Al-'Alaq* in the final edition by the prophet Muhammad, describes the Qur'an's initial revelation taking place at "night." *Surah Al-Fajr* narrows it down to "predawn," and *Al-Falaq* pinpoints it at the time when the "first sliver of light splits the darkness," approximately 3 am. For the day of revelation being a Friday, see: Muslim (854); An-Nasa'i (1429); An-Nawawi (4/482); Al-Arna'ut (1050).

Note that because many Quranic chapters were revealed in phases (sometimes over years), I refer to the order of Surahs by pinpointing the timing of their initial phase. Beyond that initial marker, when necessary I made allusions to other passages from the same Surah revealed at later times and only then inserted into the original content.

For an account of Meccan persecution, including Sumayyah's martyrdom, see Ibnu Sa'd (4/101); Ibnu 'Abdil-Barr (4/1589, 1864); Ibnu Mindah (1/92); Al-Balathiri (1/157); Al-Majlisi (18/241); As-Suhaili (2/337); Ibnul-Athir (2/60–76). For accounts of Al-Walid's attempted intervention and discussion of the "frowning incident," see Ar-Razi (11/52–53); Al-Ujhuri (742); As-Suhaili (2/216).

For accounts of 'Umar's conversion, see: Ibnul-Athir (2/84–86); As-Suhaili (2/120–26); Ash-Shawkani (3/502); Ibnu Daqiq Al-'Id (2/424); Ath-Thahabi (3/375); Al-Hakim (6897); Al-Bayhaqi (420); Ad-Daraqutni (1/123); Al-'Asqalani (1/198); Al-Busairi (7/166); Ibnu Sa'd (3/267); Az-Zaila'i (1/199).

CHAPTER 5

For accounts of the migration to Abyssinia; popular uprising against the boycott; the deaths of Abu Talib and Khadijah; and the subsequent visit to Taif, see: Al-Bukhari (434, 1341, 3884, 4230, 4232, 4772); Muslim (24, 528, 2502, 2499); Ahmad (1740, 1742); Ibnu Hibban (982, 3181); Al-Haithami (6/27); Abu Na'im (1/114–15); Ibnul-Athir (2/76–82, 87); Al-Halabi (1/456–

87, 488–512); As-Suyuti (1/149); As-Suhaili (2/90–119, 223–34); Ahmad (1740); Al-Wadiʻi (96, 1672); Al-Albani (126); Al-Arnaʾut (1/216, 429, 2486).

For discussion of the Qurʾanic account of Joseph see: Ar-Razi (6/416–523); Al-Baghawi (2/433–506); Az-Zamakhshari (2/415–481); *Al-Musʻifu fi Lughati wa Iʻrabi Surati-Yusuf.*

The original name of Surah 17 was "Surah Bani Israel" and appears in numerous Hadith, including Al-Bukhari (4994) and At-Tirmithi (3402). In fact, Ibnu Hajar Al-ʻAsqalani declared that "the *Surah*'s name during the time of the prophet Muhammad, as well as that of the generations that came after him was *Surah Bani Israel*"—see *Fath-ul-Bari* (8/388). Ibnu ʻAshur said, "It was called Bani Israel, during the time of the followers of the prophet"—see *At-Tahriru wat-Tanwir* (5/15). Imam As-Sadiq, a prominent descendant of Muhammad, referred to the chapter as Surah Bani Israel, see *Nur-uth-Thaqalain* by Al-Juwaizi (4/115). Finally, Muhammad himself referred to it as Bani Israel—see Az-Zamakhshari (2/854) and *Ruh-ul-Maʻani* by Al-Alusi (15/5).

Note that the Qurʾan never uses the root *J-H-D* (*Jihad*) in the context of war, instead it employs the root *Q-T-L* (*Qital*). The root *J-H-D* appears only in reference to the exertion of extensive energy and effort, connoting a struggle in achieving an arduous task. See: Ibnu Manthur (2/239–241); Al-Fairuzabadi (249–250); Al-Azhari (6/26–27); Al-Khalil (160). For discussion of *hijrah* see Al-Bukhari (3906, 3911, 3925); Muslim (2381); At-Tabarani (611, 3605); Al-Bazzar (1746); Al-ʻAsqalani (7/307, 735); Al-ʻIraqi (2/342, 7/239); As-Suhaili (2/187–212); Al-Bayhaqi (1/298); Ahmad (23061); At-Tirmithi (3690).

CHAPTER 6

For discussion of Medina's environment, culture, and landmarks see the book *Maʻalimu Tabah* ("The Unique Sites of Medina").

The root of *Baqarah, B-Q-R,* indicates leaving a lasting impression/impact:

- *Baqaral-Amra*: "He explained the nuances of the matter making it relatable and applicable for lasting impact."
- *Baqaral-Ardha*: "He highlighted the various segments of the land, outlining their distinct elements, characteristics, and freshwater sources."

- *Baqaral-mas'alah*: "He deeply examined the problem to arrive at its deep causes and effects."
- *Tabaqqara fil-kalam*: "His eloquently articulated and well-presented words left an impact stirring the audience to take action."
- *Al-Baqir*: "The scholar whose depth and breadth of nuanced understanding leaves a lasting impact."

The word *Baqarah* is typically translated as "cow," yet it has a more precise meaning in the context of the Surah. As in the case with *Iqra,* which can figuratively mean "read" (and which in the post-Qur'anic era almost always means "read" or "recite"), the word *Baqarah* is figuratively used to refer to the bovine species used to plow the earth. However, the root *B-Q-R* originally referred to the deep and lasting impact of the plow or the goring effect of bovine horns, not the cow or ox itself. See: Ibnu Manthur (1/470–472), Al-Fairuzabadi (318–319), Al-Azhari (9/119–120).

For accounts of the Abyssinian delegation see: Al-Bukhari (907, 4894); Muslim (892, 1941, 1943, 1945, 1946); Ahmad (860, 12564).

For discussions of *Surah At-Tawbah*, the Qur'an's severest passages, concerning the Meccan massacre of Muhammad's pagan allies in breach of the Treaty of Hudaibiyyah, see: At-Tabari (11/351–53); Al-Wahidi (10/301–3); Ash-Shinqiti (5/285–86); Ibnu Kathir (4/114); Al-Qurtubi (8/78); Ibnul-Jawzi (2/238–39); Ibnu Abi Hatim (6/1758); Az-Zamakhshari (2/249); Abu As-Su'ud (4/45) and Ibnu 'Ashur (10/120–24).

Ibnu 'Ashur comments that "the Qur'an sanctions the execution of the guilty from the Banu Bakr because they massacred the unarmed Banu Khuza'ah in cold blood and betrayed the peace treaty" (120–21), "yet the passage continues by stressing (*tawkid*) that pagans who kept the pledge are not to be harmed." See: Ibnu 'Ashur (10/123); Az-Zamakhshari (2/249); Abu As-Su'ud (4/45).

For discussion of compilation, arrangement, and editing of the Qur'an, see At-Tabarani (315, 8322); Al-Bukhari (893, 4986, 7191); Ahmad (2922, 17918, 17947); Al-Haithami (7/51, 8/260); Ibnu Kathir (4/516); Abu Hatim (13456); Ibnu Sa'd (410); Ash-Shawkani (3/267); Al-Baghawi (2077, 3456); Al-Hakim (2/668); Ibnu Hibban (6919); At-Tirmithi (3103, 3086); Ahmad (76); Al-Marwazi (45); An-Nasa'i (7995); Ahmad (399, 499); An-Nasa'i (8007); Abu Dawud (786); Ibnul-'Arabi (2/445); Al-'Asqalani (1/44).

Zaid ibn Thabit remarked, "While with the Messenger of God, we compiled the Qur'an from many sheets into one." See: Ahmad (5/184); Al-Hakim (2/668); Ibnu Hibban (1/320); At-Tirmithi (5/734).

Zaid said, "I was a scribe of revelation . . . writing it on palm fronds," and later, "compiling [the Qur'an] into one volume from the lower cuttings of palm fronds [al-'usb], white stone slabs [al-likhaf], cloth and raw animal skin sheets [ar-riqa'], cured leather parchments [qita'-ul-adim], camel-saddles [al-aqtab], camel rib bones [al-adhla'], and shoulder bones of sheep and camels [al-aktaf]." See: Al-Bukhari (4986, 7191); Ahmad (76); Al-Haithami (8/260); At-Tirmithi (3103); Al-Marwazi (45); An-Nasa'i (7995).

'Uthman and Ibnu 'Abbas narrated how specific passages were compiled in the Qur'an, observing that some chapters would be revealed with a large number of passages, yet at other times only individual passages would be revealed. In those cases, Muhammad would say, "Place this passage in the *Surah* that has such and such passages and place it between such and such passages." See: Ahmad (399, 499); An-Nasa'i (8007); Abu Dawud (786); Ibnu Hibban (6919); At-Tirmithi (3086); Ibnul-'Arabi (2/445); Al-'Asqalani (1/44).

CHAPTER 7

For an account of events from Muhammad's death till the Abbasid period, see *Tarikh-ul-Khulafa* by As-Suyuti (6–422); *Al-Fihrist* by An-Nadim; Al-Bukhari (1242, 2704, 3670, 3700, 7207, 7217, 7219, 4454); Muslim (1759); As-Suhaili (4/438–61); Ibnu 'Asakir (67/98); Al-Bazzar (1/98, 193); Ibnu Hibban (6607, 6919); Ibnu Kathir (7/60–194); At-Tabarani (1628).

For further reading on the incidents relating to Musailimah, see Al-Bukhari (3620, 4072, 4078, 4373, 4378, 7034, 7461); Muslim (2273). For the content of Musailimah's letter and alleged revelation see Ibnu Hajar Al-'Asqalani in *Al-Matalib-ul-'Aliyah* (2/374); Al-Busairi in *Al-Ithaf* (8/5); Al-Baqillani, *I'jaz-ul-Qur'an;* Ibnu Kathir.

'Umar is a complex individual from early Islamic history. He is looked on with suspicion by most Shi'ah sects, whereas he is seen as a saintly figure by most Sunnis. Both groups agree that he had a temper and a complicated personality, as can be witnessed from his conversion (see *Muhammad the World-Changer*, pp. 142–145). Due to this disparity, he has been the perfect victim for false attribution of oppressive decrees, that clearly contradict his established record of justice; transparent and accountable governance; entrepreneurship and humility.

'Umar has been wrongly accused of expelling Jews from Arabia—despite the fact that Jewish rulers still governed in Arabian cities like Tayma into the late twelfth Century CE (as reported by the Jewish-Spanish traveler Benjamin of Tudela). He is also falsely accused of propagating edicts limiting the rights of non-Muslims. These are all later fabrications used by zealous Muslim movements to justify their oppressive policies as a counter to the Reconquista and Crusader aggression.

The writings of the Patriarch of Jerusalem Sophronius the Sophist serve as a non-partisan witness to 'Umar's character and foresight. The Patriarch reports that 'Umar declined the Patriarch's gracious offer to pray at the Church of the Holy Sepulchre by saying: "I fear that if I pray here, future generations may use this as a justification declaring, ''Umar prayed here so we must turn it into a mosque.'"

When 'Umar led the prayers on the Temple mount in Jerusalem, eyewitnesses state that "he recited the entirety of *Surah Sad* in the first part of the prayer and *Surah Bani Israel* in the second." *Surah Sad* mainly speaks about David and Solomon, respectively the establisher of Jerusalem and builder of the ancient Temple. The Surah also relates how David often prayed in *Al-Mihrab*, which the 'Ulama clarify as *Quds-ul-Aqdas* ("The Holy of Holies"), upon which the Dome of the Rock was subsequently built to honor its sanctity. While *Surah Bani Israel* narrates the double destruction of Jerusalem and its Temple, it also prophesizes their restoration—which 'Umar saw himself fulfilling. In fact, 'Umar personally led the cleanup of the Temple mount that had been littered with ruins and refuse. See: Ibnu-Kathir (7/60–61); Al-Qurtubi (18/155); At-Tabari (2/448); Ibnul-Athir (2/347); Ibnul-Jawzi (4/193).

Since the words of the prophet Muhammad carry so much weight and can have a serious impact (both positive or negative) upon people of the Islamic faith and others, fabrication and false attribution to the prophet are viewed as a major offence. Fabricated *hadith* have repeatedly been leveraged to justify and promote hatred, injustice, or oppressive practices. In a foresighted moment, the prophet Muhammad himself warned his followers, "Do not falsely attribute things to me, for a lie about me is not like a lie about someone else . . ." See Al-Bukhari (106, 107, 1291, 3461).

An example of a fabricated hadith attributed to the prophet is, "Do not allow women in places of prominence and do not teach them literacy." This chauvinistic falsehood was flagged by Ibnul-Jawzi in his compilation *Al-Mawdhu'at* "The Fabricated Traditions" (2/268). Ibnul-Jawzi commented: "This hadith has no validity." Ibnu Hayyan stated: "This false hadith cannot be used as validation for anything."

Mu'awiyah remains the subject of much debate and controversy, his legacy clouded and complicated. Some proclaim him a saint while others demonize him. I chose to humanize him in my books. The character of Mu'awiyah has strengths and weaknesses: an entrepreneurial and shrewd politician, he also engaged in nepotism and underhanded dealings. As Ibnul-Jawzi said in *Al-Mawdhu'at* (2/18): "A group who alleged to follow the prophetic tradition falsely invented fabricated *hadith* in praise of Mu'awiyah, just as a group among the Shi'ites likewise invented Hadith condemning him. Indeed, both groups are clearly committing a formidable error." See also *Minhaj-us-Sunnat-in-Nabawiyah* (4/446).

Regarding the incident of the scholar witnessing the false attribution of a prophetic saying to him, the entire narrative is reported by Al-Khatib Al-Baghdadi:

One day, Ahmad ibnu Hanbal and Yahya ibnu Ma'in performed their prayers at the mosque of Ar-Rasafah when an orator stood up and began reciting: "I heard Ahmad ibn Hanbal and Yahya ibn Ma'in relate a hadith on the authority of 'Abdur-Razzaq, who in turn heard it on the authority of Ma'mar, who heard it from Qatadah, who heard it from Anas, who declared: "The Messenger of God said, 'Whoever says: *La ilaha illallah*, then God will create for every word he utters a bird with a beak of gold and feathers of pearls.'"

He continued with his ludicrous story which comprised twenty pages. Upon this Ahmad ibn Hanbal and Yahya ibnu Ma'in began to look at each other with bewilderment and confusion. Then Ahmad asked, "Did you narrate this hadith?" Yahya replied, "I never heard this hadith before this present moment."

The two remained quiet until the man had completed his story. The orator then sat down to receive contributions and gifts. At that moment, Yahya ibnu Ma'in beckoned to him with his hand. So the orator went to Yahya assuming he was going to give him money.

Yahya then asked him, "Who narrated this hadith to you?"

He replied, "Ahmad ibnu Hanbal and Yahya ibnu Maʿin."

He retorted, "But I am Yahya ibnu Maʾin and this is Ahmad ibnu Hanbal! We never heard this story among the hadiths of the Prophet. As a matter of fact, it is nothing but a falsehood! Its authorities are not us!"

Then the orator asked, "Are you Yahya ibnu Maʿin?"

He answered, "Yes!"

He went on, "I constantly hear that Yahya ibnu Maʿin is a fool, a fact which I never realized until this moment."

Then Yahya ibn Maʾin said to him, "How did you know that I was a fool?"

He replied, "You act as if there is no other person by the name Yahya ibn Maʿin and Ahmad ibn Hanbal. In fact, I have narrated hadiths on the authority of seventeen individuals by the names of Ahmad ibnu Hanbal and Yahya ibnu Maʿin!"

Shocked, Ahmad placed his sleeve over his face in forbearance and whispered to Yahya, "Let him leave." See *Al-Jamiʿu li akhlaq-ir-Rawi*, vol. 4 p. 233.

Al-Khatib Al-Baghdadi related this incident to illustrate the understanding nature and humility of the ʿUlama, even when encountering aggravating situations like this one. Other notorious fabricators include Ibnu Abil-ʿAwja, who once boasted, "I fabricated four thousand hadiths!" See *Ibnul-Jawzi* (1:37).

For a description of Baghdad, including the reference to the doors of the Temple of Solomon, and the inscription on the foundational stone, a description of Bayt-ul-Hikmah, and Al-Maʾmun's declarations, see Yaqut-Al-Hamawi's *Muʿjam-ul-Buldan* (1/458–467); Ibnu Kathir (9/520–23); Al-Yaʿqubi (3/172); At-Tabari (8/478); Ibnu Qutaibah (387); As-Suyuti (306–333); Al-Fihrist by Ibnun-Nadim (129); Ibnul-Athir (6/282).

CHAPTER 8 & EPILOGUE

Most of the historical details mentioned in Chapter 8 and the Epilogue can be easily accessed via a plethora of written sources, and as such no specific references are provided.

The quote "A thousand days of tyranny are better than one day of chaos," appears in many forms, yet with the same meaning. These include "Sixty days under a tyrant are better than one night of lawlessness," and "A century of a ruler's tyranny is better than a year of the people's tyranny against one another." Ibnu Taymiyyah in his *As-Siyasat-ush-Shar'iyyah* ("Policies of Governance") writes: "A century of tyranny is better than a day of chaos."

Ibnu Taymiyyah's statement has often been misapplied to dissuade Muslims from taking agency to advocate for justice under oppressive conditions and instead tolerate abusive authority—even though Ibnu Taymiyyah severely criticized tyranny and stressed the responsibility of rulers to be diligent and just.

The *'Ulama* neither justified nor promoted tyranny. Quite the opposite. Traditional scholars valued justice, human dignity and compassion, yet remained wary of the immense harm spawned by chaos and anarchy. Their proclamations focused on the lesser of two evils and sought to dissuade aggressive revolutions propelled by vengeance and animosity rather than a genuine desire to improve society and establish a just government.

SCHOLARLY CHAIN OF TRANSMISSION

In conclusion, I humbly present one of my chains of transmission, offered as an illustration of the traditional scholarly links underlying authoritative material presented. Significant names mentioned in this book are emphasized in bold. Since each link in this unbroken chain is the foremost and universally recognized Qur'anic authority of his time, and connected directly to the prophet Muhammad, it is known as a Gold Chain (*Silsilat-un-Thahabiyyah*).

- ◆ Muhammad Sukkar (d. 2008, *Shaikh-ul-Qurra'* "Foremost Qur'anic authority"- Damascus),
- ◆ Mahmud Fa'iz Ad-Dair'atani (d. 1965, *Shaikh-ul-Qurra'*-Unparalleled Master of the *Qira'at* and leading authority on the Arabic language-Damascus),
- ◆ Muhammad Salim Al-Halawani (d. 1944, *Shaikh-ul-Qurra'*-Damascus),
- ◆ Ahmad Al-Halawani (d. 1889, *Shaikh-ul-Qurra'*-Damascus),
- ◆ Ahmad Al-Marzuqi (d. 1846, *Shaikh-ul-Qurra'*-Egypt & Mecca),
- ◆ Ibrahim Al-'Ubaidi (*Shaikh-ul-Qurra'*-Syria),
- ◆ 'Ali Al-Badri (*Shaikh-ul-Qurra'*-Syria),

- Muhammad Yusuf Afandi Zadeh (d. 1754, *Shaikh-ul-Qurra'*-Constantinople),
- 'Ali Al-Mansuri (*Shaikh-ul-Qurra'*-Syria),
- Sultan Ibnu Ahmad Al-Mazzahi (*Shaikh-ul-Qurra'*-Syria),
- Saifuddin Al-Fadhali (*Shaikh-ul-Qurra'*-Egypt),
- 'Abdurrahman Ibn Shahhathah Al-Yamani (*Shaikh-ul-Qurra'*-Egypt),
- Nasiruddin Muhammad Ibnu Salim At-Tablawi (d. 1559, *Shaikh-ul-Islam* and *Shaikh-ul-Qurra'*-Egypt),
- Zakaria Al-Ansari (d. 1519, *Shaikh-ul-Islam* and *Shaikh-ul-Qurra'*-Egypt, prominent student of **Ibnu Hajar Al-'Asqalani**),
- Muhammad Al-'Uqaili An-Nuwairi (*Shaikh-ul-Qurra'*-Damascus),
- Muhammad Ibnul-Jazari (d. 1430, *Shaikh-ul-Qurra'*-Unparalleled Master of the *Qira'at* & leading authority on the Arabic language-Damascus),
- 'Abdur-Rahman Ibnul-Mubarak (d. 1379, *Shaikh-ul-Qurra'*-Baghdad),
- Muhammad Ibnus-Sa'igh (d. 1325, *Shaikh-ul-Qurra'*-Egypt),
- 'Ali Ibnu Shuja' (d. 1263, *Shaikh-ul-Qurra'*-Egypt),
- Al-Qasim Ibnu Firruh Ash-Shatibi (d. 1222, *Shaikh-ul-Qurra'*-Unparalleled Master of the *Qira'at* & leading authority on the Arabic language-Alexandria, Egypt-born in Xàtiva, Spain),
- 'Ali Ibnu Huthail Al-Balansi (d. 1186, *Shaikh-ul-Qurra'*-Valencia, Spain),
- Sulaiman Ibnu Najah (d. 1118, *Shaikh-ul-Qurra'*-Valencia & Córdoba, Spain),
- **'Uthman Ibnu Sa'id Ad-Dani** (d. 1066, *Shaikh-ul-Qurra'*-Unparalleled Master of the *Qira'at* & leading authority on the Arabic language-Córdoba, Spain),
- Khalaf Ibnul-Qasim (d. 1015, *Shaikh-ul-Qurra'*-Córdoba),
- Ahmad Ibnu Usamah At-Tujibi (d. 964, *Shaikh-ul-Qurra'*-Morocco),
- Isma'il Ibnu 'Abdillah An-Nahhas (d. 905, *Shaikh-ul-Qurra'*-Egypt),
- Yusuf Al-Azraq (d. 862, *Shaikh-ul-Qurra'*-Denia, Spain-born in La Vall d'Alcalà),
- 'Uthman Ibnu Sa'id Warsh (d. 812, *Shaikh-ul-Qurra'* & foremost Master of Arabic language-Egypt).
- Nafi' Al-Madani (d. 785, *Shaikh-ul-Qurra'*-Medina),
- 'Abdurrahman Ibnu Hurmuz (d. 739, *Shaikh-ul-Qurra'*, Master of Language and Hadith sciences-Medina-Teacher of the legendary **Imam Malik**),
- **Ibnu 'Abbas** (d. 687, *Shaikh-ul-Qurra'* and Master of Exegesis-Mecca),
- **Ubayy Ibnu Ka'b** (d. 649, *Shaikh-ul-Qurra'* and senior Qur'anic scribe-Kufah),
- **The Prophet Muhammad** (d. 632).

The torch of Qur'anic authority has travelled significant distances over the past fourteen centuries. Like a raincloud, its nuanced expertise replenishes all without discrimination. But its lifegiving waters can only spark actual growth and blossoming if human beings take practical steps to unleash their potential and transform their state of being—thereby changing the world.

INDEX

as slave in Egypt, 104–8, 117–18, 204

Jundub Ibn Junadah (renamed Abu Tharr), 111

Ka'bah shrine (Mecca), 7, 18–19, 38, 55, 56, 79, 87, 89, 102, 136–37, 153, 180, 181

Khadijah (wife of Muhammad), 46, 65, 102

Khalifah (caliph), 40, 166, 168

*Kharijite*s, 176, 178

King James Bible, 8–9

Kubbara (unbearable frustration), 18–20, 26, 175

Kufah (Iraq), 21, 169–70, 177–78, 183–84, 188

Kufic script, 170, 174

Kurush (Cyrus the Great), 42, 132

Lam (imparting wisdom), 28

Levites, 137–41, 155

Maccabees, 42–43, 129–30

magnifying glasses, 202

Mahdis (messianic figures), 212

Malachi, 42

Malik (infusion of fresh energy), 77–78, 142

marriage, 20–21, 115–17, 120, 145–47

Mary (Maryam, mother of Jesus), 43, 89–90, 101, 138, 144, 156

Mathhab ("navigation method"), 183–84

Mecca/Meccans

  Al-Masjid Al-Haram (mosque), 119

  battles and raids with Medina, 11, 131, 139–41, 147–48, 150–54, 161–62, 207

  camel caravan to Damascus, 57–58, 63–65, 69, 139, 151

  conquest of, 11

  contradictions and inconsistencies of, 26–27, 59

  Dar-ul-Arqam (secret academy), 68, 79–80, 86–88, 90, 92, 103, 177, 180

  description at emergence of the Qur'an, 55–61

  early rejection of the Qur'an and, 3, 18–21, 52, 60–62, 81

  famine aid from Medina, 136–37

  Hashemite concentration camp outside, 99–100, 102

  idolatry/polytheism in, 34–36, 56–58, 84

  Ka'bah (shrine built by Abraham), 7, 18–19, 38, 55, 56, 79, 87, 89, 102, 136–37, 153, 180, 181

  leadership fears of Muhammad and the Qur'an, 77, 89–90, 96–98, 99–100, 111, 112, 131, 146–47

  macho/nomadic culture of, 55–61, 76, 93

  as mercantile economy, 55, 57, 126

  Mount Hira, 1–3, 7, 54, 65–66, 76

  Muhammad escapes, 70

  Muhammad's family roots in, 63, 64, 85–86, 91, 131

  origins of Qur'an in, 1–3, 54, 55, 75–76

  slavery/enslaved people in, 55, 63, 64, 80–81, 91, 111, 147

  stagnation of, 35, 37–38, 56–61, 62, 65, 78–79, 213

  supporters of Muhammad, 76–78

  treaty with Medina, 147–49, 150–53

  Zamzam well, 59

medical innovations, 203

Medina (formerly Yathrib), 10

  assassination of Mumahhad's disciples, 161–62

  battles and raids with Mecca, 11,